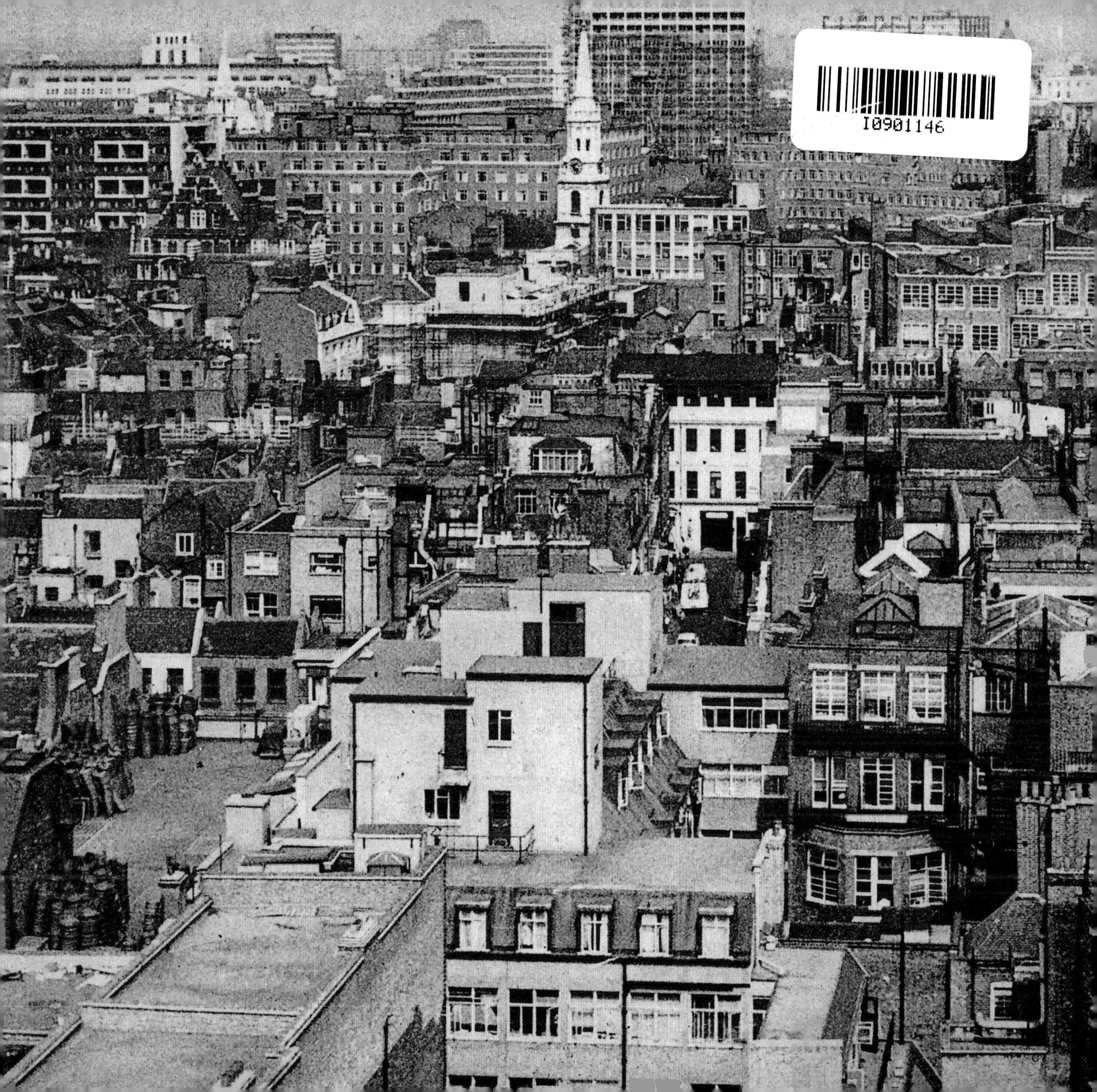

INTRODUCTION

Frank Norman and Jeffrey Bernard had fun with this book, which presents a unique view of Soho in the 1960s. Frank wrote the words and Jeffrey took the photographs. They were eminently qualified to produce it being old Soho hands. Frank had lived and played there since the 1940s and Jeffrey was to base his 'Low Life' column for *The Spectator* there. He already had an uncanny eye for detail.

Frank was a well-established and successful author with his autobiographical books *Bang to Rights*, 1958; *Stand on Me*, 1959; *The Guntz*, 1962, and his play *Fings Ain't Wot They Used T'Be*, 1959, to his credit. Frank wrote *Soho Night & Day* in the same economical, first-person style that he brought to his memoirs. It is more of a personal reminiscence than a guidebook, a snapshot of a wonderful place, at a certain time, now separated from us forever by the vault of time.

Soho Night & Day is two old friends working together on the best kind of project. Jeffrey Bernard remembered, 'He [Frank] wrote it and I took the pictures, it was something of a farce. We'd wander around Soho all day and night, having hospitality heaped on us by publicans and restauranteurs who wanted to appear in the book, and I think we were drunk for a year.'[1] In Jeffrey's case, the money was already gone before they began. In 1962, when they were first paid a £100 advance on the book, Jeffrey lost his share on just ten turns of the roulette wheel in ten minutes at a gambling club. He was, at the time, married to the long-suffering actress Jackie Ellis, who was supporting them both. 'You could hear the slap my lady gave me the length of Greek Street,' he later wrote. She left him soon afterwards.'[2]

Frank valiantly covers all the guide-book categories: a brief history, the restaurants, the markets, the clubs, the pubs and so on. You could use it as a guide to all the most interesting places in Soho back then, but Frank was much more at home in the world of Soho villains than in the Italian delis of Old Compton Street. The schpielers (illegal gambling clubs), the ponces, the strip clubs and pornshops are lovingly recorded in his deceptively straightforward style. He was writing the tale of the tribe; his tribe. For years he was a homeless layabout in Soho, and he recalls his Soho youth with obvious nostalgia, 'I remember it as being the best place in the world for being on the bum.' So, this is not your usual guidebook, it is more an autobiography.

'My London is Soho,' he wrote. 'That square mile which has by turns destroyed and enriched my soul and pocket … I arrived in Dean Street a beautiful and naïve boy of sixteen years, had a light ale in the French pub under-age and have remained underage ever since. From that day forward I have not glanced back and am now a Soho addict beyond cure or redemption. I perpetually complain about how much the old place has changed in recent years…'[3] That was written in 1969, just three years after this book was first published.

He wouldn't recognise the place now: Wheelers, Jimmy's, Trattoria Terrazza, The 2is, The Moulin d'Or are all gone, but Quo Vadis is still there, so is l'Escargot, and The Gay Hussar only closed in 2018. The Mandrake, the Colony, the Gargoyle, The Caves de France and Murray's are gone but the French House survives and thrives. These days 'old Soho' is represented by places like Andrew Edmunds' restaurant or the Groucho Club, both opened in 1985, that didn't even exist when this book was written.

Gone too are the days when Elizabeth David could suggest that particularly hard to find ingredients for her recipes could be obtained from 'specialist food shops in Soho' for there are none. For decades now there has not been a single butcher, grocer, or fishmonger in Soho; all driven out by the greed of landlords. Berwick Street market is now largely given over to street food stalls with only a couple of fruit and vegetable stalls remaining.

But these changes were yet to come. Frank gives us an authentic portrait of Soho from half-a-century ago. He is painfully honest. He doesn't see many Soho pubs worth recommending, with the exception of The French Pub, the York Minister, to which he devotes considerable space. He obviously likes Gaston Berlemont, the proprietor. In fact, the French is one of the few places that remains more or less untouched since Frank described it, and still does have the 'spirit' of Soho.

Much has been written about Muriel Belcher's Colony Room but this account is from a friend whom she knew and trusted. She was included to give an accurate and balanced picture of Soho even though a tourist would not have been able to visit the Colony as it was a members' only club.

He actively warns visitors against Soho's gambling clubs as they are certain to be ripped off. Most strip clubs are 'crummy' apart from a few continental-style hi-end night clubs, and as for sex, the visitor might as well forget it although much is promised.

Much of the book is a soliloquy, a series of fond recollections about a place that appeared then about to disappear. He was writing at the time when Soho was most under threat from the combination of Westminster Council and property developers: old houses were being torn down and replaced by ugly high-rise blocks. It seemed as if the old Soho would disappear completely and finish up looking like a council estate. In fact, there were many battles to come and most of the new development was stopped, but you can understand his consternation and dismay because when this book was written Soho's Georgian buildings, its rogues and villains, its wide-boys and tarts, were all being wiped out in the name of 'progress'.

Also unusual in a guidebook, towards the end of the book Frank ignores the tourist reader and issues a word of warning to his fellow Soho-ites against fraternising with the law, as the friendlier they get, the more they have on you. These were the days of massive corruption in the Met and no-one was safe from being fitted-up. This concern is perhaps to be expected from the author of *Bang to Rights, a prison memoir.*

Despite the disappearance of the food shops, thanks to the activists, Soho looks much the same now as then, and you can still look down Dean Street and imagine Frank and Jeff standing, a little tipsy, debating which pub to go to next. And follow in their footsteps…

Barry Miles

1. Pomeroy, Gerry, *A Day in the Life of Jeffrey Bernard*, BBC-2 Arena, 1987.
2. Lord, Graham, *Just the One, the Wives and Times of Jeffrey Bernard. 1932-1997*. London: Sinclair-Stevenson, 1992, p115.
3. Norman, Frank, *Norman's London*, London: Secker & Warburg, 1969, p248-9.

Soho Night & Day

Frank Norman & Jeffrey Bernard

ACC ART BOOKS

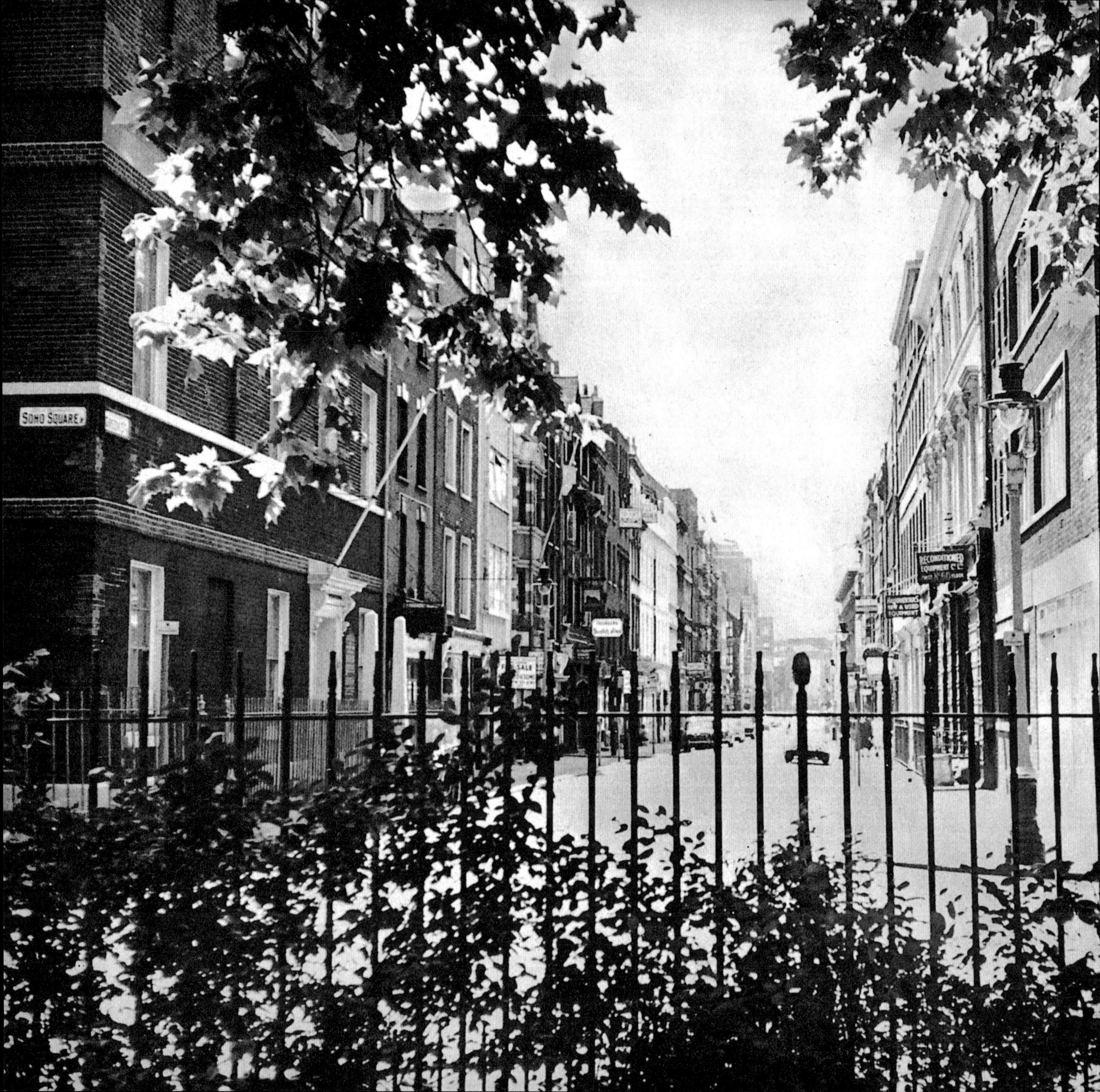
SOHO SQUARE
RECONDITIONED

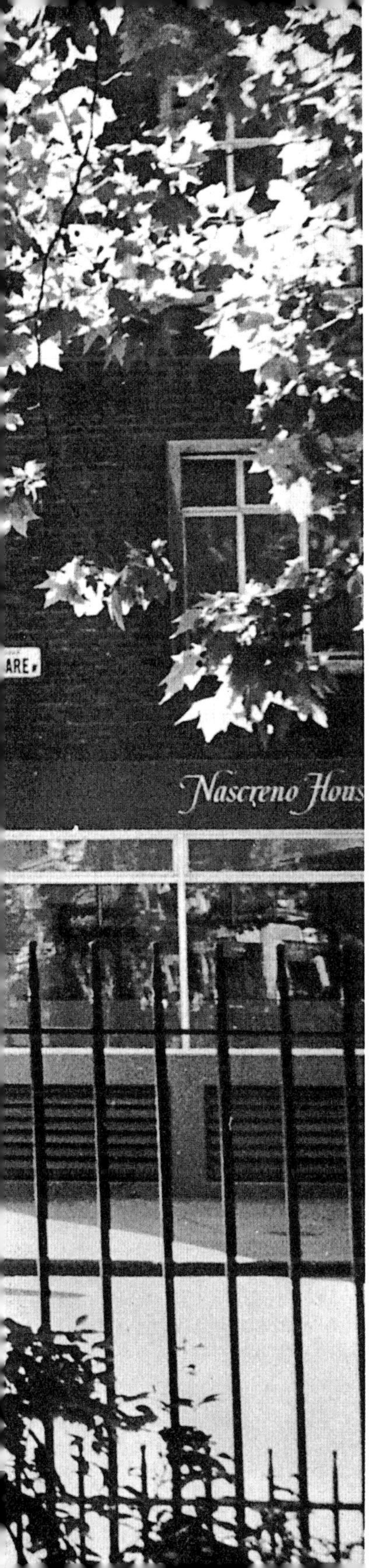

WHAT THE HEADMASTER SAID

During my last term at school the headmaster summoned me to his office. As usual I thought I must have misbehaved myself in some way and was about to get yet another six of the best. I tapped on his door lightly and heard him bellow come in. I opened the door with some trepidation and entered the room; he glanced up at me from behind his desk, for some reason he had a smile on his face. Now it must be said that I had never seen him smile before, and the sight of it disturbed me greatly, and frightened me far more than his usual scowl. 'Come in boy, come in!' he beamed, 'I won't eat you.' I approached him slowly, not getting too close in case he should give me a sudden cuff around my earhole. 'Sit down lad,' he grinned. Gingerly I sat down on the edge of a hard wooden chair facing him, for a time he ignored me while he scribbled some notes on a sheet of foolscap paper, occasionally glancing up at me over the top of his glasses. When he had finished he sat back in his chair and smiled on me benignly and I was filled with terror.

'Well son,' he began, 'as you know you will be leaving us at the end of the term.'

'Yes sir,' I squeaked.

'I have always made it a practice to have a little talk to each of you lads before you go out into the world to earn your livings,' he cleared his throat.

'Yes sir.'

'Don't interrupt, boy.'

'No sir, sorry sir.'

'The purpose of my sending for you is so that I can set you straight about the world you will find when you leave school.'

'Yes sir,' I said again.

'Don't keep saying "yes sir", boy,' he snapped, but he continued to smile. 'Now when you leave school you will find that a great many temptations will fall in your path.' He cleared his throat again.

'I feel that it is my duty to warn you firstly against loose women for they will cause you a great deal of trouble. . . . Stop smiling boy!'

'Sorry sir.'

'I wish also to warn you against drink for it will surely end in your ruination, and further I would warn you against gambling, it is a curse that has ended many a man in the bankruptcy courts.' He rumbled on about sex, sin and corruption for a good half hour and then with a handshake dismissed me from his presence.

At the time I was fourteen years of age and the war had just ended, and I was let loose on the world. I must own that every single word my worthy headmaster had to say has turned out to be God's honest truth. Loose women can indeed get you into a load of trouble and drink can destroy you both mentally and physically and as for gambling it is a curse that can end you in the poor house. However, there was one thing that my headmaster did not tell me and that is the best place in the world to find these things is Soho—that I found out for myself.

SOHO IN HISTORY

I do not intend to dwell on the history of Soho, because in the first place I am not a historian and in the second place there have been a great many books written on that subject. I am concerned more with the Soho of today and the recent past. But in point of fact what is happening to Soho today is not so different from the early beginnings when it was a small village with green fields all around and the hunting cry was SO HO! SO HO! from which Soho got its name. In these days Old Compton Street, Greek Street, Wardour and Dean Streets had not been laid out. In 1762 Sir Joshua Reynolds, Sir George Savile and others were given the job of laying the paving stones on Soho streets. Their job was not difficult for they had only the flat ground to contend with. Today Soho is being laid out again, but the job is now more difficult for first the old buildings must be demolished.

Soho Square was laid out in 1681, and later the Duke of Monmouth built a great house in the Square which some legends attributed to Wren and it became fashionable to live there. Many famous people have lived in Soho, including Sir Francis Compton, Mozart at 20 Frith Street and Hazlitt died farther along at No. 6 and was buried in St Anne's churchyard which is now a car park. There are few of the old houses still standing and only one preserved with some semblance of its former magnificence and that is No. 1 Greek Street, better known as the House of Charity and now known as the House of St Barnabas. Built between 1746 and 1748 it became the home of a Richard Beckford who was Member of Parliament for Bristol. He was a very rich man and lavished a great deal of money on the decoration of the interior, but did not enjoy it for long for he died after he had lived in the house for only two years. According to the rate books in the Westminster Library there were several tenants after Beckford died until it was taken over by the charity in 1862. Today the house is run for the benefit of unmarried mums, saved suicides, epileptics and the like. All the inmates are women and I gather that there is great excitement when the police arrive with a 'nice' girl who they think is too good for the cells. The police are also not above carting off Irish ladies who have had a drop too much of the hard stuff and see the words 'charity' and 'Saint' together and reckon that they are home and dry. However, they do not find themselves 'home' but they do find themselves 'dry'. The warden is a very pleasant and patient lady and can hardly be blamed for the poorhouse atmosphere about the place, for all such places have an atmosphere of poverty about them.

At the back of the house there stands a French Gothic chapel, the foundation stone of which was laid by Mrs Gladstone in 1863; it has been described as a miniature cathedral and it is said that it stands on the exact site of Dr Manette's lodgings in *A Tale of Two Cities*.

In 1760 Teresa Cornely bought Carlisle House in Soho Square and it is thought that Casanova with whom she was having an affair which had gone on for years, gave her the money to do so. She ran it as a sort of night club for The Nobility and Gentry, giving balls and masquerades and charging her guests two guineas. They were so successful that she increased her price to five guineas for one gentleman or two ladies. A newspaper scribe of the time wrote the following piece about one of her parties on May 19, 1770.

> 'Mrs Cornely's taste never appeared with greater *eclat* than in the arrangements of the lights, and the economy of the supper and dessert, where plenty and elegance went hand in hand. The new rooms were capacious and genteel, and well adapted for such an occasion. Among the characters and best supported was Lord Ogleby by Mr R——. He kept up the genuine spirit of the character with the greatest propriety the whole night without a masque; his gallantry to the ladies, which was rather *eutr'e*, afforded much diversion. . . . Mr Oliver changed his dress from a Ballad-singer to a Doll, and was very droll. Cardinal Wolsey was a great teaser to many of the insipids, and displayed much wit. Abraham Snip, by Mr Vaughan, was justly regarded as one of the most capital characters in the room.
>
> Miss G——, in Leonora, looked charming; she sung the favourite air in the Paddock with great sweetness. The situation of her pretty tame bird was envied by many. . . . The Lady ran mad for the loss of her lover was a character well sustained for some time; but she soon recovered her senses: no other madhouse could have administered more effectual remedies . . .'

If some one gave such a party in Soho these days, the chances are it would be raided by the law. Today the old houses of Soho echo to the sound of office typewriters, telephone bells, adding machines and photostat machines. It is hard to imagine the days gone by when 'great personages' flitted about from one stately home to the next without the slightest fear of being run over by a taxi or a newspaper van.

Another Soho-ite of days gone by was Wordsworth, who was painted by Pickersgill, one of the most prolific painters of his age, who in the course of his career exhibited no less than 400 portraits at the Royal Academy. Wordsworth wrote to Henry Crabb Robinson in 1833: 'In passing through Soho Square, it may amuse you to call in upon Pickersgill, the portrait painter, where he will be gratified to introduce you to the face of an old friend.' A few months later Robinson went to visit Pickersgill at his studio and wrote in his diary: 'I went with Mrs Aders to Pickersgill's, to see his portrait of Wordsworth. It is in every respect a fine picture, except that the artist has made the disease of Wordsworth's eyes too apparent. The picture wants an oculist . . . .'

People from all walks of life have lived and still do live in Soho. Lords and Ladies, Admirals and Generals, Writers and Artists, Bums and Layabouts of every nationality in the world. Few people are actually born there but many die there from many causes, from gun shot to a sudden heart attack, from drinking too much brandy or breathing petrol fumes.

It is hard today to imagine a charming picture of the Soho end of Oxford Street as described by a Madame von la Roche, a German woman who came to London in 1786.

> 'We strolled up and down lovely Oxford Street this evening, for some things look more attractive by artificial light. Just imagine a street taking half an hour to cover from end to end, with double rows of brightly shining lamps, in the centre of which stands an equally long row of beautifully lacquered coaches, and on either side there is room for two coaches to pass one another; and the pavements, inlaid with flag-stones, can stand six people deep and allows one to gaze at the splendidly lit shop fronts in comfort.'

Some hopes today! I have known it take half an hour or more to drive from one end of Oxford Street to the other in a high powered sports car on a clear day. Soho like almost all other parts of London has lost all signs of leisure and easiness: everything moves at such a rate that one does not know whether one is coming or going. Soho today is essentially a place of business: there are Clubs, Bookshops, Film Distributors, Strip Joints, Clip Joints, Pubs, Gambling Rooms and especially Restaurants. The charming lanes as described in the history books have turned into a maze of one-way streets, lined with parking meters and 'no parking' signs. The houses of Carlisle, Monmouth, Falconberg and Compton have either been smashed to the ground to make room for Council flats or are now used as offices of one kind and another.

Yet all the same Soho has an atmosphere not to be found anywhere else in London. The elegance of the early days has gone long ago but the Soho of today has much to offer. There are so many sides to Soho and so many things going on that it is difficult to know where to begin. In any house on any street there may be many tenants; on the top floor a tailor, on the second floor a prostitute (not of the type that saved Thomas De Quincey with a reviving drink), on the first floor a film cutting room and at street level a Chinese Restaurant. God only knows what might be going on in the basement, a gambling den perhaps or maybe the occupant is an aged old widow desperately trying to survive on a meagre pension.

In every street many businesses rub shoulders with each other, trying to do each other out of trade; a night club next door to a bakery, a strip joint next door to a dirty book shop, a bank next to a publishing house with a big overdraft, a pub next to a film distributors, or an Italian restaurant next door to an Indian restaurant.

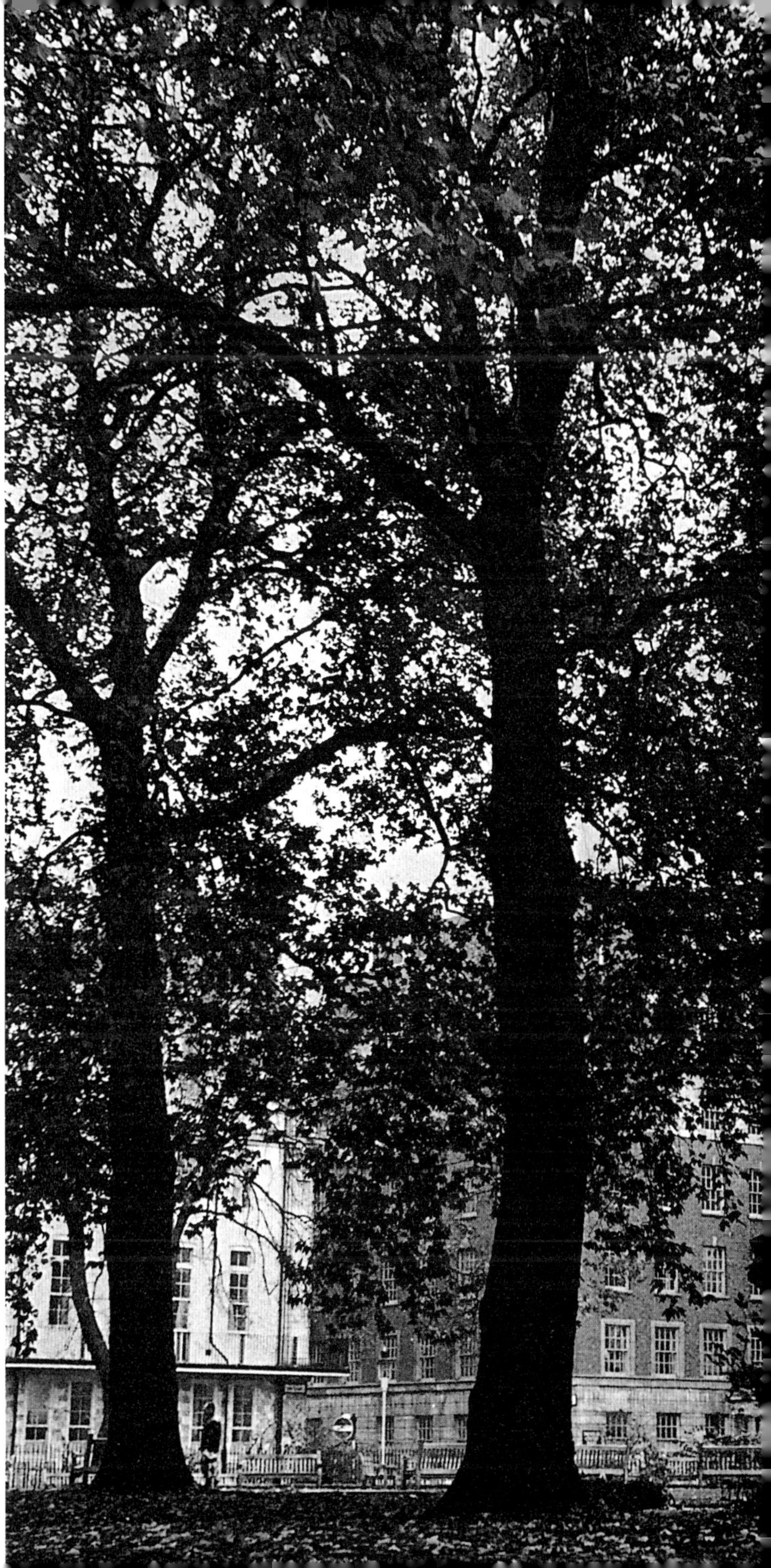

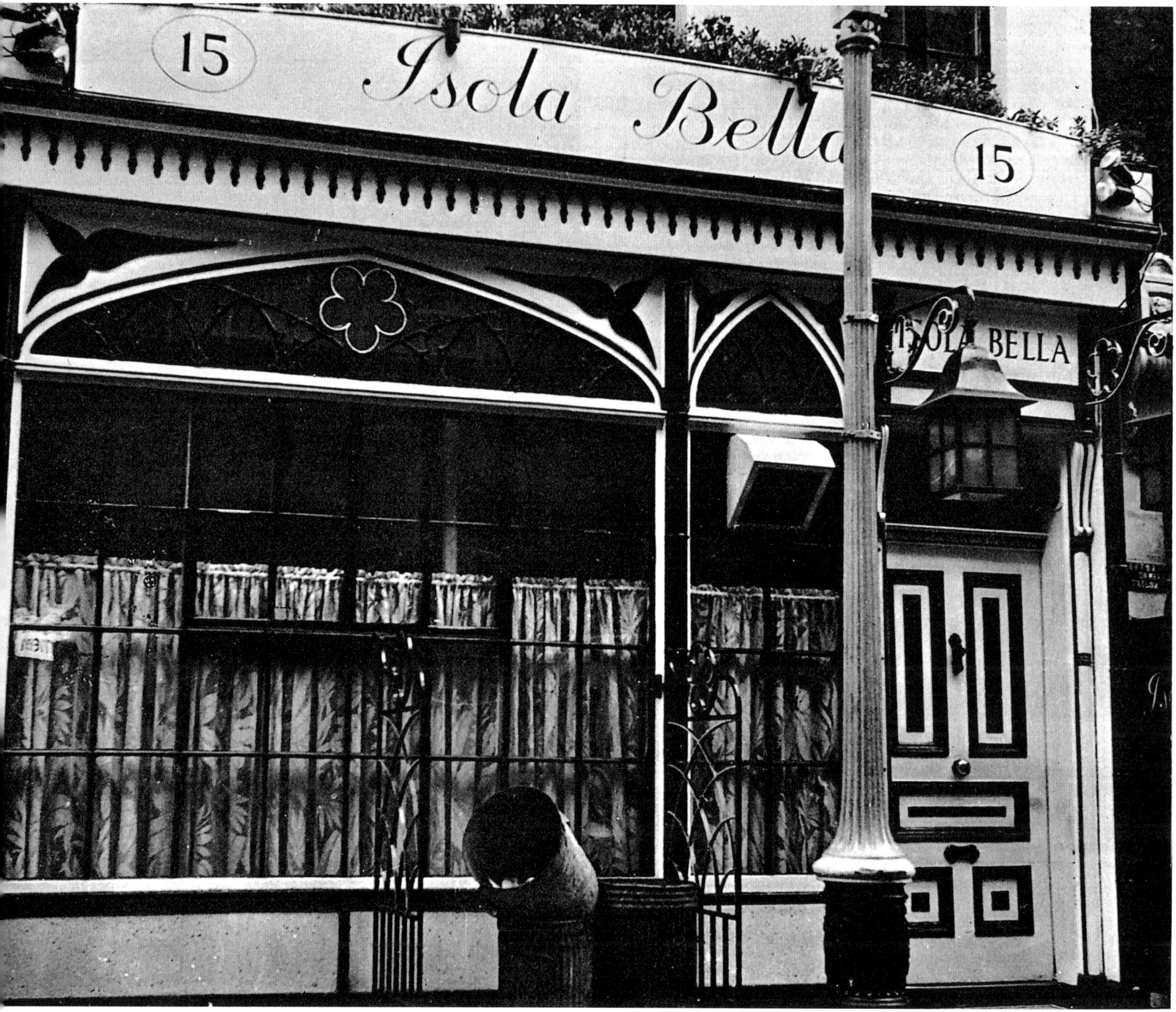
15
Isola Bella
15
ISOLA BELLA

SOHO RESTAURANTS

As there are more restaurants in Soho than there are anything else in Soho, I think it might be best to deal with them first. Hundreds of tons of food are sold in Soho's many restaurants every day, cooked by an army of chefs and served by another army of waiters wearing shiny soup stained monkey suits. Actually Soho's restaurants are not posh in the sense that The Caprice or The Mirabelle is posh. The main interest of a Soho restaurateur is that the food that he serves is of the best. There are not many dishes that cannot be had in these restaurants: Chinese, Indian, Italian (these days more than anything else), German, Hungarian, French, Spanish, Greek, and, except at Mrs Beaton's restaurant at No. 4 Greek Street, I cannot remember ever having had any English. With the exception of Wheeler's in Old Compton Street it is almost impossible to find an English waiter, for very nearly always you will find that the waiter who serves you is of the same nationality as the food on your plate. For the most part the waiters are either middle-aged or old, with flat feet and grey faces topped with silver hair. It is not easy to get youngsters to take up the trade. This I do not find very surprising because all they have to look forward to if they take a job as a commis waiter is long hours and not too much money at the end of the week, whereas if they get a job in a factory they will get more money and not have to work such long hours to earn it.

I was recently talking to an old waiter friend of mine, who has worked in Soho for over forty years, and he told me that in his opinion the days of the good restaurant are numbered. The younger generation, it appears, have not got as sensitive palates as their fathers and grandfathers. These days people go into cafeterias and devour anything and everything that is put in front of them, and never give it a second thought.

Apparently in the old days a father would take his son to his favourite restaurant and introduce him to the head waiter. He would then teach his son how to eat and what wines to drink with what dish. He would also teach him how to detect a good wine from a bad one, and also how to tip; my old friend tells me that young men these days either tip far too much in order to impress their girl friends or through sheer ignorance, or else they will tip far too little because they are mean or also through ignorance. It certainly is a far cry from the elegance that was once Soho.

Though most of the restaurant people do their level best to cook you the best meal they possibly can, in the cleanest conditions possible and with a maximum of service, there are some who have been spoiled by success, as a result of which the food has gone off and the staff have become rude and indifferent to complaints. How they manage to stay in business I do not know, but imagine that it must be for the same reasons as when a bad play runs 'Because people go to see it'. One such restaurant that I visited in connection with the writing of this book (it shall be nameless) invited both myself and my illustrator to dinner, a pleasure unasked for, in order that we might take some pictures and also talk a little about the restaurant in the hope that I would be able to collect some material for the text. Upon our arrival at the appointed time (I remember it was New Year's Eve) we were greeted coldly by our host and then completely ignored by him. After a while our host sent over his brother-in-law or it may have been son-in-law, who curtly asked us our business. I explained somewhat uncomfortably that we had been asked to come by the owner, whereupon we were informed that he was far too busy to see us now. I glanced across the room to where he was sitting drinking a large glass of brandy, and remember thinking that he did not look as busy as all that. Thinking the relation had not understood what I had been saying, I explained again that we had in fact been invited and that we had turned down another dinner invitation in order to come. This moved him neither one way nor the other. His attitude became somewhat offensive and we became exasperated and left. This sort of thing is by no means uncommon in Soho these days: some tradesmen are liable to be short with customers and goods are sometimes of poor quality and fantastically expensive. However people come from far and wide to shop in Soho shops and in some cases it seems to me that the ruder tradesmen are, the better the customers like it, but then of course I suppose that is not all that surprising these days.

After interviewing several restaurant owners, I was not really very surprised to find that almost all of them had the same tale to tell. They came to this country from Greece or France or where-

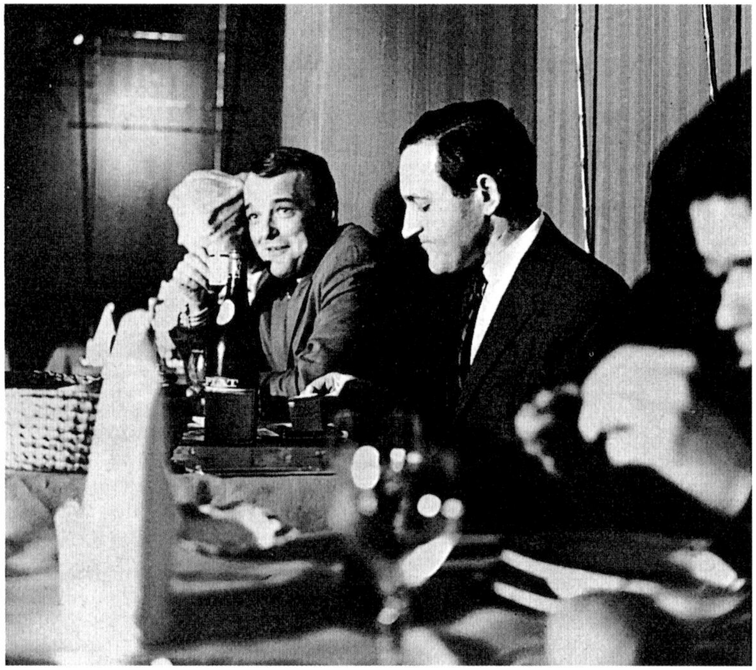

ever, without a penny to bless themselves with, got jobs washing dishes, and then became waiters until eventually they had saved enough to open their own restaurant, only in a small way at first but gradually building their business up, until today they have a very large restaurant serving two or three hundred lunches and dinners, and some of them have even got a whole chain of places.

Are all of these stories true? I wonder. Some of them come very pat. But one such story which certainly *is* true is that of Mr Leoni of the Quo Vadis which is situated half-way up Dean Street. He came to London from Cannero, Italy, in 1907, at the age of nine, and got himself a job scrubbing pots in a kitchen. By slow stages he worked his way up until nineteen years later, that is to say 1926, Leoni, now a young man, opened his own restaurant, the Quo Vadis. In those days he only had seven tables and used to take about twelve and twopence per day. Slowly but surely he built his business up until today he has the whole of the three floors of the building in which he first had these seven tables. He serves about 450 lunches and dinners in season and about 250 out of season. Mr Leoni is not in the least bit spoilt by his success. He tells me that a customer who wants some beans on toast and a glass of water is as welcome as the customer who wants a three course meal and a bottle of wine.

When we went along to see him, without any hesitation whatever he asked us to dinner. He said that if it was all right with us he would choose our dinner for us and see to the cooking of it himself. We agreed and I must say that we made no mistake in doing so. We sat down at the table and were served with melon followed by Scampi Brochet which is served with a delicious tomato sauce–the head waiter then brought us a bottle of Sabioncella '52, a very delicate white wine, and for our main course we had *poulet supremo Dario* which is the most delicious way of cooking chicken I have ever tasted in my life. For afters we had Bambolino Orange which I might say I had some difficulty in getting down on account of being extremely full by this time: with our coffee and brandy we were given an extremely good cigar. Eventually it was time to go, so we thanked Mr Leoni very much for the meal. As we were about to leave he said: 'If you don't feel well in the morning look in at the Italian Hospital in Queen Square, and just mention my name and they will take care of you.' Upon asking him why, he told me that he did the catering for the hospital. I can only think that the patients must live like lords and come out twice as fit as they were when they went in.

Mr Leoni employs a staff of about seventy, seven of whom are members of his own family. He told me with a smile: 'If they don't work then they don't get no spaghetti.' There are twenty men working in the kitchen which is absolutely spotless: 'My kitchen is not as clean as the Savoy's . . . the Savoy's is as clean as mine,' he said.

His remarks on customers are somewhat mixed, but then of course this is not surprising, because although it becomes less and less obvious we are still individuals. He says that in his opinion the English are without doubt the greatest gourmets in the world. I must say that I was very surprised to hear him say this because the fact is we have the reputation for being the worst. I mentioned as much to him, whereupon he became even more insistent. 'The English business man comes into my restaurant at lunch time,' he said. 'He may be with a client and the reason for the lunch is to discuss business. But he will not discuss the business over the meal, he will do that in the bar before they go and sit down at their table to eat.' On the other hand he tells me that an Italian or Frenchman will not stop talking business throughout the whole of the meal, and therefore does not enjoy it nearly as much. Though I must say that I have not found this to be always the case, it is very nice of Mr Leoni to have such a high opinion of us.

Until recently another restaurant, as new as Quo Vadis is long-established, was the No. 4. This was run by two friends, Bill Stortan and Michael Stafford, who are two Australians who have been over here more years than they care to think about. Michael opened the No. 4, which is No. 4 Greek Street, about three years ago, and was joined by Bill Stortan eight months after he opened. (As a matter of interest Bill had already got a great knowledge of the restaurant business from another place that he ran in Chelsea called La Popote.) Their aim was to offer their customers simple food served in elegant surroundings, and I must say that they succeeded in doing so very well indeed. The restaurant was on two floors, the ground floor and the basement. The ground floor, being the main room, was decorated by Jay Hutchinson, in a very dark shade of green with gold trelliswork and gold roses, and was extremely dark and intimate. Though I liked this room for dinner I found it a little too much for lunch. The basement however was not quite so overpowering: the room was known as Mrs Beaton's Tent and was designed by Loudon Sainthill. In my opinion the No. 4 was one of the only restaurants in Soho if not the whole of London where they knew how to cook vegetables which are eatable. I think this was because Bill is in fact a very good cook in his own right, and in fact many of the dishes were made from

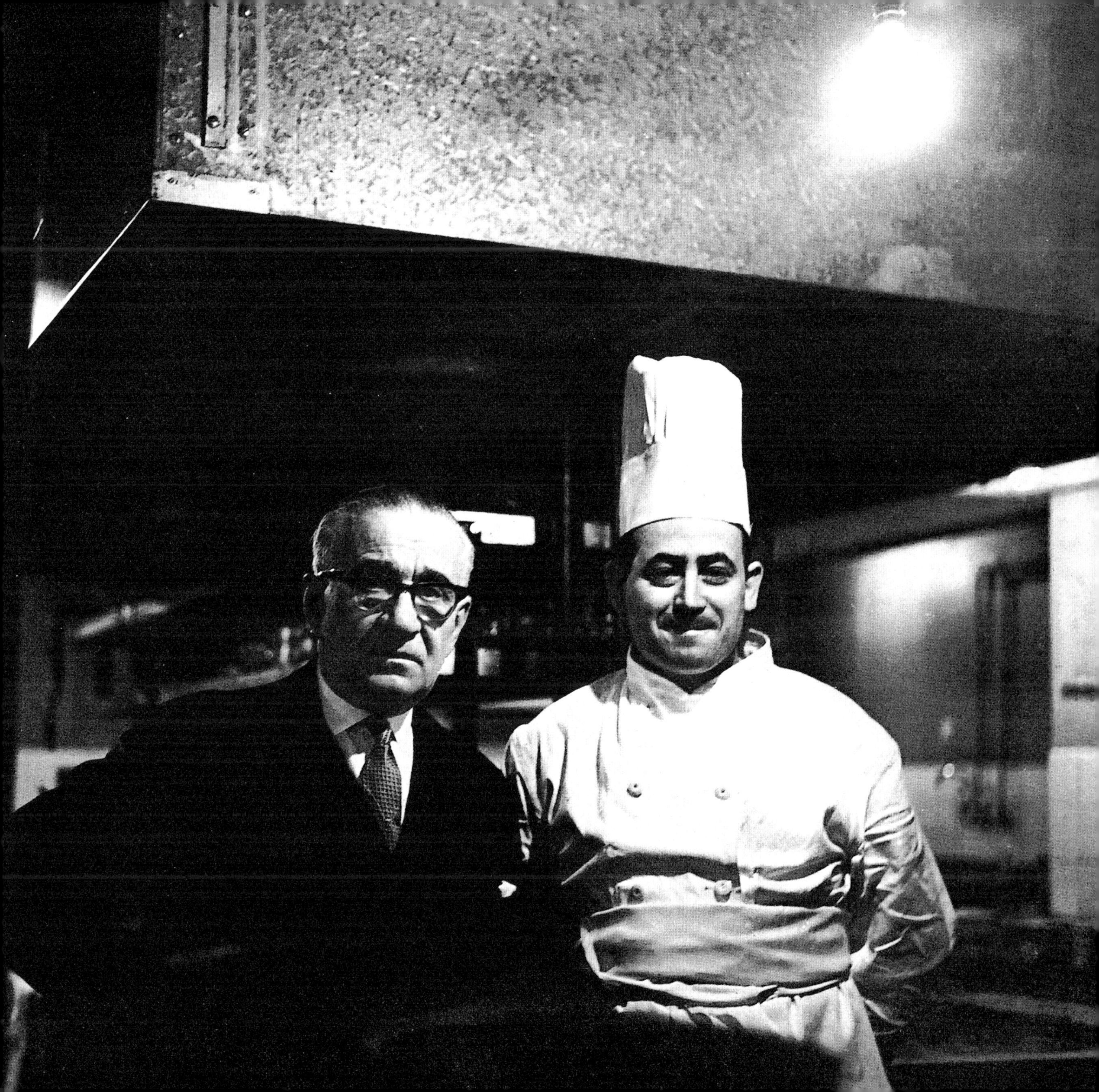

his own recipes, such as Bill's Sea Food Soup, Scampi Bill and others. However, most of the dishes were plain and simple, such as Steak and Kidney Pud, Fish Pie and Shepherd's Pie, though I must admit that I have never come across a shepherd who puts a bottle or two of red wine into his pie. Speaking of wines the No. 4 had an excellent wine list, some of which are rather rare. Personally I am not all that good at telling one wine from another, not being brought up in the way I mentioned earlier, but anyway Chateauneuf du Pape 1960 could be had at twenty-five and a tanner a bottle and Sancerre clos du Chêne Marchand 1961 at thirty-seven and a tanner, both of which I am given to understand are very good indeed.

On Soho, Bill and Michael feel that the rebuilding is spoiling the place, because although many of the old buildings are somewhat unsanitary when they are gone much of Soho's character will go with them. Perhaps this is why Bill has closed down the No. 4 and has opened a new place in Fulham Road called the Hungry Horse.

One of the biggest restaurants in Soho is Wheeler's in Old Compton Street, and the governor, Mr Bernard Walsh, is one of the greatest characters of the old school. He was born in Whitstable where his father had a small fish shop of the cockles and whelks variety. In 1928 he came to London and bought the Old Compton Street premises as a sorting house for the oysters he sold to the big hotels. At that time he used only the ground floor, but gradually people started to drop around in the mornings for a few dozen oysters to cure their hangovers, so he built a bar. And that was the beginning of one of the biggest chains of fish restaurants in the world, anyway the most famous. Having built the bar he took to boiling a few lobsters and serving a little smoked salmon, the customers bringing their own wine. Then came the war and a fortune poured into his lap. The reason was simple. During the war all restaurants were given a five bob limit: this however excluded unrationed foods and oysters were not on anyone's ration books. To be fair it must be said that Mrs Walsh ran the restaurant whilst Bernard was away in the forces. The war over, Bernard Walsh really got a move on: he opened the second floor and began to serve cooked food. Slowly but surely he opened up one floor after the other until the Old Compton Street restaurant became the biggest fish restaurant in town. As business flourished he bought other restaurants, first the Wheeler's in St James's, then the Ivy, then the Braganza, and so on until he now owns six places in London and two in Brighton. He also owns half a dozen racehorses which I'm afraid are inclined to eat well rather than run fast. At the Soho restaurant about 400 meals a day are served and 2,000 oysters are opened–it is a success story indeed. When I first began to go there it was rather more a meeting place than a restaurant, painters such as Francis Bacon and Lucien Freud and writers such as Colin Macinnes and many others could be seen daily sitting at the bar drinking gallons of white wine and eating dozens of oysters. Unfortunately those days have passed, I do not really know why but they have; nowadays we all still go there but only individually. In the season it is like being in Sardi's in New York, for the whole place is packed out with American tourists, who are all searching for a little local colour and it must be said that although the Soho layabouts do not go to Wheeler's as avidly as they used to, it is still quite a nice place to go.

On the top floor there is a room, in which the Thursday club is held, needless to say every Thursday. The members are gentlemen only, and its purpose I have never been able to find out, unless it is so that they can have a get-together in order to drink vast quantities of brandy and eat great plates of Lobster Thermidor. I am given to understand that Prince Philip is a member, though I cannot say that I have ever seen him there.

Fortunately, not all the restaurants in Soho are as expensive as the ones that I have mentioned up to now. This is just as well because not everyone has the kind of money that it takes to have dinner or lunch in them. Jimmy's Greek Basement is a great deal cheaper, the decor may not be as smart as the more expensive places and the waiters may not have as much polish but the food, though not as elaborate, is very good and wholesome. One has to shout one's order at the man behind the bar, the menu is limited to stewed beef, roast lamb, chicken pilaff and Kebab. As one sits down at one's table a waiter comes over and dumps down a great wad of bread and a green pepper in front of you. For the most part the clientele are Greeks as is the governor, but many other working-class people use it as a haunt. One can take one's own wine and the bill which is never given but only spoken never comes to more than about five or six bob. The main thing I like about Jimmy's and places like it is the atmosphere, the people are down to earth and unaffected, which is something that cannot be said for many of the phoney nits that one comes across in the posher places, where often the management's interest is only in whether or not you are able to pay your bill. In Jimmy's you take your turn whether or not you are rich or skint and they do not stand for any up-stage behaviour. My own feeling is that it is a shame that there are not more such places, because to quite a large extent Soho has been taken over by smarties who have no interest in the place whatever, apart, that is, from what they can get out of it, by feeding the middle class, who are a group of people who seem these days to have given up fighting against things that they do not like.

Getting back to the better restaurants where more expense accounts lunches (the 1965 budget has curtailed them somewhat) are served than any other part of town one can get a lunch for five or six pounds for two on your credit card, or cash in a luncheon voucher for four bob. If you stand around in a Soho street between 12.30 and 1 p.m. you will see Rolls-Royce cars stop outside good restaurants, they are driven by liveried chauffeurs who jump out and open the doors so that elegant ladies escorted by fat gentlemen may alight, the fat gentlemen get fatter and the ladies take good care of themselves. Show biz girls arrive with their agents or lovers for a meal at an Italian restaurant before going off to do a matinée at one of the theatres in Shaftesbury Avenue, or else they will go and buy a new pair of dancing shoes at Gamba's on the corner of Dean Street, and bums will bum a lunch from someone or other who has the price of it; the more successful bums may manage to get a free lunch every single day.

To be quite honest it is only in very recent years that I have been an eater of good food and yet I have been around Soho since I was sixteen years of age, during which time I have spent more time in places like Jimmy's Greek Basement than I have anywhere else. Also I cannot say that I like the thick sauces as much as all that, though they are there in abundance to be eaten until they come out of your ears. It is interesting to note that few of the Soho people go to the Soho restaurants, either because

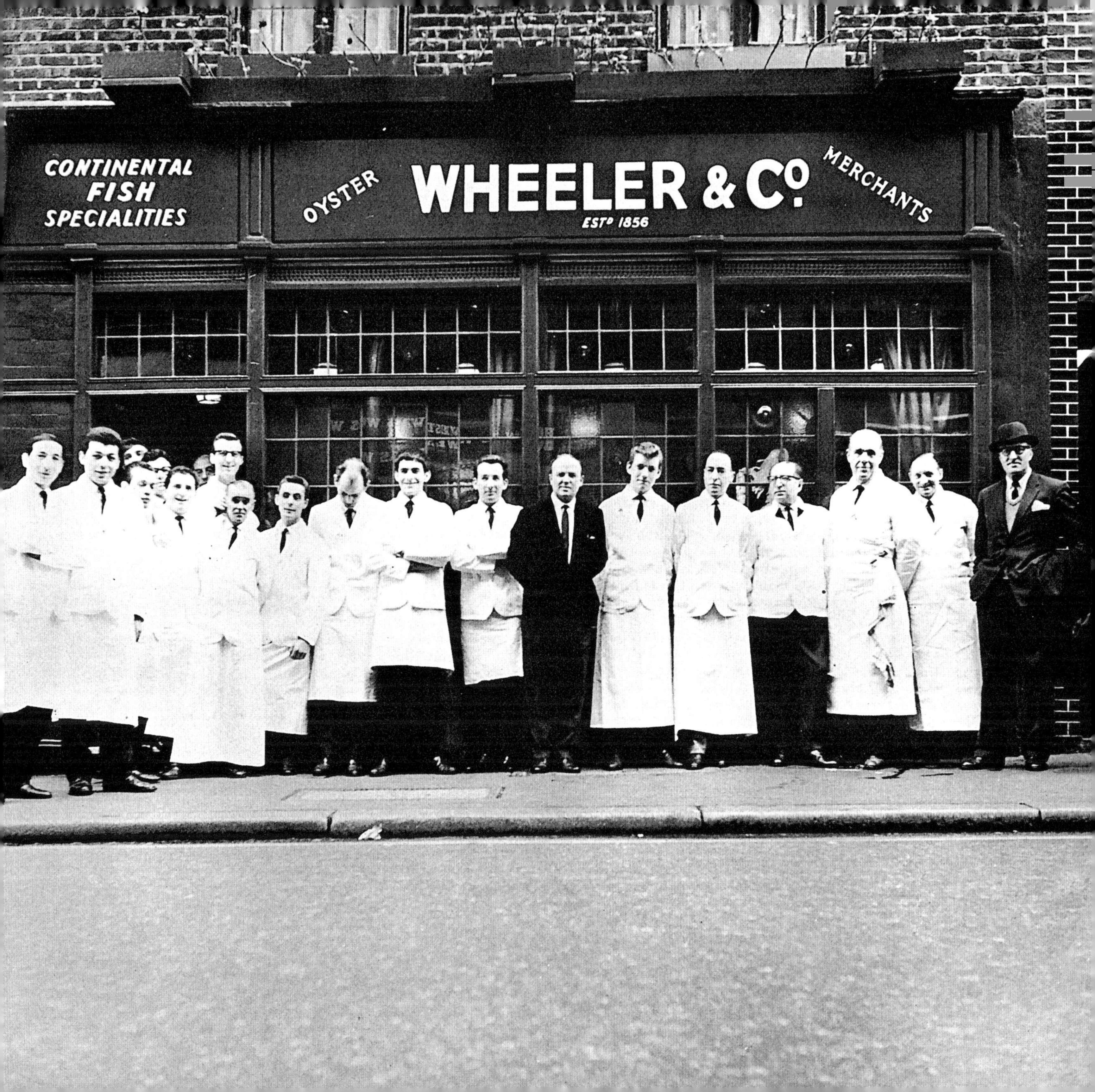
CONTINENTAL
FISH
SPECIALITIES
OYSTER
WHEELER & Co
ESTD 1856
MERCHANTS

they do not have time or because they think them too expensive. This includes the food suppliers and hardware salesmen, of whom there are a great many. In fact, the majority of the customers come from farther afield, from Golders Green, Kensington, Knightsbridge and Mayfair. It would be safe to say that these are the Soho restaurateurs' mainstay. However, in the season Soho restaurants are besieged by tourists from every country in the world, especially America, so much so that it is often impossible to get a table unless you book well in advance by phone.

Considering the tremendous business that the restaurants are doing, it may sound surprising that many of the restaurateurs never seem to stop moaning about how bad things are. Personally I do not think that this is from greed but rather simply for something to talk about. A French and Italian restaurant owner may meet in Berwick Street market early in the morning and ask one another how things are. 'Things is terrible,' says the Italian, 'how are things with you?'

'Terrible also.'

'But every time I look in your window you are always full up?'

'That may be but I'm still doing terrible.' The conversation will go on like this while they pick out some onions or some garlic. In point of fact they are both doing well enough, and their sons are at boarding school or at Oxford. When they have finished moaning about how bad things are, they may begin to talk about their sons who are at those posh schools, learning to be doctors, and lawyers. It is all a far cry from the days when they first arrived in this country with nothing to their names but the tattered shirts to their backs. Some of them might have been simple immigrants and others may have been political exiles, who have been here thirty years but still cannot return to their own countries for fear of being shot. They have now almost forgotten the plains of Spain where battles raged. Also forgotten are the mountains of Italy, their life now is the restaurants, their trips to the market and trying their best to serve their customers well. They employ their fellow countrymen who no doubt will one day open their own restaurant next door, and so it goes on day in, day out, year in, year out, the struggle to make a living, the struggle to get rich and richer still. Each night their wives will count the takings; she has been sitting there all day making out the bills, she knows exactly how much each one should come to. The waiters cannot live without tips; generally, all the tips go into a box and there is the big share-out at the end of the week. The money is not shared equally: the head waiter gets the most, the next senior waiter gets the next most and so on right down to the boy commis waiters who get the least. I suppose their ambition is to become head waiters themselves.

One of Soho's oldest restaurants is Moulin D'or which was opened in 1914 by George and Ernest Stone and their mother who has since died. Though they still do very well their place has seen more romantic days. Situated in Romilly Street it was once the meeting place of people such as Douglas Fairbanks jr., Field Marshal Montgomery, in fact famous people from all walks of life, their guest book is full! In spite of rationing they managed to keep their place open throughout the whole of the last war, and somehow or other managed to get hold of enough food to serve their customers. The thing I really like about the Moulin D'or is its old world charm, the decor is modest and there are always flowers on the tables. George and Ernest are both elderly gentlemen, and can

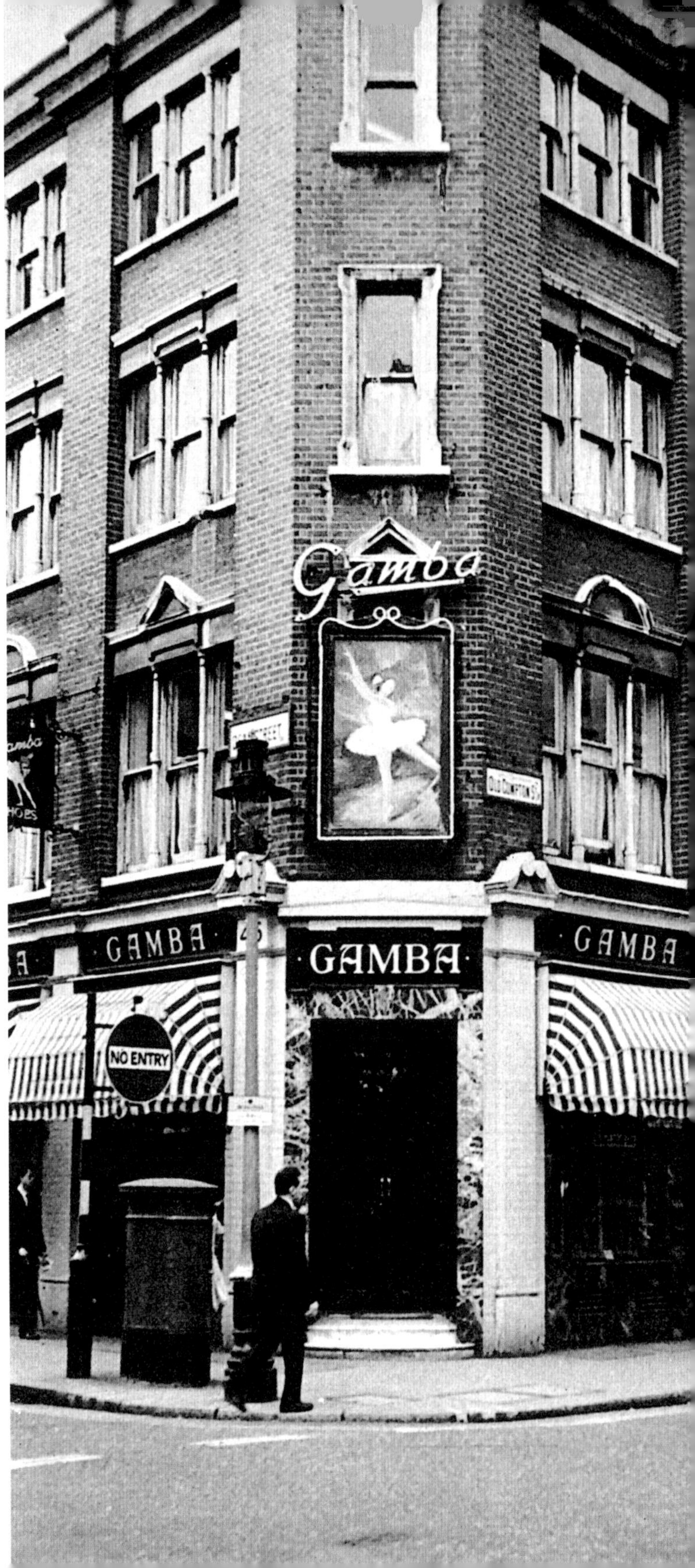

remember a time when Soho had much more of the village atmosphere about it. When I went along to have a chat with the brothers we got around to talking about Soho of the more recent past. George in particular feels that Soho 'has never been more sordid or filthy'. When I asked him why he felt this, he said that before the street offences act of 1959 which made soliciting in the streets a serious offence the sweet prostitutes would roam the streets with impunity from lunch time till dawn saying: 'Short time darling?' to any man that passed by. But they had charm and looked pretty. George told me of one little French girl who had a little room on the opposite side of the road from his restaurant. In the winter she would get up early in the morning and brush the snow from the pavement outside her door so that her clients would not get snow on their shoes and take it into her room. Such charming acts are no longer to be seen around Soho, the girls have become hard from fear of being arrested and have gone underground. Personally I am in complete agreement with George Stone, things around Soho are not nearly so nice now that the girls have gone and I think that the Home Secretary should be hailed as the Patron Saint of ponces for he has made their work much easier and much less risky. It is no longer necessary for them to skulk about in dark shop doorways to keep an eye on their girls, in order that they do not get troubled by the law or any nasty clients.

Another complaint of the Stone brothers, and they are not alone, is the sudden restrictions of one kind and another which are being inflicted on restaurateurs by the police and the fire officers. Many restaurants, the Moulin D'or is one of them, have been ordered to build fireproof walls in the oddest places such as half-way up the stairs for instance. This rebuilding has to be done at the owner's expense and to the specifications of the fire officer. As has been pointed out to me (in spite of the fact that it was obvious) these buildings have been standing for hundreds of years without being burnt to the ground, so why all of a sudden is everyone panicking; personally I think building fireproof walls etc. is tempting providence. Another stupid law is that your bottle of wine that you are having with your lunch must be taken off the table on the dot of three o'clock, though you may still have some in your glass until 3.30 p.m. On days when I have had to have a late lunch, head waiters have apologetically poured out four glasses of wine for me so that they could take the bottle away by three o'clock. The first time this happened to me I thought he had gone mad, my life I don't know why they can't leave people alone, after all one does not get such treatment in Paris or New York, it is little things like this that make the public angry and restaurateurs exasperated because of the pettiness of it all. One of these days I am going to have a quick look in Trenchard House, the coppers' doss house just off Berwick Street, and see what is happening there. I should not like to find them breaking the law at all.

I should think that there are more than 100 restaurants in Soho so it would be impossible to go into all of them. There is The Escargot, a famous old place which has recently had a face lift. Around the corner there is the Café Blue where you can get yards and yards of spaghetti with rich brown sauce and round the corner again you come upon an Indian restaurant, in fact, wherever you look in Soho you will see a restaurant, Trattoria or a Coffee House.

TRATTORIAS AND COFFEE HOUSES

Of the many Trattorias that have opened in the last few years, Mr Leoni, of the Quo Vadis, says that he does not think of them as restaurants, but more as cafes. Though I think that in a lot of cases he has a point, there are however a few exceptions. Probably the most successful is the Trattoria Terrazza in Romilly Street, which opened five years ago and is run by two Italians called Mario and Franco. It is not always easy to tell why one place becomes an immediate success and another place is a flop, I suppose it is something to do with luck and something to do with magic. Anyway from the moment the Trattoria opened it was instantly popular, it is patronized by writers and painters, film directors and extras and also a great cross-section of businessmen and lovers, the atmosphere is very Italian which I am sure is part of its charm and Mario particularly is the most Italian Italian you could ever wish to find outside of Rome. The decoration is also very Italian, what with volcanoes painted on the walls and fresh grapes hanging from the ceiling. When you enter the restaurant you are greeted as though you are a long lost brother. Both of the owners have been here many years—Mario, 18 years and Franco, 24 years—so they understand the English well enough to know that if one is in a bad mood the best thing to do is to leave one alone. This too they do at the Trattoria, which is more than can be said for many places. Mario and Franco are very fond of Soho and think of it as a village, they miss people when they are not around, and are genuinely interested in what one is doing, this, of course, can be a bore, but I do not find it so with Mario and Franco. The place has recently had a face lift, but has lost none of its garlic flavour.

Though I do not think there are as many coffee bars as there are restaurants there are certainly a great many, in every street you will find at least two or three. Actually they are very nearly all restaurants these days, for although they sell quite a lot of coffee they also serve just as many meals, such as Eggs and Chips, Sausage and Chips, Spaghetti and Chips (which must be disgusting), in fact, like the title of the play, 'Chips with Everything'. The most famous is the 2i's which is at the Wardour Street end of Old Compton Street. Run by Mr Tom Littlewood it has been the springboard for many pop, rock and skiffle stars. Tom Littlewood

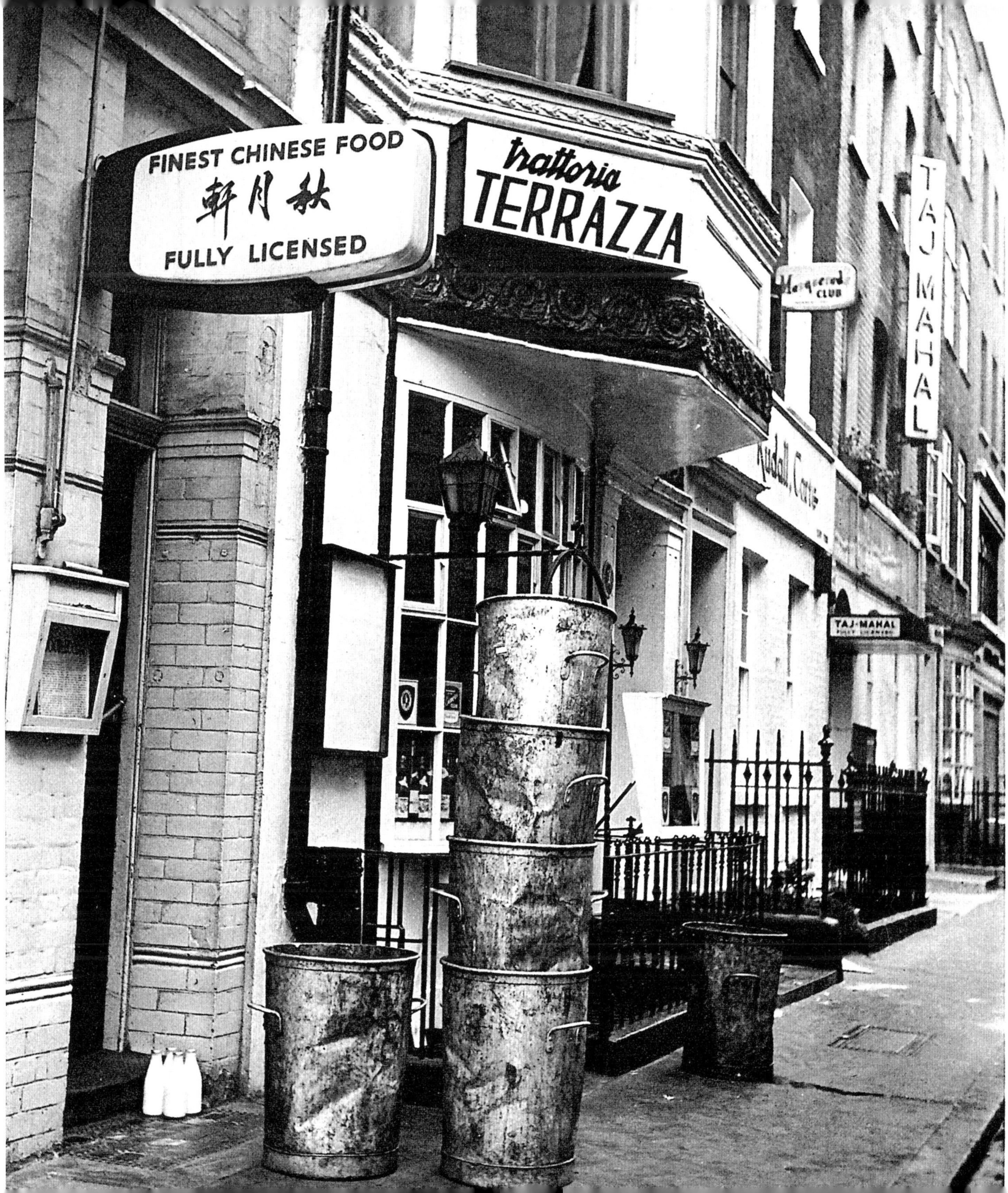
FINEST CHINESE FOOD
軒月秋
FULLY LICENSED
trattoria
TERRAZZA
TAJ MAHAL
TAJ-MAHAL

is an ex-stunt man (though I doubt the ex part of it). He is also a judo black belt which I think must come in very handy sometimes at the 2i's for I have seen some very dodgy people hanging about outside his place, but then maybe they are not dodgy at all, and it is just me. Anyway he was training at the YMCA where he met two friends, Paul Lincoln and Ray Hunter, who are a couple of wrestlers; all three were looking for something to do, so they got together and bought a cafe in Old Compton Street. At this time it was a steak house, and it was not very long before they found it very boring and decided that the thing to do was to get a Spanish guitarist in to liven the place up a bit (it was Tom Littlewood who thought of the idea). Later on they installed a Juke Box, after that one thing followed another in quick succession. Tommy Steele worked there with a skiffle group, he was a smash hit and became a star overnight. From that time on groups fought to get in. Terry Dene was the next for the glory march with Wee Willie Harris close on his heels. Then came the biggest day the 2i's has ever seen when the TV programme *Six-Five Special* was televised from the club which Littlewood had opened in the basement. Since then the 2i's has been associated with all the big names in the pop world, and has even issued its own discs. Tom Littlewood took over as full-time manager in 1958 and has run it ever since. When he isn't at the 2i's he is appearing in films, some of which have been *The Tommy Steele Story*, *Beat Girl*, and *The Criminal*, as well as many TV films. He also handles all the PRO work and having let a few thousand quid escape him he now runs his own agency and puts shows on the road. When auditioning he looks for cleancut kids who want to work hard and are lively. He has no time for layabouts, in fact there is quite a bit of the youth leader about him. His latest discovery at the time of writing is sixteen-year-old Stewart Halbert from Paisley (should he become a teenage idol, it will doubtless be by another name). Stewart appears to have all the right attributes: he is a plumber and idolizes Elvis Presley and shaves every other day. On my visit to the 2i's I met a brunette whose ambition is to become a Screaming Lady Sutch and I was not surprised to learn that her hobbies were guitars and horror films. She assured me that she loves everybody and that it is quite safe for her to be around Soho on her own because 'No one ain't never said nuffingk inoffensive to me.' After that remark I can only wish her the very best of luck.

Among the stars who have appeared at the 2i's, apart from those already mentioned, are Cliff Richard, Adam Faith, Emile Ford, Connie Francis and of course, needless to say, The Beatles. In spite of the great success of this place I have always found it very sad whenever I have passed by on the other side of the road; it seems to me that the hordes of young kids who hang about outside on the pavement just waiting about for they don't know what, are a miserable lot. I once took my courage in my hands and asked them about themselves, mostly they didn't know anything about themselves, but a few said that they reckoned that the 2i's was a good place for pulling birds. Mind you I do not remember myself having much incentive for anything when I was their age, except perhaps for a bit of earnest laying about. But in point of fact the boys and girls who hang about inside the 2i's are very respectable and work in shops and offices during the day. Tom Littlewood will not stand for any villainy in his place such as punch-up merchants or purple heart bandits; these people get an extremely short shrift.

SOHO 'MYSTERIES'

Not all the coffee houses are as respectable as the 2i's and not all the restaurants are as smart as Wheeler's. Soho is a place of great contrasts; it is as easy to have a woman as it is to buy a loaf of fresh French bread. Many of the cheap prostitutes come to London with every intention of getting a job and leading a respectable life; however, things can often be difficult for a young girl who does not know her way around and does not have any friends. Such girls if they are unlucky, will run into some ponce who will stick her out on the game before she has a chance to realise what is happening to her.

I visited a ponce's lair on the top floor of an old house in Dean Street which shall be nameless for reasons of my health. It is a little restaurant-cum-den of iniquity where hard cases gather for the purpose of discussing birds, gambling, tealeafing and villainy of one kind and another while they eat plates of egg and chips. I was sitting in this place sipping a cup of terrible coffee and feeling rather uncomfortable, because of being watched by a bunch of tearaways sitting at a table by the window. Suddenly the door opened and two young whores came in; I do not know how old they were but I do not think that they had thirty years between them. They sat down at the table next to mine, ordered some tea and then began to paint their nails. For some time I sat watching them, wondering who they were and where they had come from. The tearaways sitting by the window were also clocking them, the two birds had the unmistakable stamp of the no-homer. Their clothes were cheap and old and their hair was dyed, one red and the other blonde, both with black roots, their finger nails which they were painting red were the filthiest I have ever seen, they talked to each other in broad North country accents. Nothing ventured nothing gained, I leaned over and asked them if they would care for a cigarette. They accepted in a vicious sort of way. I offered them my packet and gave them a light. For a time they fell silent, eyeing me sullenly, no doubt trying to make up their minds whether I was a possible client or a copper.

'Have you been in London very long?' I ventured after a while.

'What's it got do with you?' said the tougher one of the two; the other one gave me a blank look and then continued painting her filthy nails.

'Sorry,' I went on nervously, 'I didn't mean any offence.'

'If you must know we've been down here for two weeks,' said

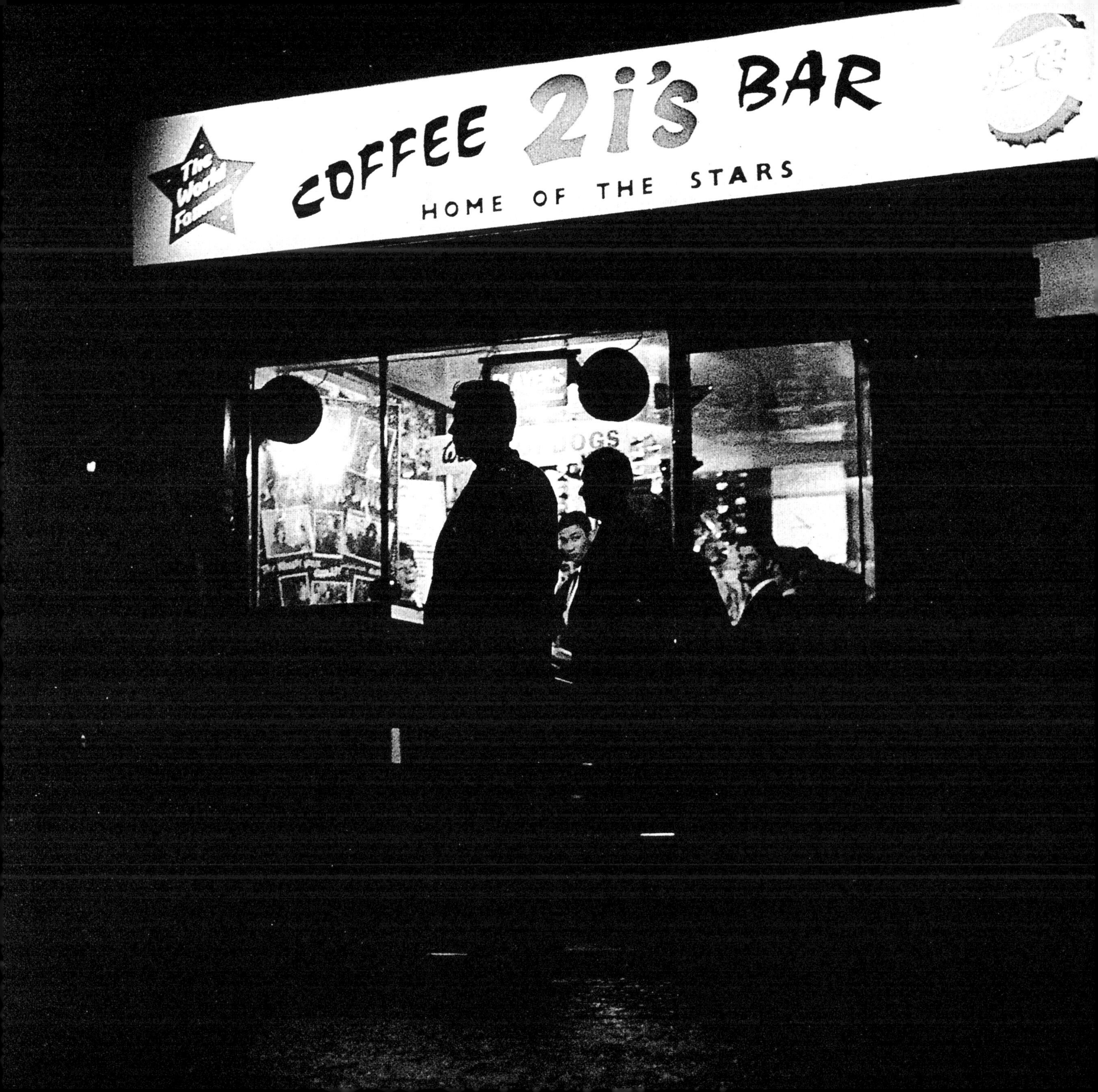
The World Famous
COFFEE 2i's BAR
HOME OF THE STARS

the less tough one, and I could tell that two weeks had been a long time.

'What are you doing?' I asked.

'Isn't he nosey?' said the tough one. 'What has it got to do with you?'

'I didn't mean any offence,' I said again. 'I just wondered if you had got a job or what, that's all?'

'If you must know we have been looking for a job, but there aren't any about,' she went on. 'How about buying us some more tea?' I beckoned to the greasy waiter behind the bar who came over to my table, and I ordered them some tea. The tearaways over by the window had now lost interest in me and were chatting away nineteen to the dozen about something that I would have loved to hear about, but could not because they were too far away. The waiter brought the teas and put them down in front of the girls who put about six spoonfuls of sugar in each. Before I had a chance to question the birds any further the door opened and two young dark haired boys came in, and walked straight over and sat down at the same table as the girls. I sat back and said no more, the boys glared at me with black eyes. 'Who's the geezer?' asked one of them. 'I don't know,' said one of the girls. I grinned sheepishly, and they ignored me.

'What are you two doing laying about in here?' asked one of the boys angrily.

'It's too cold to go out,' replied the tough girl.

'Listen, I don't care if it's cold or not,' said the other boy. 'You wonna get out and earn. Otherwise it will be the worse for you.' The little girls looked frightened. 'But there are policewomen around all over the place,' said one of them.

'If you're cunning you won't get caught,' replied one of the boys.

'Now get out, and don't come back till you've got some money,' said the other. Wearily they put their powder compacts into their plastic handbags and got to their feet and left the room. 'They won't reign long,' I thought as I watched them go out of the door.

And that is the way it is liable to be with young mysteries arriving on the manor when they are homeless and friendless. Often the only thing that can save them is if they are picked up by the law and sent back to where they came from. Sometimes a father will scour the streets of Soho in search of his erring daughter. The chances of him finding her are not very good, but should he find her the chances are she will tell him to go away and leave her alone and stop trying to run her life for her. Whereupon the unhappy parent will become so distressed that he will go to the police for help. The police go out and arrest the girl and put her in charge of the courts, who will no doubt consider her in need of care and protection; she will then be handed over to the probation officer or else put in a home. The girl will then hate her father for the rest of her life; it is all a very strange thing. For if one of these girls is heading for disaster nothing in the world will deter her from destroying herself, and all the begging and pleading of a father or mother will not make any difference. Maybe it is the boys, and maybe it is the bright lights and perhaps it is even some sort of rebellion against the times in which we live. These girls have been coming to Soho ever since I have been around, and no doubt they will still be coming around long after I am dead and gone. I left the cafe feeling somewhat brought down, and I noticed that there was blood on the stairs, it had been fairly freshly spilt.

HAMBURGER BARS

Apart from the restaurants and coffee houses, there are also the hamburger bars and bacon and egg cafes. Although they are quite popular with the passing trade, I cannot find much nice to say about them. The decor is loud, shiny and tasteless, the waitresses are liable to be very short tempered with the customers. On one of my rare visits to one of these places I ordered an egg and bacon and a cup of coffee. Imagine my surprise when I was given the bill straight away before I had hardly got my order off the end of my tongue. I then waited twenty minutes for my order to arrive, when it came the egg was overdone and the bacon underdone. This made me a little cross because I had in fact asked her to have it cooked the other way around. I saw little point in complaining for had I done so, I feel sure that I would have felt a sharp edge of someone's tongue. That is the trouble these days, people seem to stand for anything at all from anyone at all. In one of the old established Soho restaurants such behaviour on the part of a waiter or waitress would not be tolerated. The only thing that can really be said for the hamburger and egg joints is that they are cheap in every sense of the word. The frightening thought about all this is that these are the places of the future, for slowly but surely the restaurants where you can get personal service in an atmosphere of congeniality are being pushed out. As the redevelopment surges ahead and the buildings looking like corn flake packets on end go skyward the Soho people die, one day a destruction company will smash St Anne's church tower to the ground and it will be the end of Soho as a place of character as sure as the death of Scott Fitzgerald was the death of the jazz age.

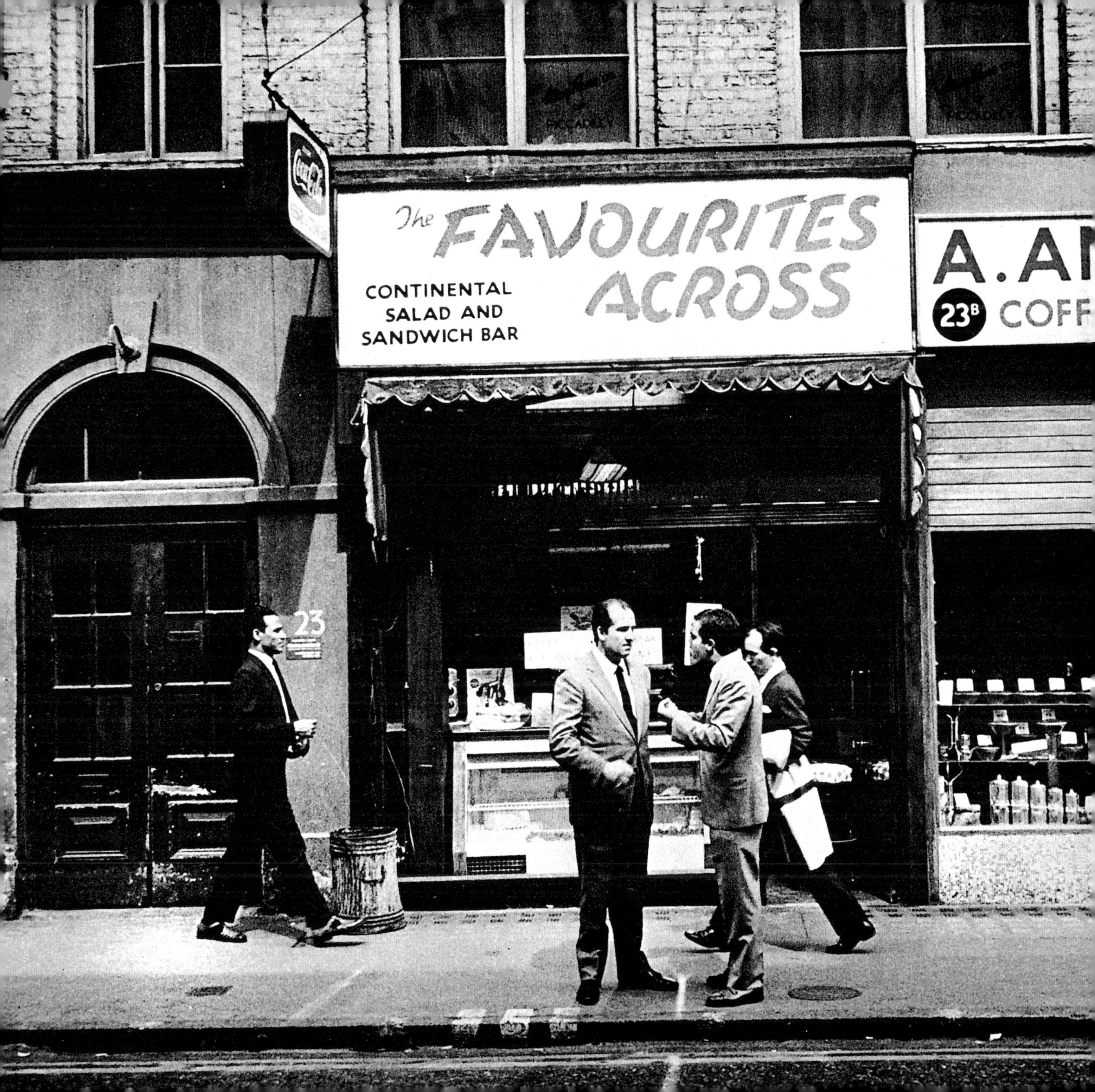
The FAVOURITES ACROSS
CONTINENTAL
SALAD AND
SANDWICH BAR
A.A
23B COFF
23

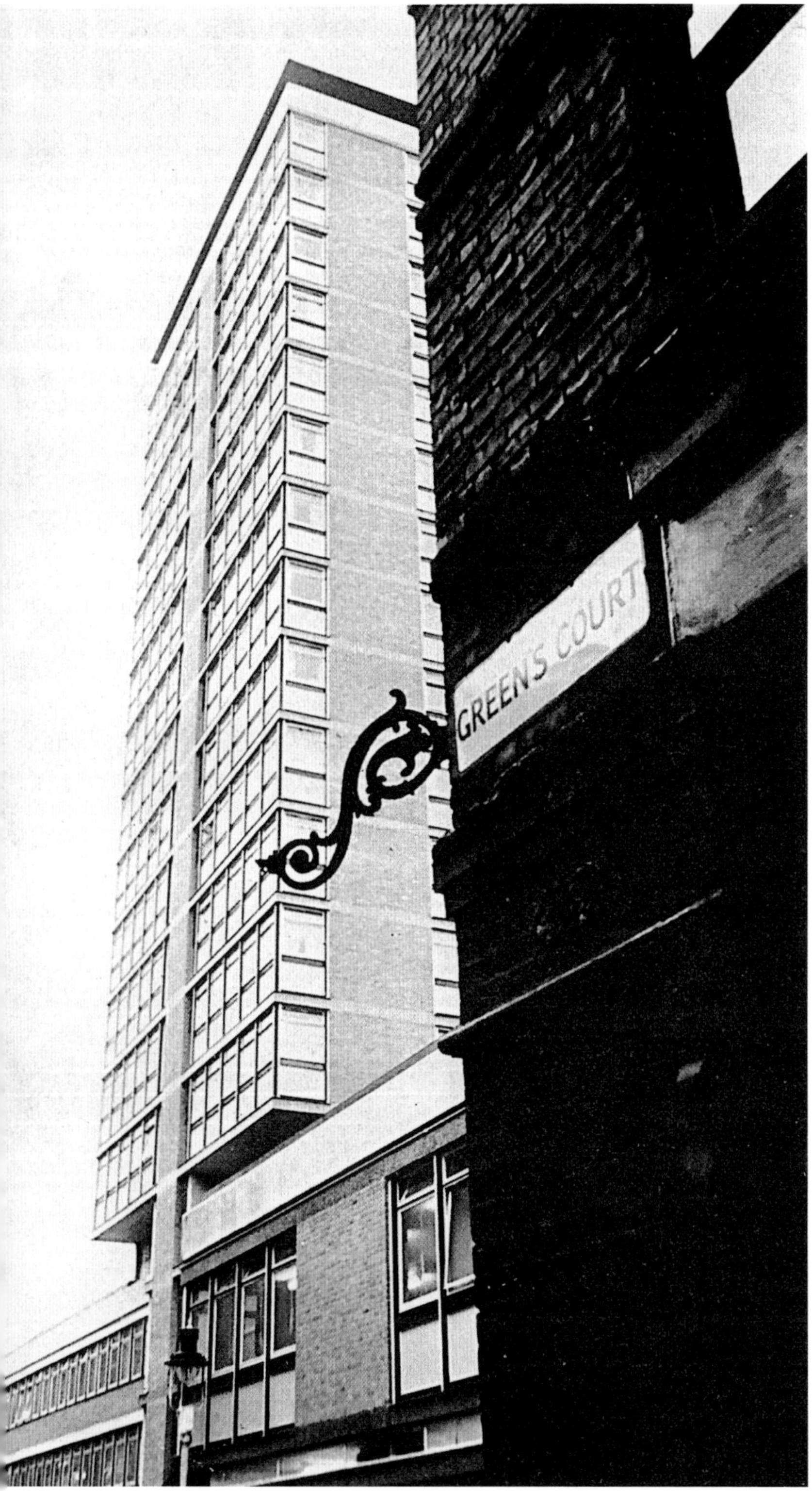
GREENS COURT

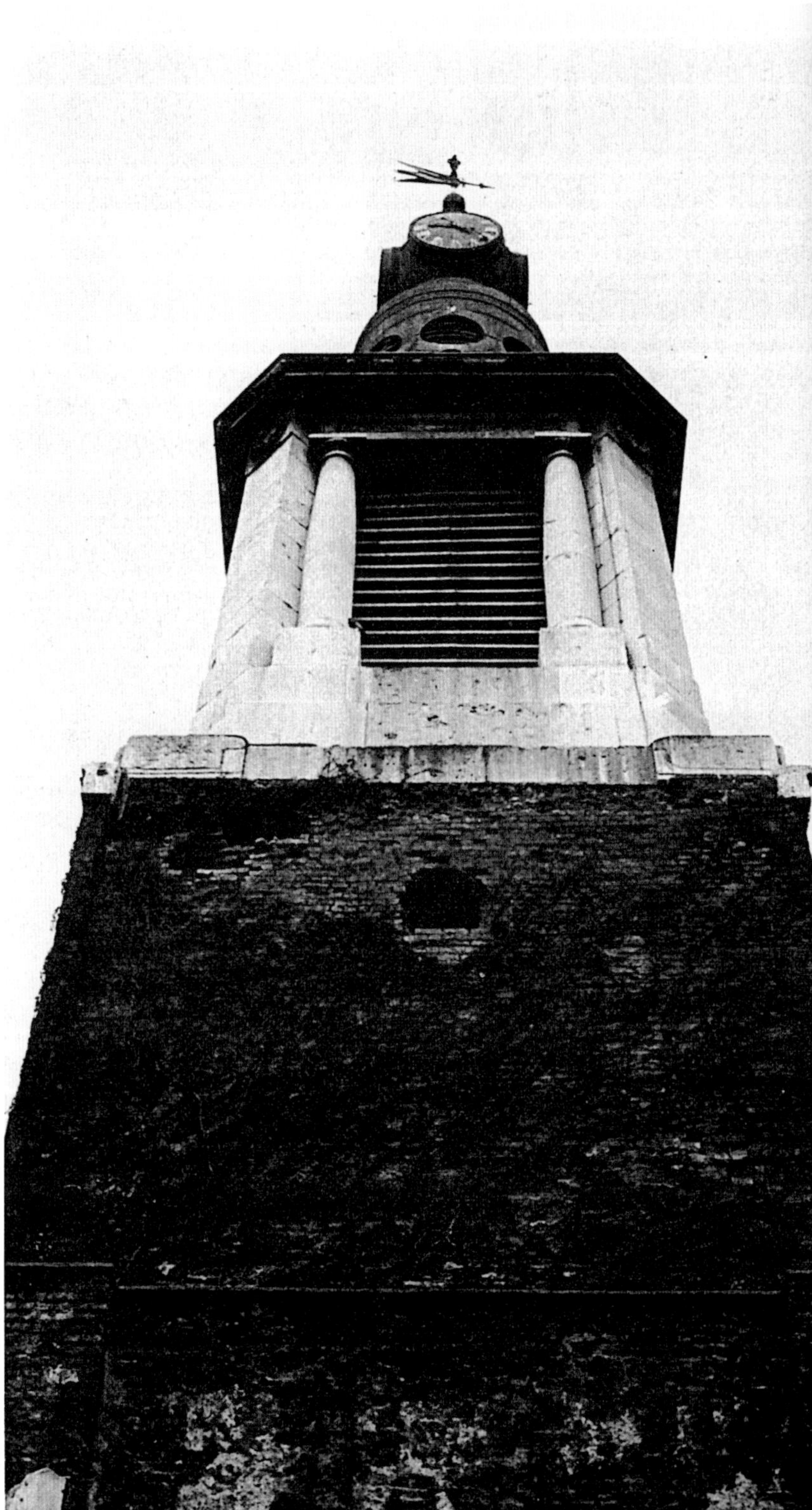

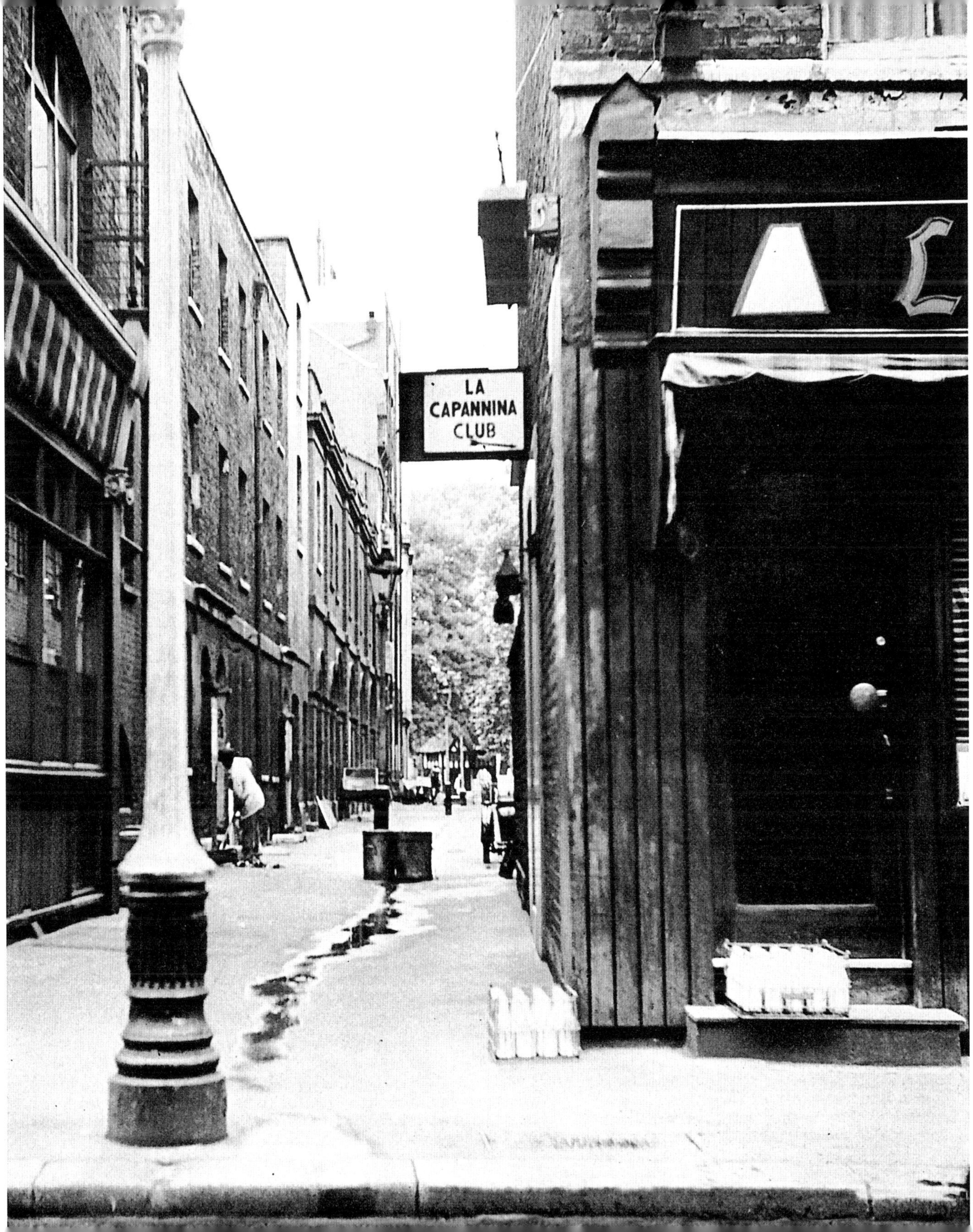
LA
CAPANNINA
CLUB

THE MARKETS

Where you have restaurants you must obviously have raw food. In fact most of the restaurateurs buy their raw materials in bulk from the big meat, fish, and vegetable markets, such as Smithfield, Billingsgate and Covent Garden, but for the smaller restaurant owner Berwick Street market and the local butcher and fishmonger is good enough. The main Soho market is in Berwick Street where one can buy anything from a pin to a pound of carrots; it is probably the most colourful part of Soho, of a lunchtime. One can hardly walk along the street for shoppers jostling each other as they hunt for bargains.

Most of the stalls sell vegetables but there are also jewellery stalls of the paste variety, fly pitchers flogging nylons from suitcases and keeping an eye out for the law, hardware shops where you can buy anything from a tin opener to a bloody great casserole which can hold a hundred pints of soup. They are a pretty tough lot of business people; in fact when we wandered along the street with our cameras a very hard looking barrow boy mentioned: 'If ya takes me bleedin' pickcher I'll smash both ya bleedin' 'eads in!' We beat a hasty retreat to the nearest boozer where we took sanctuary. Fortunately, however, not everyone was as camera shy as this. In fact mostly they are a very friendly bunch, the old lady with the secondhand clothes stall has been there for fifty years as has the old flower seller. Most of the stalls are handed down from one generation to the next and I was somewhat surprised to learn that they did not mind the changing face of Soho. In Berwick Street there is a great block of council flats which houses several hundred families. One stallholder told me that since this building has gone up his weekly takings have gone up by double. When I asked him about the block of flats and places like it changing the character of the place, he said that he could not care less about that, if it was good for business then it was good for Soho. I suppose he has a point but not everyone sees it quite like that.

The local people are by no means the only people who shop in Berwick Street. Pretty office girls wearing black leather boots and tight skirts come to buy a new pair of nylons to wear to a dance they are going to on Saturday night at The Hammersmith Palais or else the latest Beatles record to play at a party. A flamboyant businessman will come to buy a flashy tie to wear on his holiday in the South of France. A housewife from Chelsea will come to get a copper frying pan or some garlic and a pickpocket will come and whiz a fat old gent's watch or wallet.

The customers mill about in their thousands looking here, buying something there, or stand and chat for a while to a friend outside a strip joint, not having the slightest idea what is going on on the other side of the wall behind them. Coppers seem never to stop pinching the street traders for obstruction: many of them get pinched once a week and have to appear in front of His Beakship the next morning to be fined yet again. At the end of each day the road sweepers and tramps come to clear up the mountains of rubbish, the tramps collect a few lettuce leaves here, a potato there, and a few squashed tomatoes somewhere else. All over the street there are masses of paper, orange boxes, rotting vegetables and the like: it is all swept into great piles and left for the dust cart to collect in the early hours of the morning after the wandering mongrel dogs have had a good rummage in it.

Around the corner from Berwick Market is Brewer Street which runs from Regent Street to Wardour Street. It is a street in which most human wants can be gratified, prostitutes hang out of top floor windows and there are strip joints everywhere you look. At street level it caters for the suburban housewife with the most marvellous selection of food that you could ever wish to revolt your friends with. You can buy squid, vast lobsters, barrels of oysters or fish called John Dory whose head is so hideous that most fishmongers protect their customers by removing it before putting it on show. Conger eels can also be got by the squirming yard. There is one shop in Brewer Street which has been advertising its last final reductions for at least three years to my knowledge. As a matter of fact it is worth missing the bargains and crossing the road to the other side where you will find Lina Stores, an Italian shop which is run by a whole family of aunts, nieces, nephews, neighbours and their children, all of whom chatter away in cockney Italian from morning till night. You can buy pasta of every shape and size in an atmosphere not to be found elsewhere this side of the Italian border.

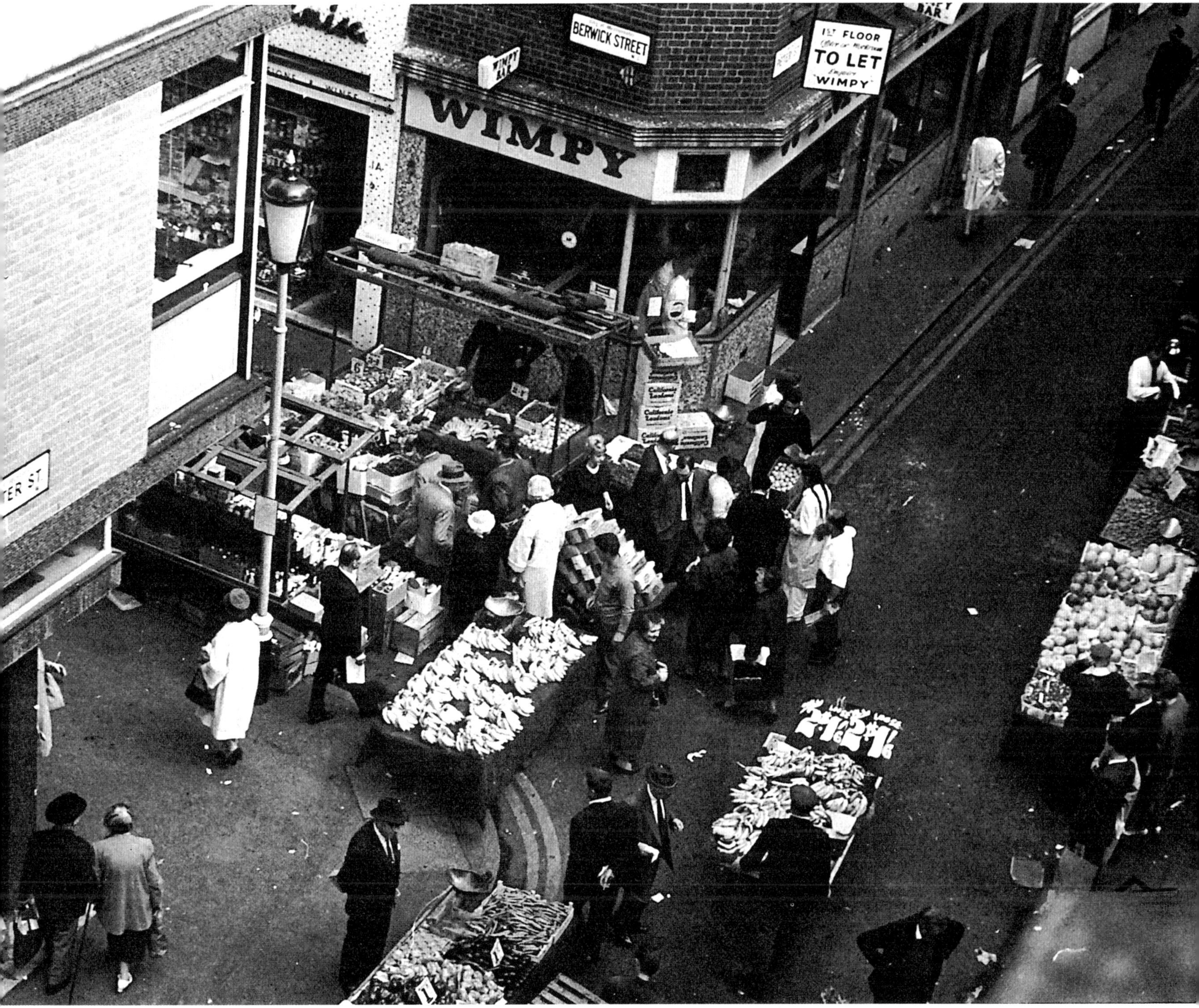
BERWICK STREET
WIMPY BAR
WIMPY
1st FLOOR
TO LET
"WIMPY"
TER ST

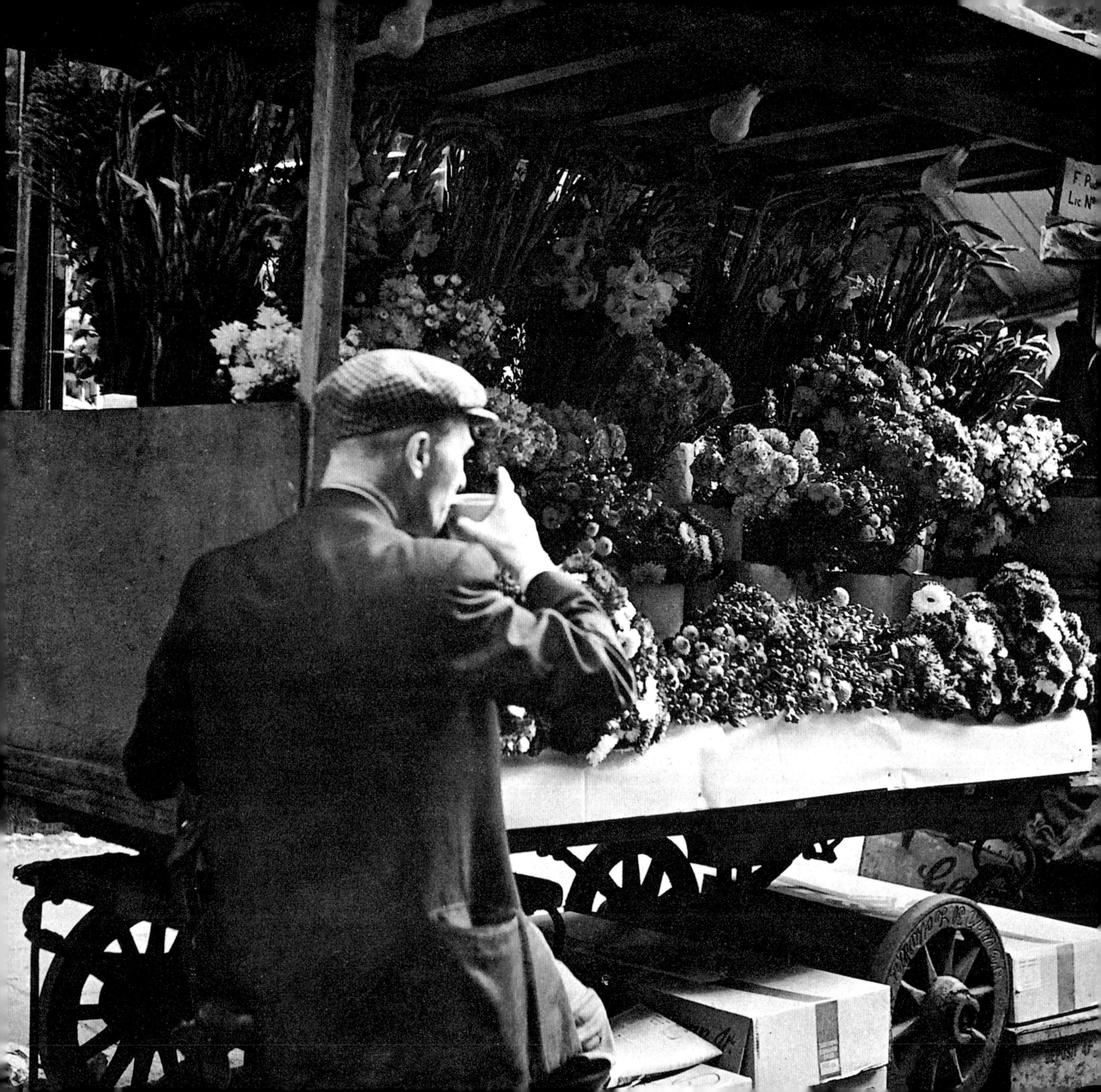

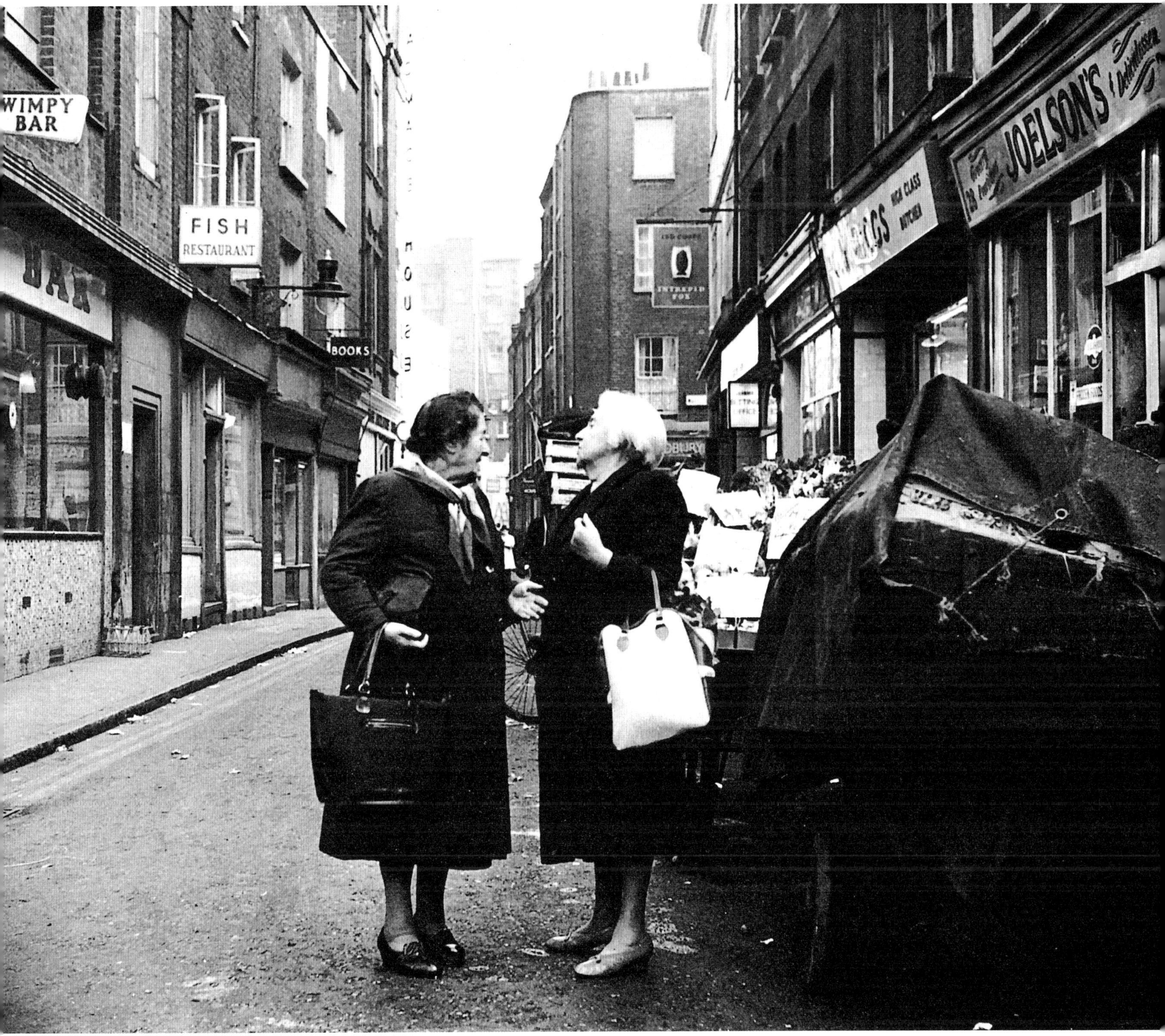
WIMPY BAR
FISH
RESTAURANT
BOOKS
INTREPID FOX
HIGH CLASS BUTCHER
JOELSON'S
Delicatessen

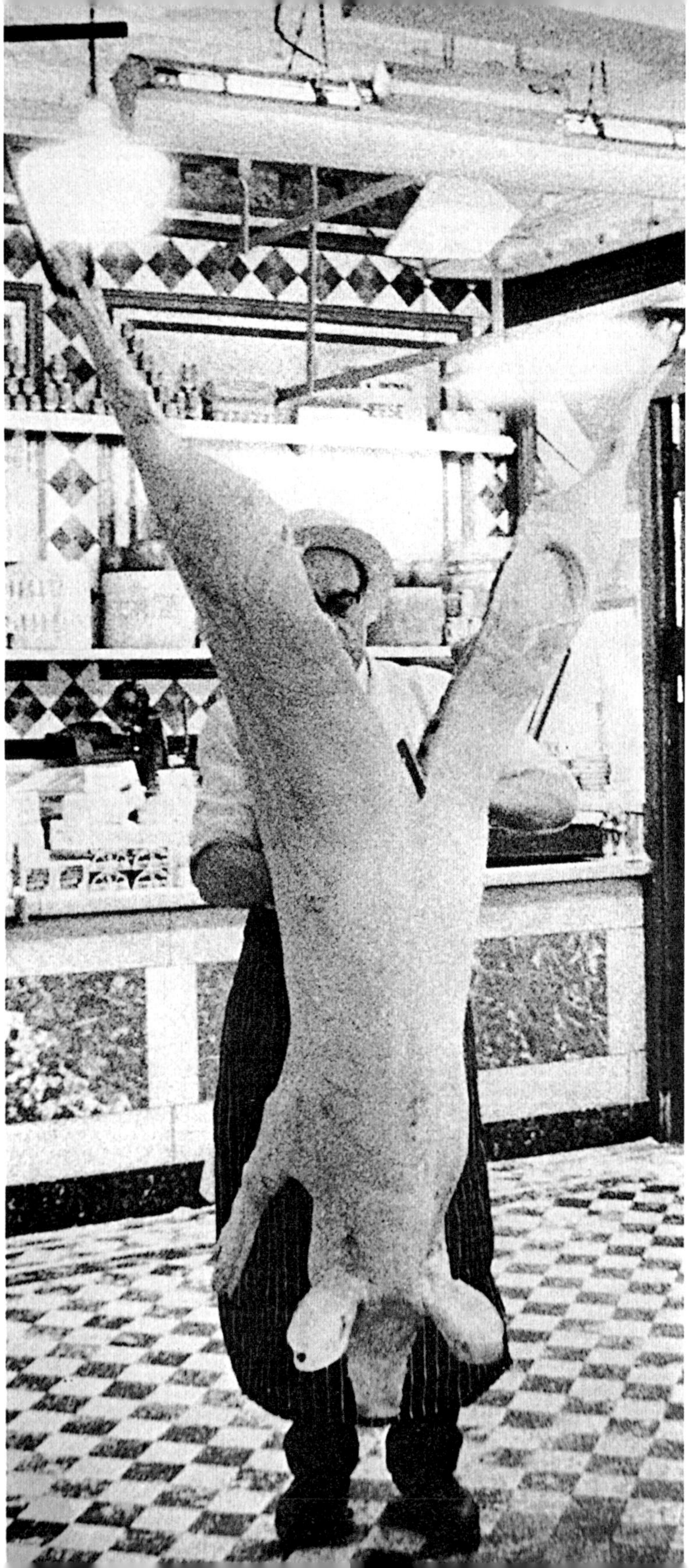

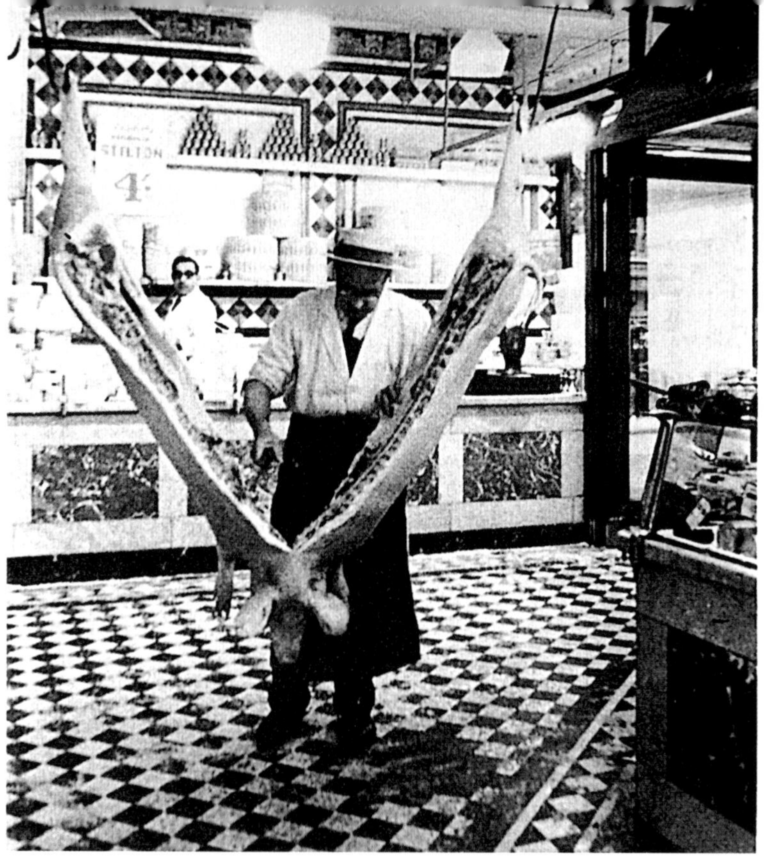
STILTON

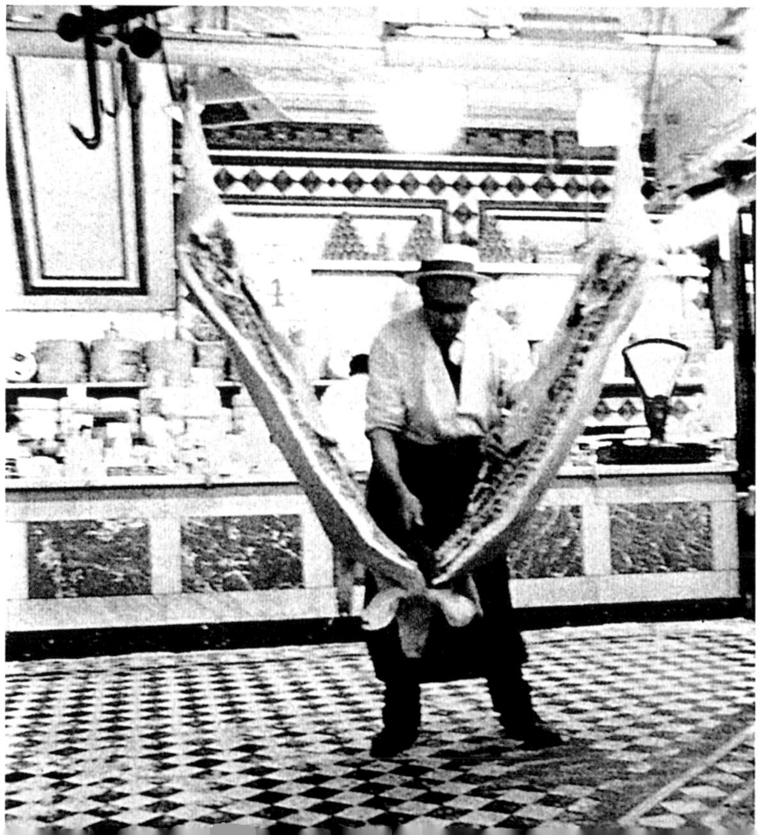

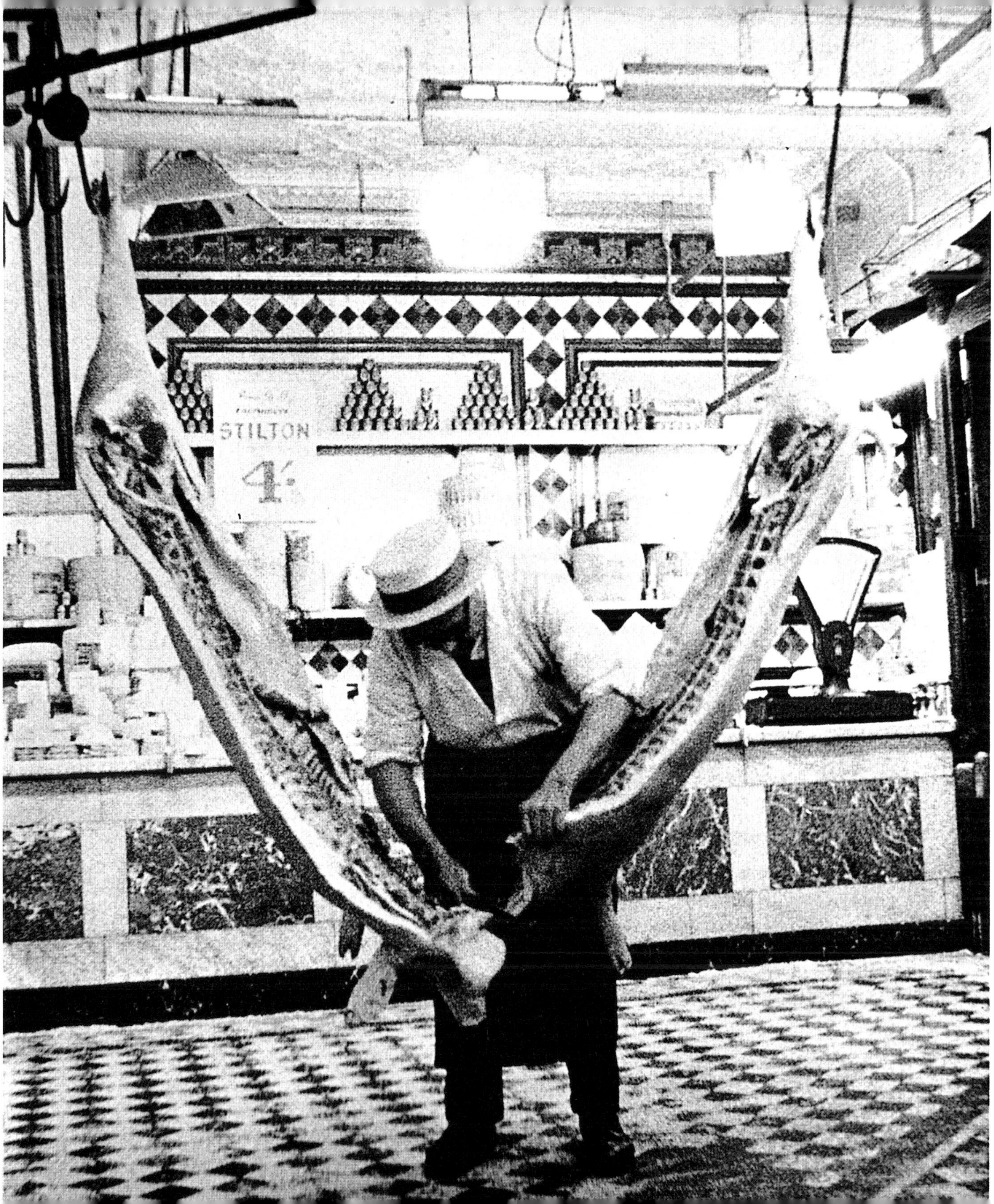
STILTON

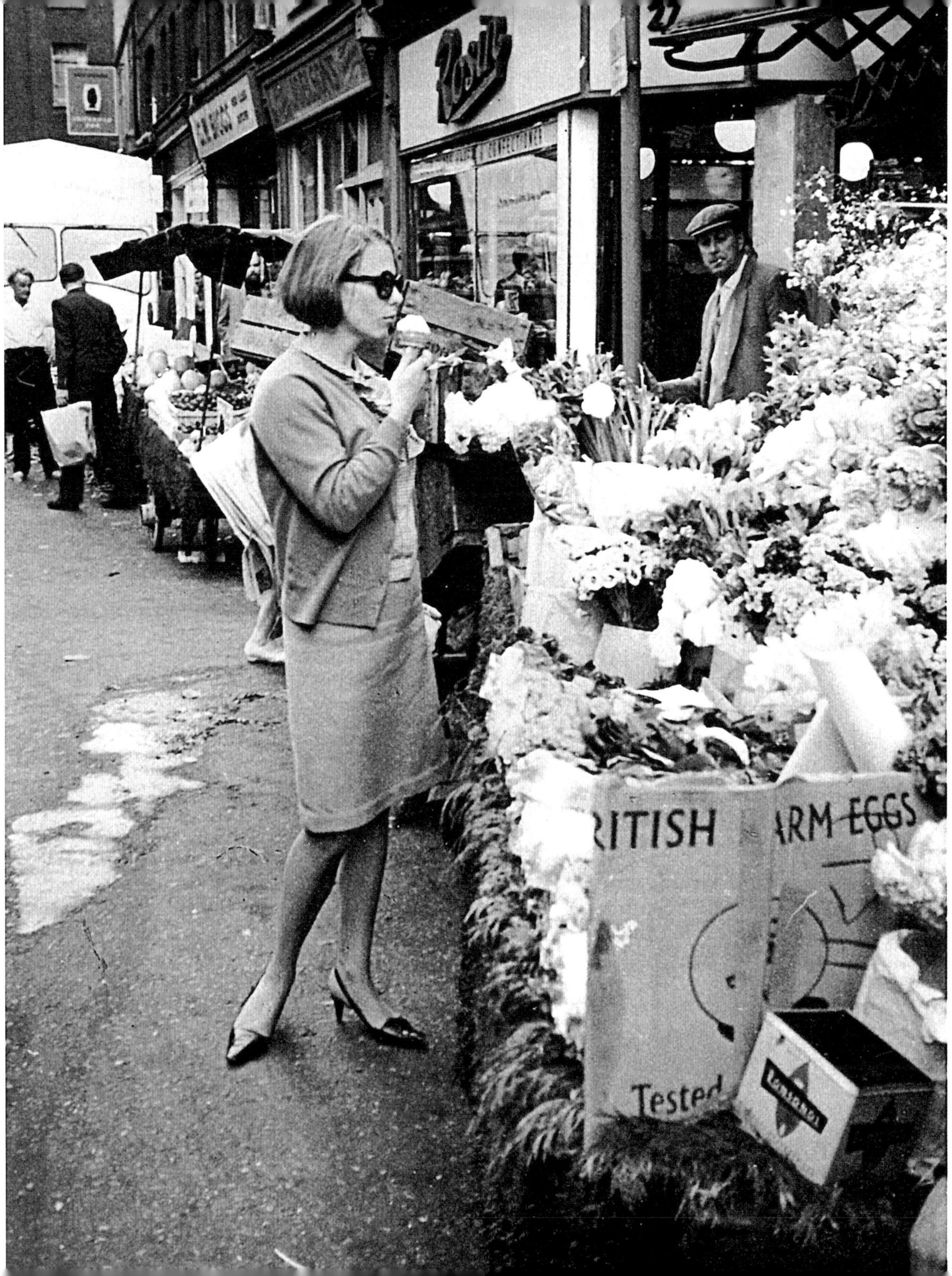
RITISH ARM EGGS
Tested

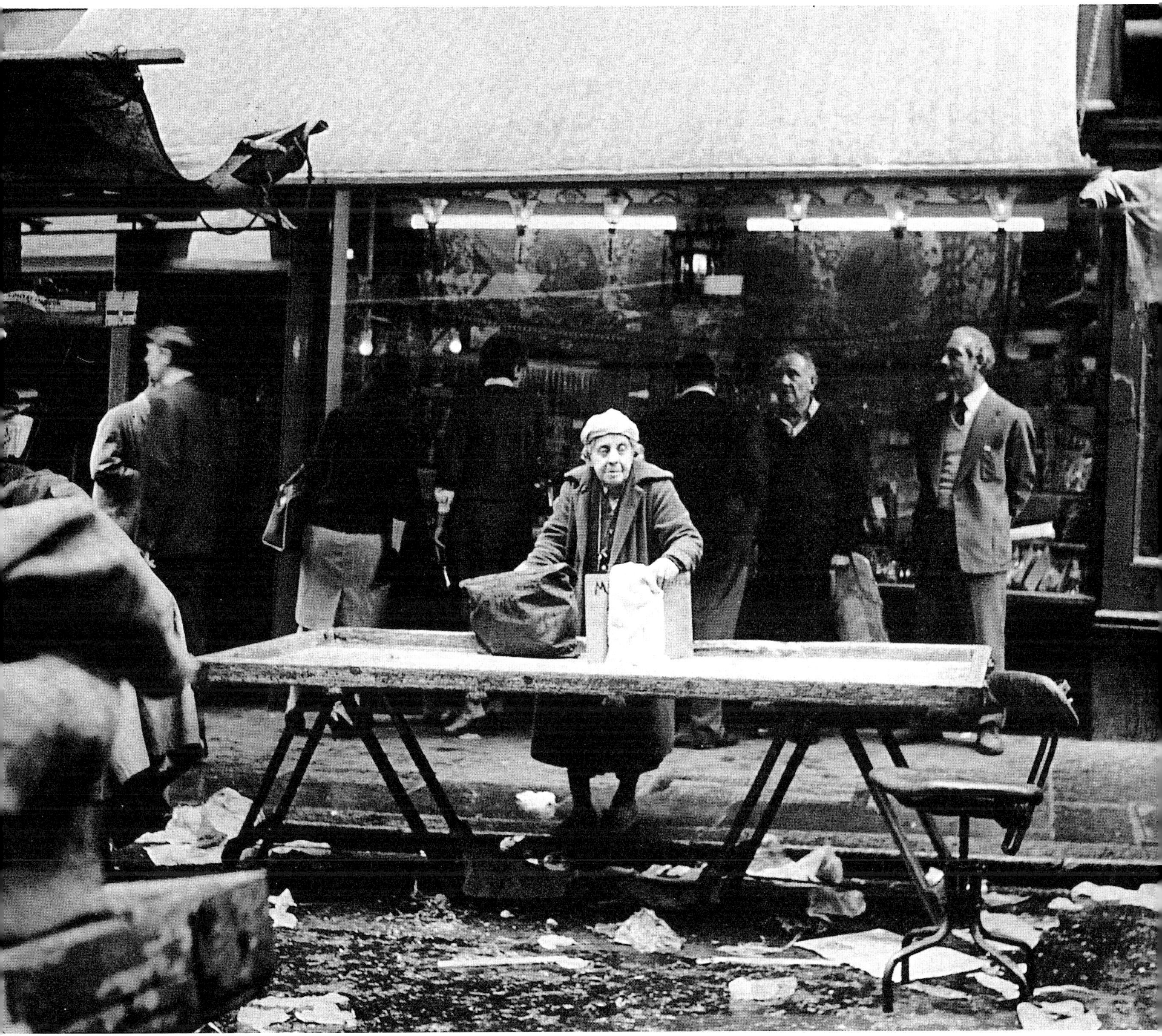

THE DELICATESSENS

Continuing on our search for food, we come to the delicatessen shops which are scattered around all over Soho. I imagine that the best known is King Bomba's near the corner of Dean Street and Old Compton Street (wherever you look in Soho there is always something to eat, it is impossible to get away from food). In these Italian and French grocers' shops you have to be very careful for they are extremely expensive and if you don't watch yourself you will find that you have spent far more money than you intended. There is cheese of every denomination and highly seasoned salami hanging from the ceiling, costing anything from two and

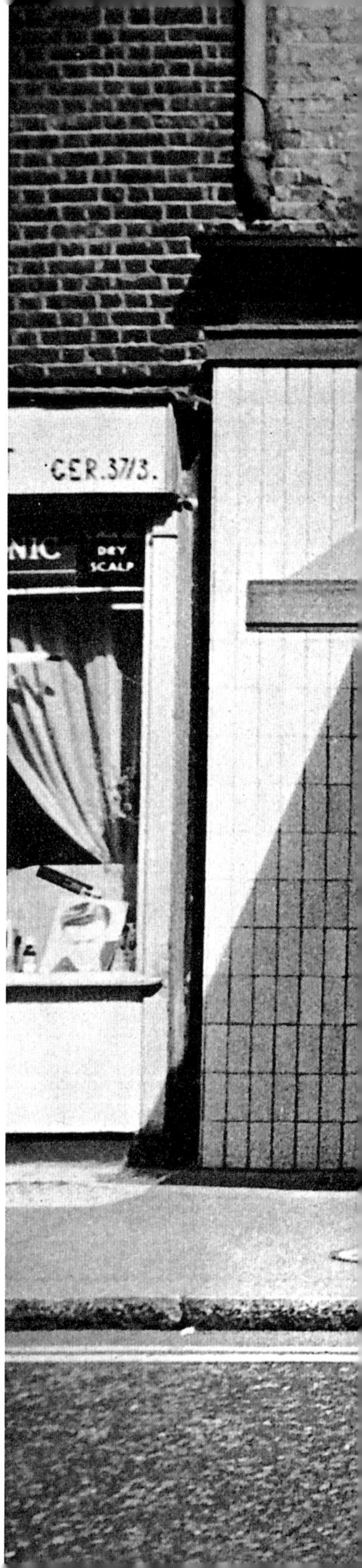

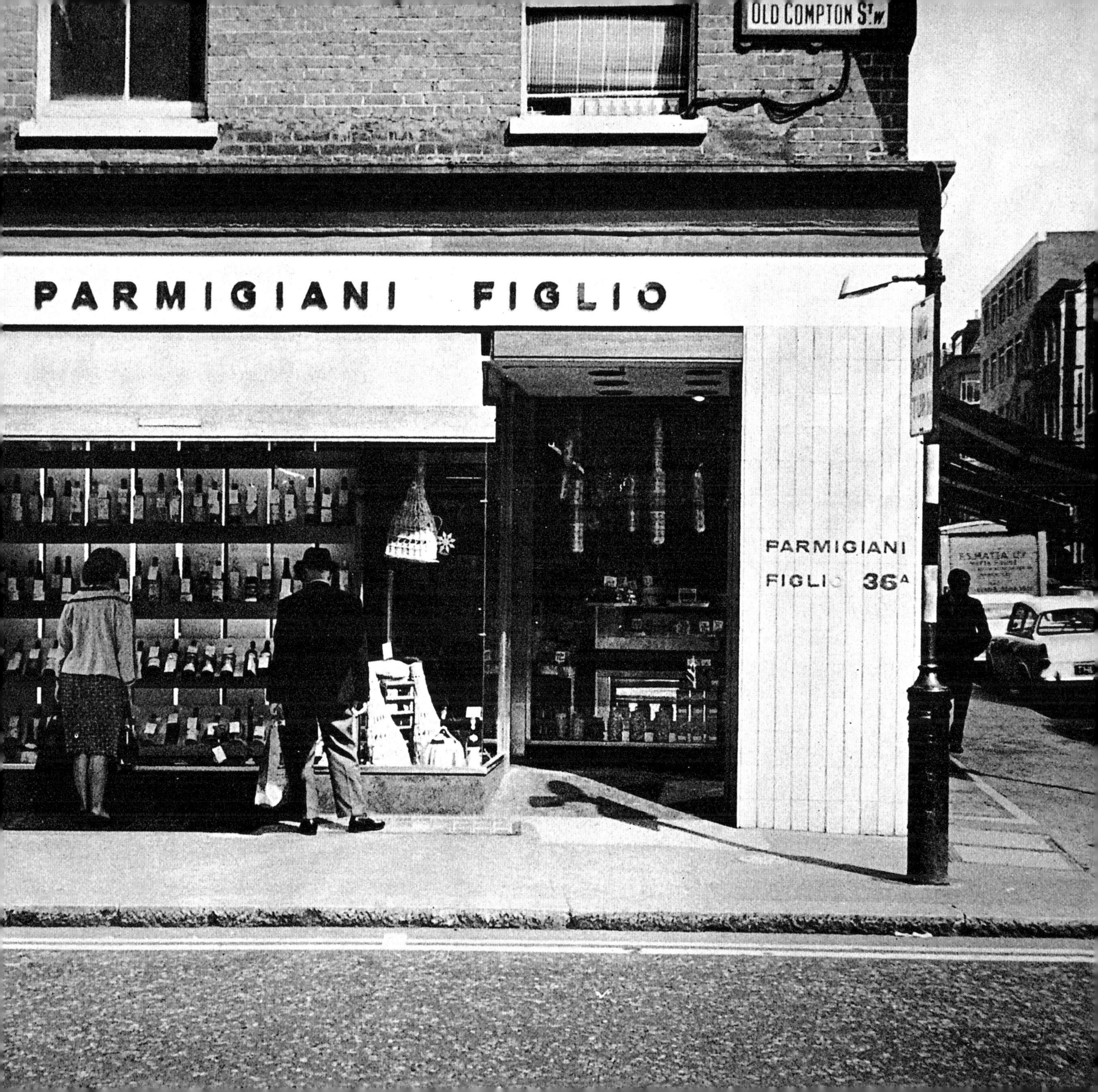
OLD COMPTON St. W
PARMIGIANI FIGLIO
PARMIGIANI
FIGLIO 36A

six a quarter to a pound a pound. The French bread is fresh and tastes almost as though it was in fact made in France. The owners of these shops have a somewhat similar tale to tell as the restaurateurs. They or their fathers came to this country and starved and then eventually opened this little shop and so on and so forth, until they are where they are today. Although there are one or two supermarkets (which have opened only in the last year or two), Soho is in fact a very expensive place to do your shopping, but then of course this is understandable because the food sold in the shops is extremely delicate and often rare: the wine, on the other hand, can be very good and reasonably priced, because many of the owners of wine shops go over to France and Italy and buy hundreds of gallons of it in bulk. This way they get it for less and sell it for less but at a vast profit all the same.

Considering the amount of food there is about it is amazing to think that there are people starving in Soho. They are not starving to death or anything as romantic as that, but let us just say that they are always in want. If you walk around the back streets behind the blazing shop fronts and the chromium-plated coffee bars you come surprisingly upon old gaslit tenements, which are both grimy and unsanitary, the tenants being in large part old people whose children have long since grown up and got married and moved away. One old lady that I know of lives in her old flat and has done so for the last thirty years or more. In point of fact her son who is now married and lives further out has offered her a room in his house, but she loves Soho so much that she will not leave, she is instead content to stay put until the day she dies. Another old man who lives in Brewer Street was in fact born in the same room that he is living in now. He is over eighty years of age and is prepared to die in the room that he was born in.

The interesting point about the poor people of Soho is that when they step outside their doors they are immediately rubbing shoulders with the rich, because the slums are so close to the smart areas that one only has to walk around a corner to find one or the other. On, say, a council estate everyone has identical standards of living: their houses or flats are identical, their children look identical, they pay the same rents, they share the same courtyards and if one of them wins the football pools he moves away as fast as his legs will carry him. To a somewhat lesser extent the same kind of thing goes on in Mayfair and Park Lane, the rich rub shoulders with the rich. But in Soho there is no routine, which is the reason why it has so much character. I mention these points at this stage of my writing because it is not really possible to divide Soho up into set patterns—the shops are mixed up with the clubs, and the market is surrounded by clip joints and barber shops, in fact Soho looks as though all its ingredients and buildings have been put into a dice shaker and tumbled out on to a baize-topped table.

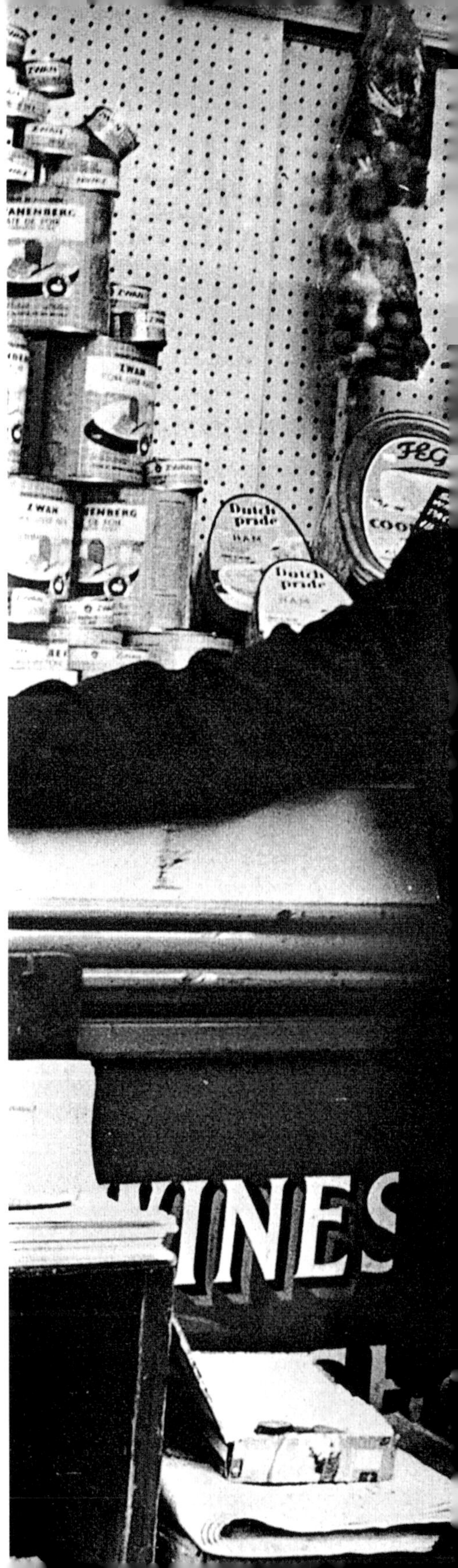

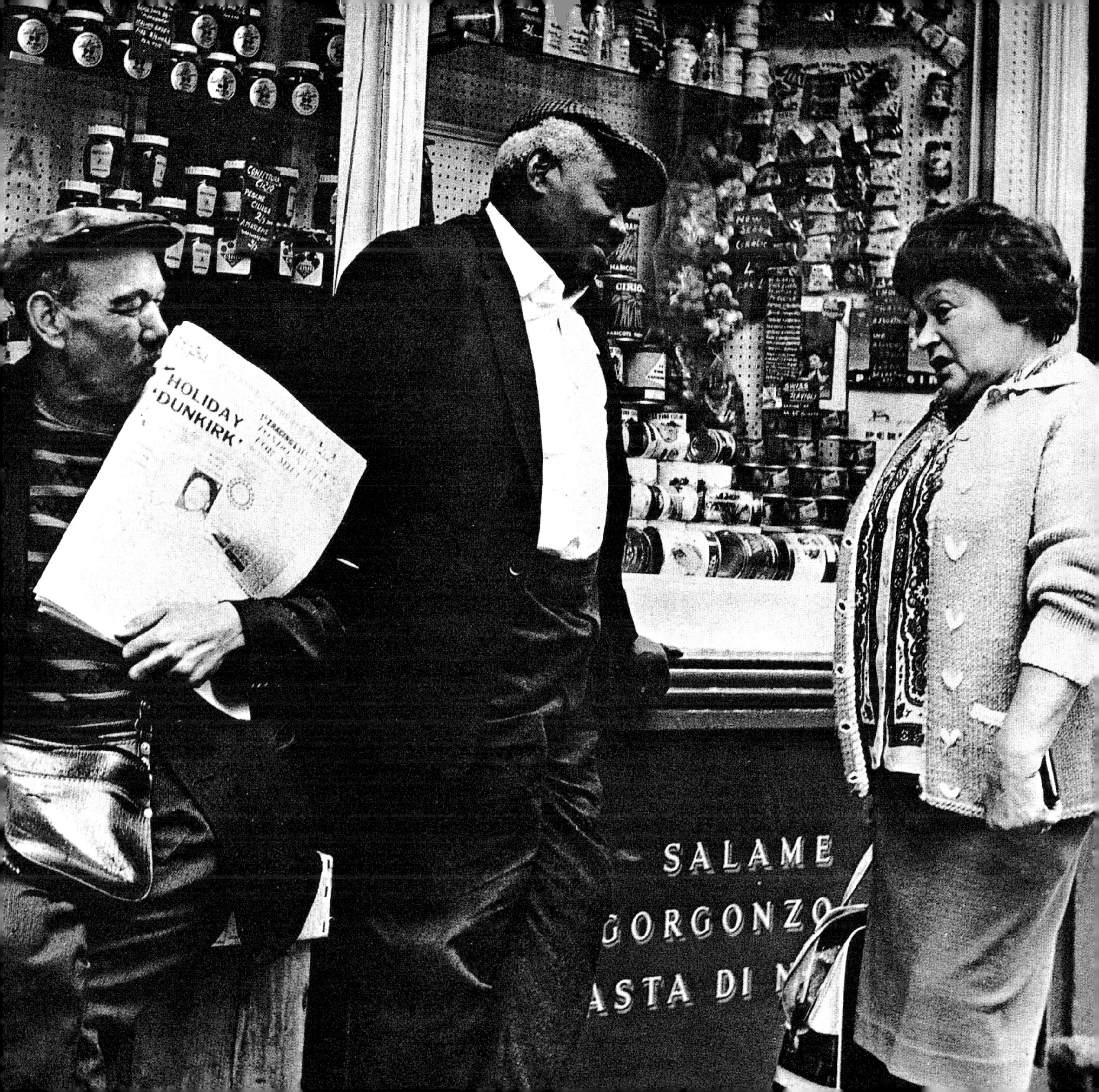

'HOLIDAY
'DUNKIRK'
SALAME
GORGONZO
ASTA DI M

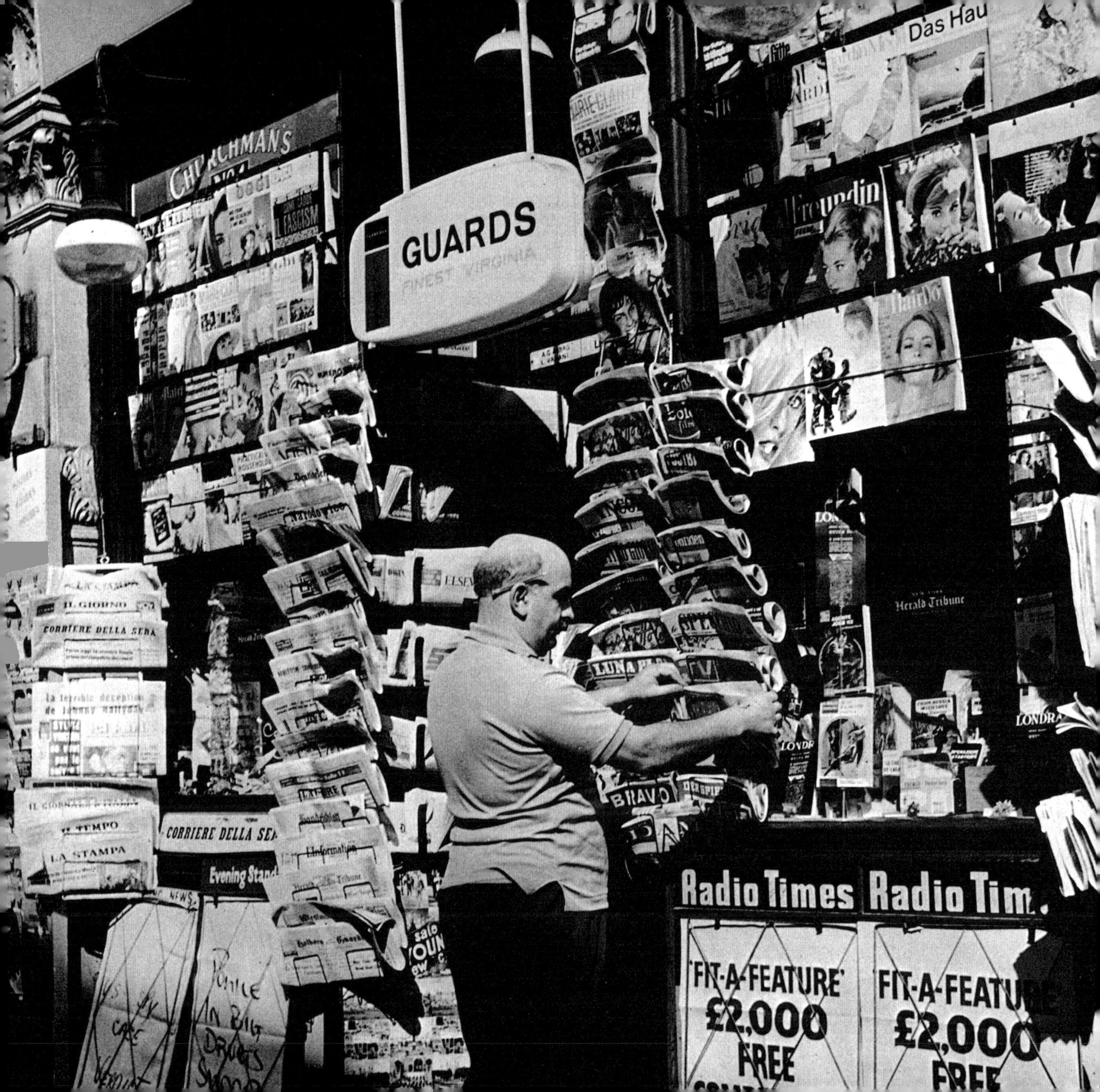

CHURCHMAN'S
GUARDS
FINEST VIRGINIA
Freundin
Hair Do
IL GIORNO
CORRIERE DELLA SERA
IL TEMPO
LA STAMPA
Herald Tribune
BRAVO
Radio Times
Radio Times
'FIT-A-FEATURE'
£2,000
FREE
FIT-A-FEATURE
£2,000
FREE

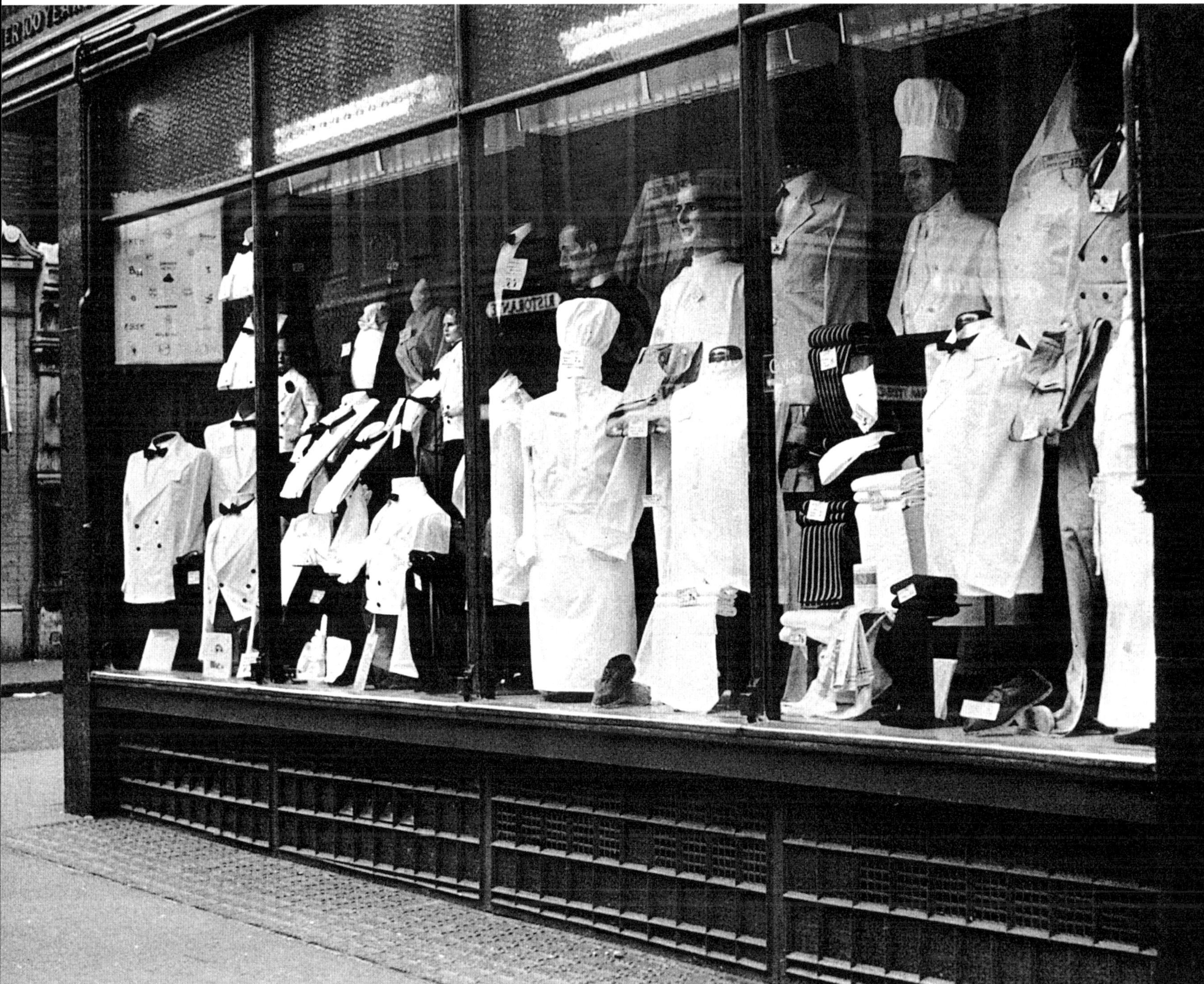

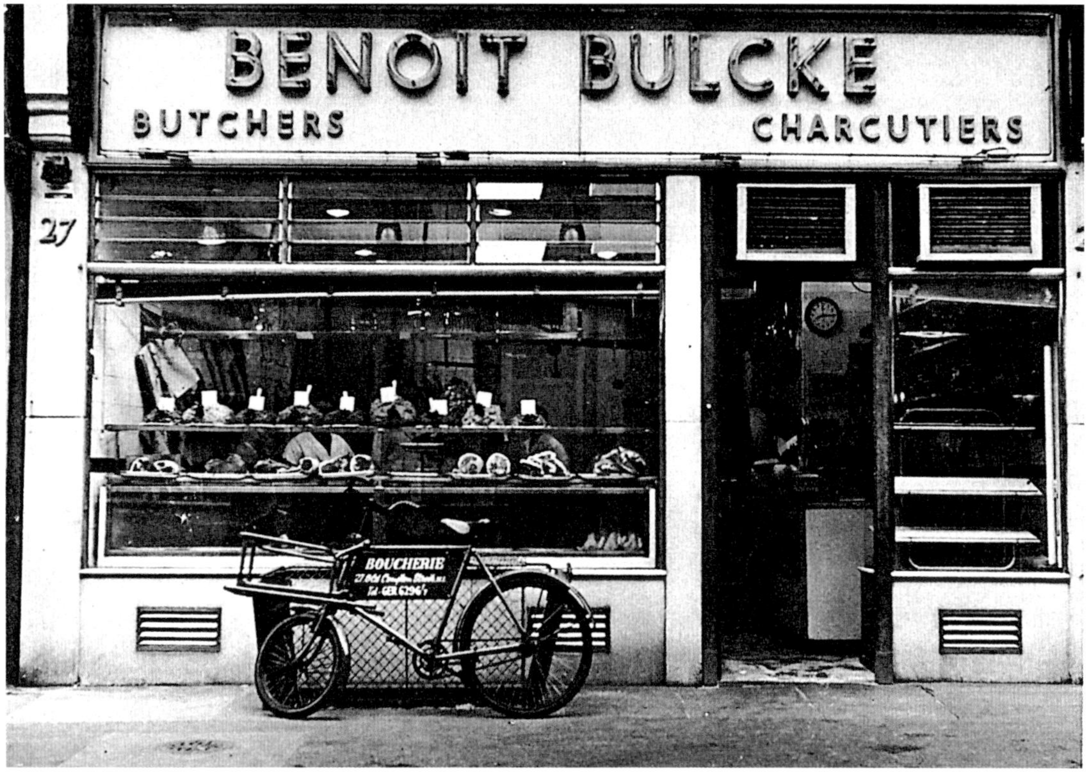
BENOIT BULCKE
BUTCHERS
CHARCUTIERS
27
BOUCHERIE

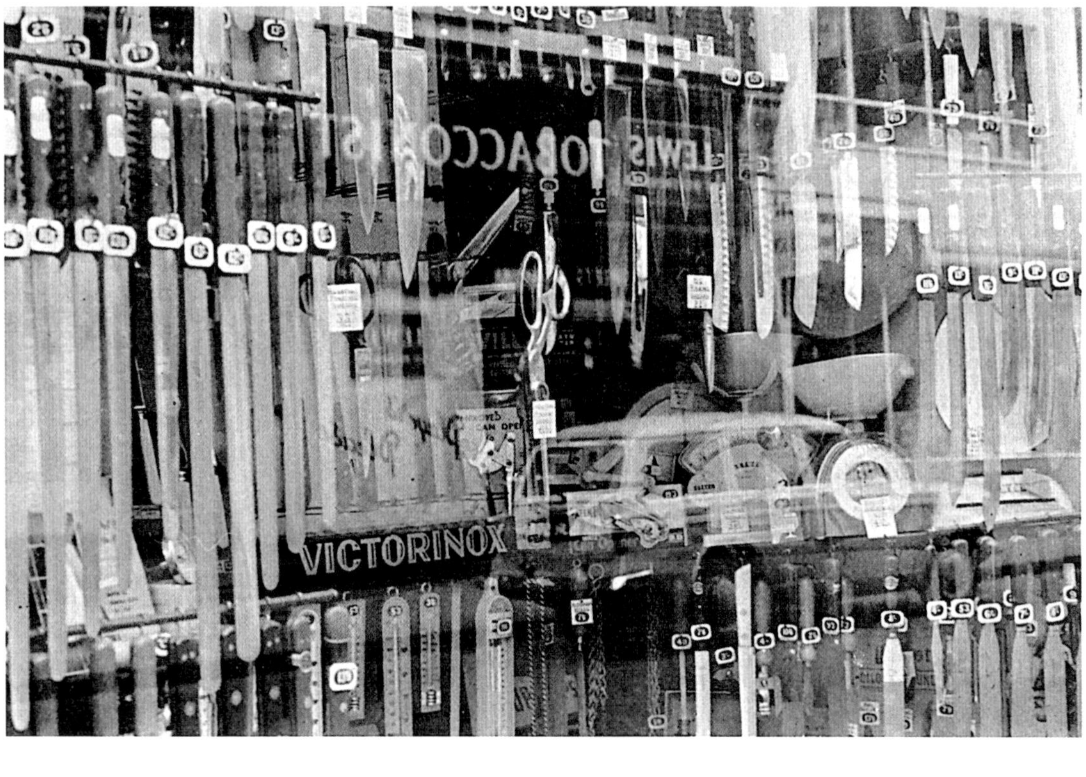
VICTORINOX

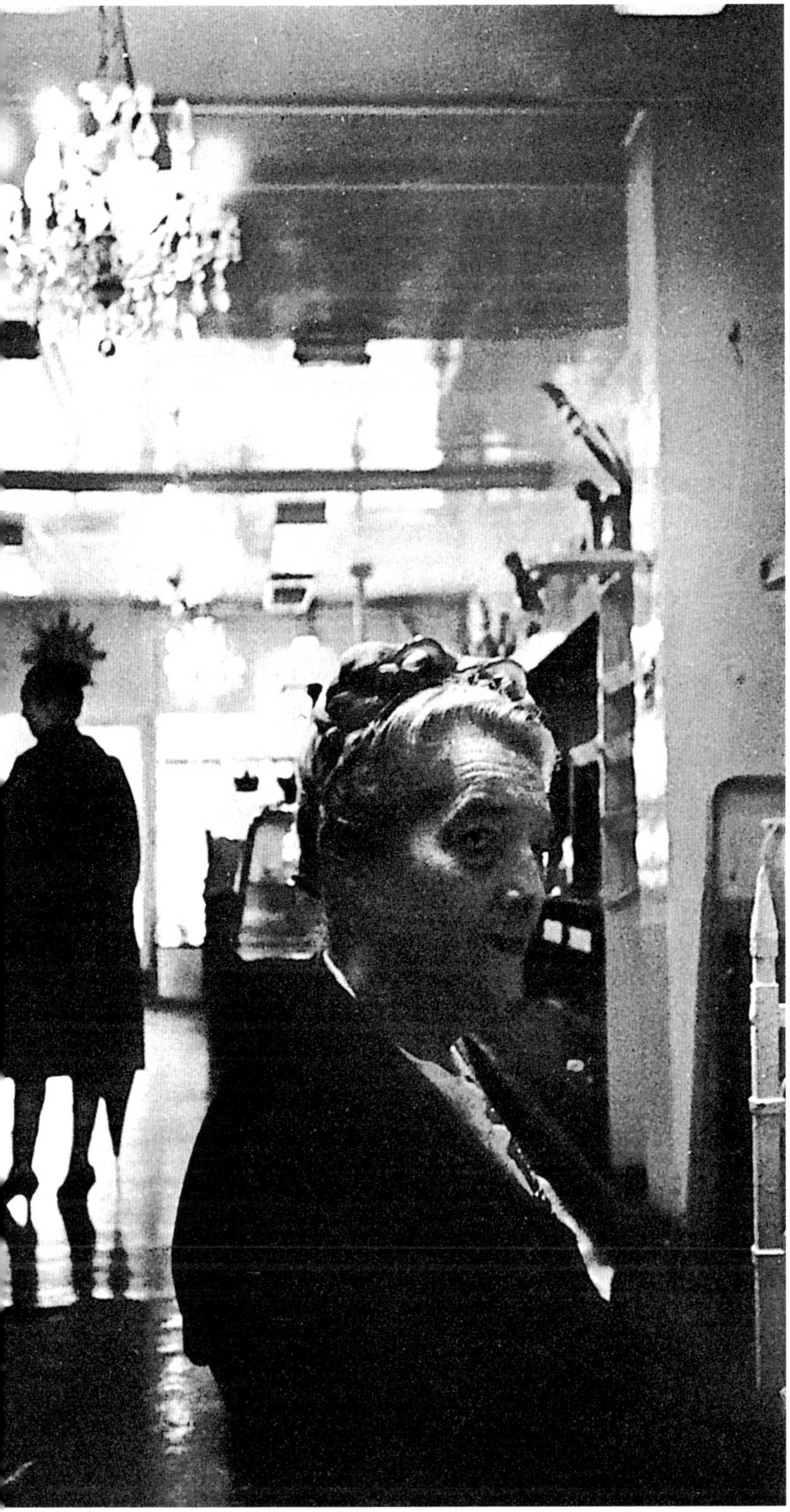

MADAME FLORIS

Without doubt the most famous shop in Brewer Street is Madame Floris's baker's shop: as far as I know it is the only shop in Soho to sport a Royal Warrant. Madame Floris came to England from Budapest in 1932 with her husband, who, after working in York for a few years, came to London and bought the now world famous chocolate shop and factory in Brewer Street from Fortnum & Mason's. After a time Madame became bored with the chocolates and in 1937 bought the bakery in nearby Bourchier Street, which has become as famous as the chocolate shop for its skill of design and delicacy of taste. When Madame Floris's husband died four years ago she decided that she would run both the chocolate factory and shop as well as the bakery. This she has done with great success ever since. Of course the bakery is her great love and she tells me that she adores the English, particularly Londoners, and even more especially the Soho people. During the war years she somehow managed to keep the bakery open in spite of the rationing. No doubt because of her great charm, she never went short of a thing.

The chocolate shop occupies the whole of the building, and is run with fantastic efficiency. There are sixty-three women employees of great skill and dexterity, and Madame Floris is as polite to the floor sweeper as she is to her chief pastry cook.

The bakery was such a success that in 1948 Madame Floris opened her own shop in Brewer Street (up until this time she had sold direct from the bakery). She now makes cakes for top people. Actually a lot of them do not look like cakes at all: there was once one for Sir Winston Churchill shaped like a map of England, and one for Leslie Caron and Peter Hall's wedding built like a Georgian Church, and for Noël Coward a stage. In fact I should think you could order a cake of any description and not be disappointed with the result. It is not often that they have a disaster but there was one occasion when a christening cake went out bearing the inscription 'My Fanny' instead of 'My Fanwyr'.

As a matter of fact I remember Madame Floris's bakery from many years ago when I was around Soho on the bum. Amateur prostitutes used to use the bakery wall for support, and if no one was looking they would use the vans as well, but that was long ago. In those days the site that is now occupied by blocks of offices and flats on the corner of Dean and Bourchier Streets was a car park (converted from a bomb site). Running under the street were the cellars of the houses that once stood there: they were the homes of all the lay-abouts, meth drinkers and bums who could find a corner.

TWO SOHO SHOPKEEPERS

One of the most interesting shopkeeping characters (well, perhaps funny would be a better word) that I went to see was Madame Cadec, who originally came to England to be a governess. During her stay she met Monsieur Cadec and married him in 1938. When he died she took over the business, altering the house around somewhat. She runs a very nice little pots and pans shop at the bottom of Frith Street. She would not like to be called an ironmonger, I am sure of that, and in any case I have yet to see anything made of iron in her shop. She specializes in copper pots and pans and has become so famous that as she says, in her French accent which is like a chef's knife: 'Now I 'ave so popular magazines like *Woman's Own* come to see me. You know people write to me with orders worth three shillings–phht–it is not worth my while such littleness and they want recipes as well!' Her arms went into the air in a gesture of French hopelessness. She has enormous vitality and warmth and lives her life with great enjoyment, as widows are inclined to do. Three or four times a year she goes off to France, touring the manufacturers, selecting and collecting, and she brings everything back in the enormous Rover car that she drives. Her shop is stacked to the ceiling with every conceivably shaped pot and pan you could ever wish to find; there are casseroles called 'Marmitso': there are also things called 'Hachoirs', which are used for goodness knows what. There are mandolins and little stone pestles and mortars for bashing peppercorns with.

Although Madame Cadec lives in Soho (she also has a house in the country) she prefers to socialize elsewhere. When I asked her about the tougher side of Soho she gave me what might be called a French old fashioned look and said that she didn't know anything about it. 'Soho exists on so many levels that it is better not to notice other people's affairs.' Madame Cadec has certainly got her head screwed on the right way all right, it is by far the best way to succeed in business without even trying. In fact she succeeded so well that since I wrote this she has much to my regret retired.

Although Soho is close-knit, that is to say jam-packed with shops, offices, and businesses of one kind and another, there is in fact little unity between the Soho business people. Like business people everywhere else they are almost entirely out for themselves alone. This was proved by the failure of the Soho Association, the reason for forming which was so that the tradesmen and residents could organize the now defunct Soho fair. The reason for its failure was age old greed. The first year of the fair was in fact very successful. Upon seeing this many outsiders tried to get in on the act, and some of the local members of the association tried to hog the fair for themselves, in a very selfish way. One of the things that made me angry when they used to have the fair was that none of the local characters were allowed to take any part in it. The poets, painters, bums and layabouts were sent packing whenever they showed their faces near any of the functions. I thought this most unfair because these are the people who can be seen in Soho every day of the week and contribute a great deal to the character of the place.

Mr Alex Strickland is a comparative newcomer to Soho and was an active member of the association. He feels that the fair was not done on a big enough scale, and its failure was due to the small-mindedness of some of the members of the association. Mr Strickland owns the Record Centre on the corner of Dean Street and Old Compton Street. He was brought up in the West End and went to the Regent Street Poly. He told me that he used sometimes to wander through the streets of Soho on his way home from school, and had always felt that he would like to be a part of it. Then five years ago he was walking along Dean Street and saw a cake shop on the corner. He was at the time looking for somewhere to open a record shop and he immediately thought that the cake shop would be an ideal site, so without further ado he bought the shop and started up in business. The Record Centre is now the most famous and successful shop of its kind in the whole of London. Mr Strickland has done so well that he has opened two other record shops which are not however in Soho. I talked to him in his Soho office which is across the way from his shop, the walls of which are hung with life-sized photographs of himself with Frank Sinatra, Eartha Kitt and many others. As we talked the three telephones on his desk never stopped ringing, with people making all kinds of enquiries, such as when is the new Beatles LP coming out or an enquiry about a Bach album which might be out of stock. Things are going so well for Mr Strickland that he is thinking of going into management, that is if he can find a good group. He tells me that he has always been interested in show business and it looks to me as though he is shortly destined to be in the thick of it.

So far as his shop is concerned Mr Strickland has always tried to push it as a Soho shop, hence the name Soho Centre. One does not automatically become a Sohoite simply by having a business in its streets, but in my opinion he has more than earned his place here and is as much a part of the place as the families who have lived in Soho for generations and contributed nothing to it. As I was leaving the office I noticed a cable pinned to the wall. It read:

> 'NEW ALBUM STOP SINATRA/BASIE CONSIGNMENT SHOULD BE WITH YOU STOP IT WAS A BALL TO MAKE STOP HOPE YOU ENJOY IT STOP REGARDS TO YOU ALL AT RECORD CENTER SINCERELY STOP FRANK SINATRA'.

I wish Mr Strickland many more of them.

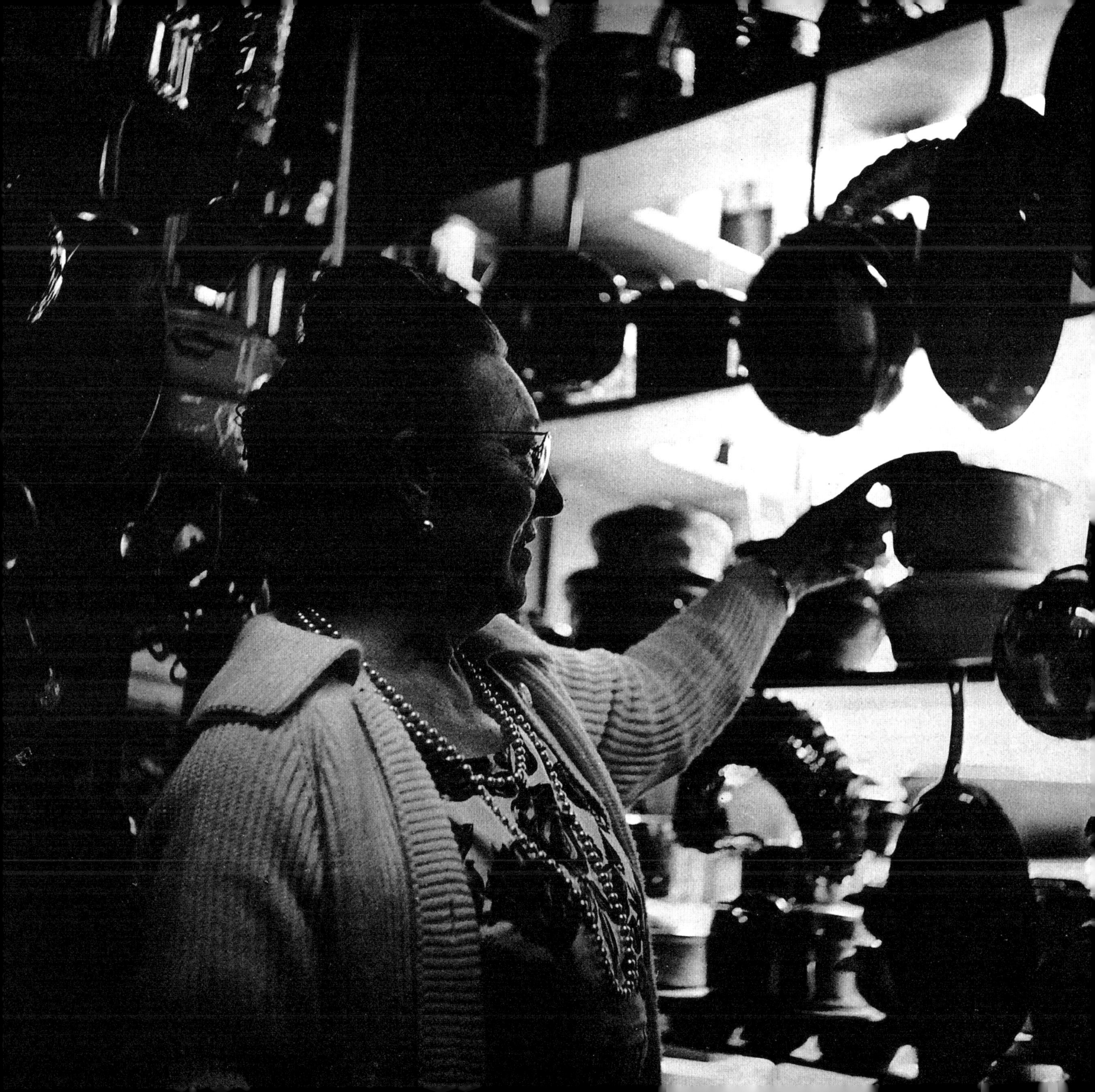

SOHO BUMS

Reverting back to the Soho of my youth, I remember it as being the best place in the world for being on the bum. In those days there were hordes of us layabouts hanging about street corners or sitting in dingy little cafes sipping cups of tea, often one between two. We sat for hours talking about the troubles of the world and other things that we knew nothing whatever about, and at night we would sleep in bombed houses or the park. Hard though this kind of life may sound it was not in fact as hard as all that, the reason being that there were so many of us doing it. There was a kind of comradeship between us: if one of the bums managed by some fantastic fluke to get a room we all stayed in it; also to a large extent the police left us alone. Today things are very different and the few bums who are around Soho are on their own, there is no comradeship and their troubles are not shared. Why this should be I cannot really say, but I do suspect that it is something to do with the Welfare State. These days you are not allowed to be on the bum, whether from choice or necessity. The government simply will not stand for people being down and out. Should you insist on being skint, the chances are you will find yourself hounded by the law until you change your wicked ways. I was talking to a friend of mine the other day who has insisted on being down and out for the whole of his life; whereas in the old days he was left in peace to starve if he chose to, today he is for everlasting getting arrested and thrown into jail for sleeping on the embankment in the wee small hours of the morning. He has had several last warnings from magistrates who tell him that he is a disgrace to society and that if he does not get a job and settle down he will be sent to prison for a very long time. Personally I consider this a diabolical infringement of people's rights, for if someone has such a lack of enthusiasm for society that they do not wish to join the game, then it is their business and they should not be penalized for it. Society's argument is that the world would be in a terrible state if everyone was like that. Everyone is not like that and the world is in the trouble it is in because of the state of society, not because of my friend who does not wish to join it.

There are a few youngsters who sometimes try to rebel by laying about in a half-hearted sort of a way, but they seem to be not so good at it as the youngsters of ten or fifteen years ago. Their dirt is synthetic and can easily be washed off, and almost without exception they have homes to go to if things get too rough. They go on the bum for kicks rather than to pursue the gentle art of avoiding work, they take purple hearts and have many possessions such as watches, cuff links and smart suits of clothes and many of them have been known to get jobs and settle down, an action which would be viewed with disgust by a hardened bum of yester-year.

The Welfare State is not I feel the only reason for the sharp decline in bummery. Another reason is the redevelopment schemes, which have caused many of the old haunts to be razed to the ground by destruction firms and built anew by construction firms, where once stood a dingy cafe now stands a towering sky-scraper, which is air-conditioned and centrally heated. As any true bum will tell you there is no fun in laying about in a place that is clean and warm, the fact is it is impossible to do so, for bums, like pigs, are only happy in shit and a bum will only thrive in places where it is cold, damp and dirty. Why this should be I cannot say, but I would hazard a guess that the reason is because clean places make them feel most uncomfortable.

As well as the tragic change in the Soho bums, many of the old places in Soho have changed, such as the Mandrake, where years ago writers, painters and poets met to talk and drink a little cider. Today the Mandrake which was in those days one room is now six rooms or more and posh food, smartly dressed customers and their girl friends are the order of the day, and instead of playing chess they pour sixpences into fruit machines. This has driven the layabouts away and the governor who once liked them is not really all that sad to see them go; making money is all important and that is the one thing that writers, painters and poets do not have a great deal of. The juke box has taken the place of the guitar and the mandolin, whisky has taken the place of cider, and successful people have taken the place of the bums: it is what you might call a major take-over bid.

The Caves de France has also taken a turn for the worse and followed the example of the Mandrake. Where once the walls were thick with dust they are now whitewashed clean, the French accordion player has long since disappeared, as have the old wine-drinking customers. Secundo Carnera, brother to the ex-heavy-weight boxer Primo Carnera, has died (he was the barman at the Caves for many years) and many a bum has died with him, if not in fact then in spirit. The French cafe at the corner of Old Compton Street and Charing Cross Road, next door to the Coach and Horses, has gone the same way, with the slight difference that it is no longer there—it is now a pornographic bookshop. I remember the time when it was packed from morning till night with Soho misfits and a sprinkling of art students from St Martin's just around the corner. After sitting in the French cafe for several hours one could wander down to the National Gallery or browse in Foyle's bookshop.

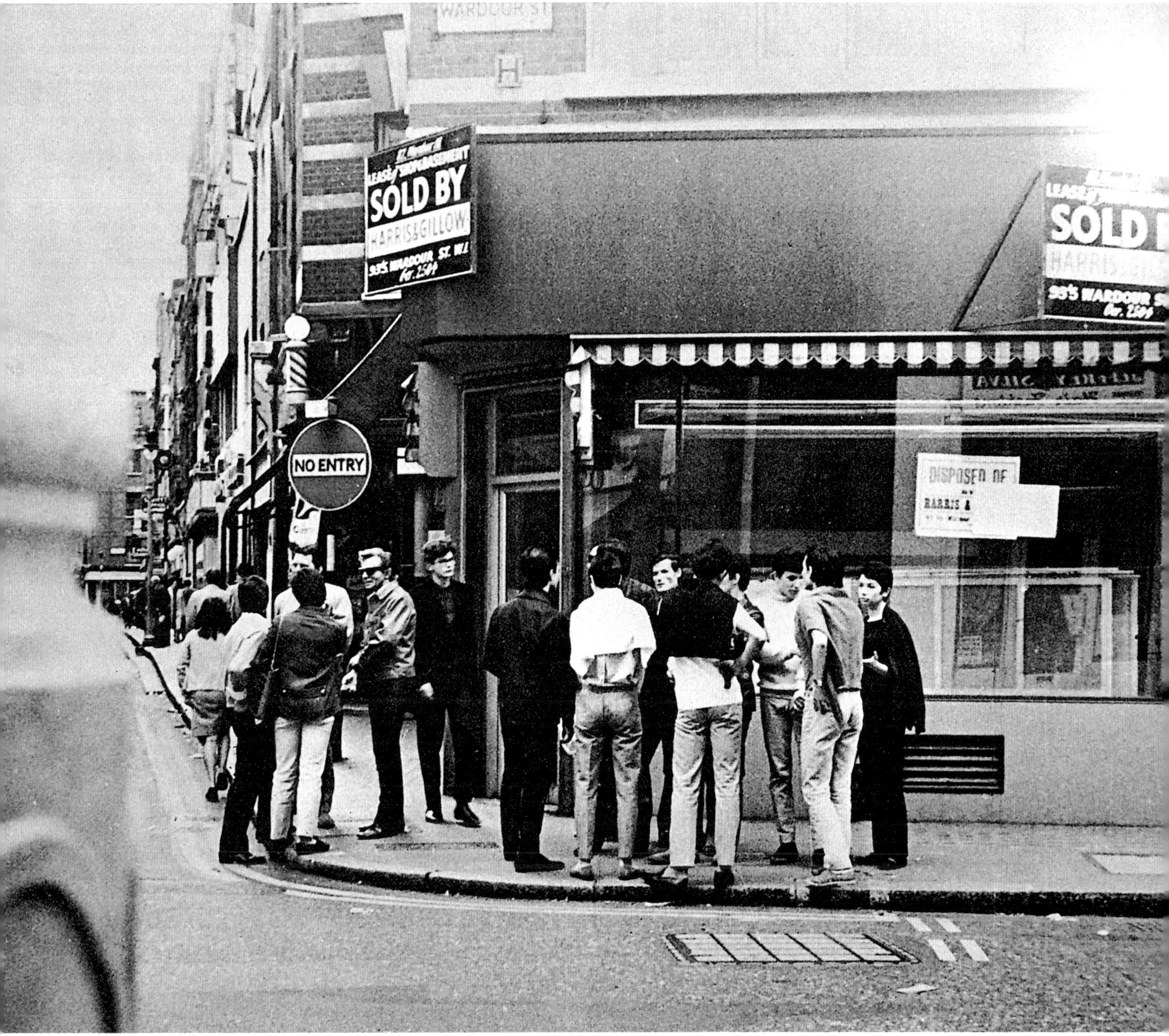
WARDOUR ST
SOLD BY
HARRIS&GILLOW
Ger. 2504
NO ENTRY
DISPOSED OF
SOLD B
95'S WARDOUR S

FOYLES BOOKSHOP

Though much of the recent history of Soho has been made memorable by misfits and failures there are also some pretty staggering successes to match them. One such is the story of Foyles. It began in 1904, when two young sons of a Shoreditch grocer failed to pass their examinations for the civil service. Somewhat disconsolate, they decided to sell their unwanted textbooks and inserted a small advertisement in an educational paper. The advert brought so many replies that the brothers were quick to notice that the book-trade offered good opportunities. The two young brothers were 19-year-old William Foyle, and his 17-year-old brother Gilbert.

Their first shop was the kitchen of their parents' home, but gradually room after room began to bulge with books so they had to find larger premises, which they did in Islington, at a rent of five shillings a week. Later they moved to a larger place in Peckham where the rent was ten shillings per week. Like all self-made businessmen the Foyle brothers worked from morning till night with no free week-ends, writing out their catalogues by hand and sending them to their customers with a request that they be returned when finished with. They lived on a diet of sausages and mash which they cooked in the back of their shops. Later came the move to the now world-renowned centre for books in Charing Cross Road.

When they engaged their first assistant the brothers really thought they were making some headway but they became very glum however when the new assistant took an early opportunity to abscond with the takings. This set them back rather badly, and they were compelled to walk to and from work for several weeks afterwards. From the start, though, they earned themselves a reputation for being able to supply books on even the most out-of-the-way subjects. It is therefore not very surprising that their business prospered. Today 30,000 letters a day reach Foyles from all over the world, the stamps from which are sold at a clear profit of about £100 per week.

In 1929 the Foyle brothers saw their dreams realized when the Lord Mayor of London officially opened their impressive new premises. Five stories high and towering above its neighbours, it may have been a tall building for those days, but in comparison to the ones that are shooting up all over Soho today it is comparatively small. However it is big enough for them to have thirty miles of shelving, which house close on four million books. To this sprawling bookshop almost all of London's visiting celebrities are at sometime or other drawn. Walt Disney has browsed among the collection of art books, world champion boxers have left with fistfuls of books on boxing and wrestling, and Eire's Éamon de Valera has frequently called to buy the latest books on mathematics. Other regular visitors have included Dame Edith Sitwell, Noël Coward, Sir John Gielgud, Paul Gallico, J. B. Priestley and Lord Harewood. By no means all of Foyles' customers however are celebrities; students, school-teachers, parsons, nuns, doctors, lawyers and of course just plain readers throng its thirty-two departments. And because people come to Foyles from almost every part of the world, skilled linguists are employed to assist them.

Among the most important branches of Foyles' business are the ten Book Clubs, boasting of a membership of nearly half a million readers. And the Foyles organization also includes a publishing house, an art gallery, a literary agency and a lecture bureau. It would appear then that the story of Foyles' growth from its humble beginnings has all the ingredients of a modern fairy tale or perhaps the commercial success story made possible by a text book from one of the shelves of this very bookshop. Yet the one touch which usually completes such stories, the vast, shiny, mechanical efficiency, which obscures the homely origin—this is missing. As I wandered around wondering what on earth I was going to be able to write about this vast organization, I felt that Foyles less than any other big business suggested streamlined organization. This impression became more acute in the secondhand book departments where vast quantities of volumes are in constant over-flow, threatening at any moment by sheer numerical bulk to overwhelm confinement, piled on floors as well as on shelves. But these conditions of informal and slightly haphazard scramble represent not breakdown in organization, they simply indicate that Foyles is still not big enough for its books. That was the problem which confronted the firm's founders in those early days in their mother's kitchen and, as Foyles continue to progress, the problem of expansion, the necessity for larger premises, is likely to be with them for many years to come.

While on my visit to Foyles I had a word with Miss Manning who is their chief buyer of secondhand books. She came to Foyles ten years ago after working on the *Financial Times* for ten years. She became old Mr Foyle's secretary and like all good secretaries it was not long before she had taken over. She comes from a long line of book lovers, both her mother and grandmother showed a keen interest in them. Miss Manning handles an average of 50,000 books a week, most of which are worth considerably less than their owners fondly imagine. Though most of Foyles' customers are honest, a great number of books are stolen; the official estimate is about 1,000 a year, but I suspect that in fact the total number is far greater. Book thieves are very often cool customers who sometimes pinch books from upstairs and carry them downstairs to the secondhand buying counter. Though this is quite a common practice it is easy to detect because new books crack when opened. Some of them specialize: one such was an old lady who used to steal bibles from a warehouse and 'Always sold them to Foyles,' as she protested when arrested.

Foyles is obviously a perfect 'passing place'. Pound notes are occasionally found between the pages of books, and one of the books on the secondhand shelves was discovered to have a revolver-shaped hole cut in it—it was empty when found.

I also talked to the manager of the rare book department, who told me that most people make the mistake of thinking that old leather-bound books are valuable. Rarity is a hard thing to define: for instance Victorian bibles are worth very little. Americans are the best customers of this department, though mostly they are looking for quaint souvenirs rather than scholarly acquisitions.

The lecture agency that Foyles founded in 1944 has a sparkling list of front rank lecturers, and has 300 discussion groups. Literary societies and luncheon clubs are on its books. Among its lecturers are Sir Leonard Hutton, Lady Violet Bonham Carter, Sir Mortimer Wheeler and General Sir John Glubb. Christina Foyle herself is much in demand as a speaker. Something of an institution too, are the famous Foyles' literary luncheons, which have been held monthly since 1931. Their guests of honour have included distinguished personalities from many walks of life, among them celebrities as diverse as George Bernard Shaw, Bud Flanagan, The Emperor of Ethiopia, Lord Avon, The Archbishop of Canterbury, Jimmy Durante, Harold Macmillan, H. G. Wells, T. S. Eliot, General de Gaulle, Eleanor Roosevelt, Hermione Gingold. A recent one to which I was invited was given for John Lennon, the *litterateur* of the Beatles, who said: 'Thank you very much,' when called upon to speak.

Today, Christina Foyle, daughter of William Foyle (one of the firm's two founders), is in control of the whole shooting match. She joined the business as a secretary when she was seventeen and founded the literary luncheons when she was nineteen. In 1938 she married Ronald Batty, who was a childhood friend and is now a director of Foyles. They have a book-lined flat above the bookshop and a charming house in Essex.

For many years William Foyle was the donor of a 'Foyle Prize' presented to the most promising student at a number of public schools and universities. And in 1947 he announced a new award which was 'The William Foyle £250 Poetry Prize', to be presented annually for the most outstanding work of poetry. Since William Foyle's death, Christina is continuing the prize as a memorial to him. Gilbert Foyle, the younger of the two founders, now lives in retirement in Eastbourne, where he takes a lively interest in civic affairs. In 1958 he presented Eastbourne Corporation with ninety-five acres of valuable downland at Beachy Head, and in 1961 he and his two sons, Eric and John, donated £36,750 for a sun lounge and cafe to be built at the Wish Tower on Eastbourne seafront. And so it goes on: grants for students, awards for good writing, money for this and money for that. It seems to me that the success of the Foyle family has been their devotion to education and literature. Their interest in the young and the up and coming is admirable. But they are also interested in every sort of everyday customers. There was for instance a certain titled lady who sent William Foyle a cheque for £500 with the request that he buy her the best and worst books ever written. And there was recently a letter from a man who lives in California and had just bought a 1929 Rolls-Royce for use in exhibitions and parades. His enquiry was where could he get clothes for himself and his family of the same vintage as his car. I think he should have written to Savile Row. There are also people who browse around in the shop each lunchtime, but do not buy anything, and I got the impression that they are as welcome as those who spend a fortune. I think that Foyles is as much a show place as any of London's museums, monuments or historic 'sights'.

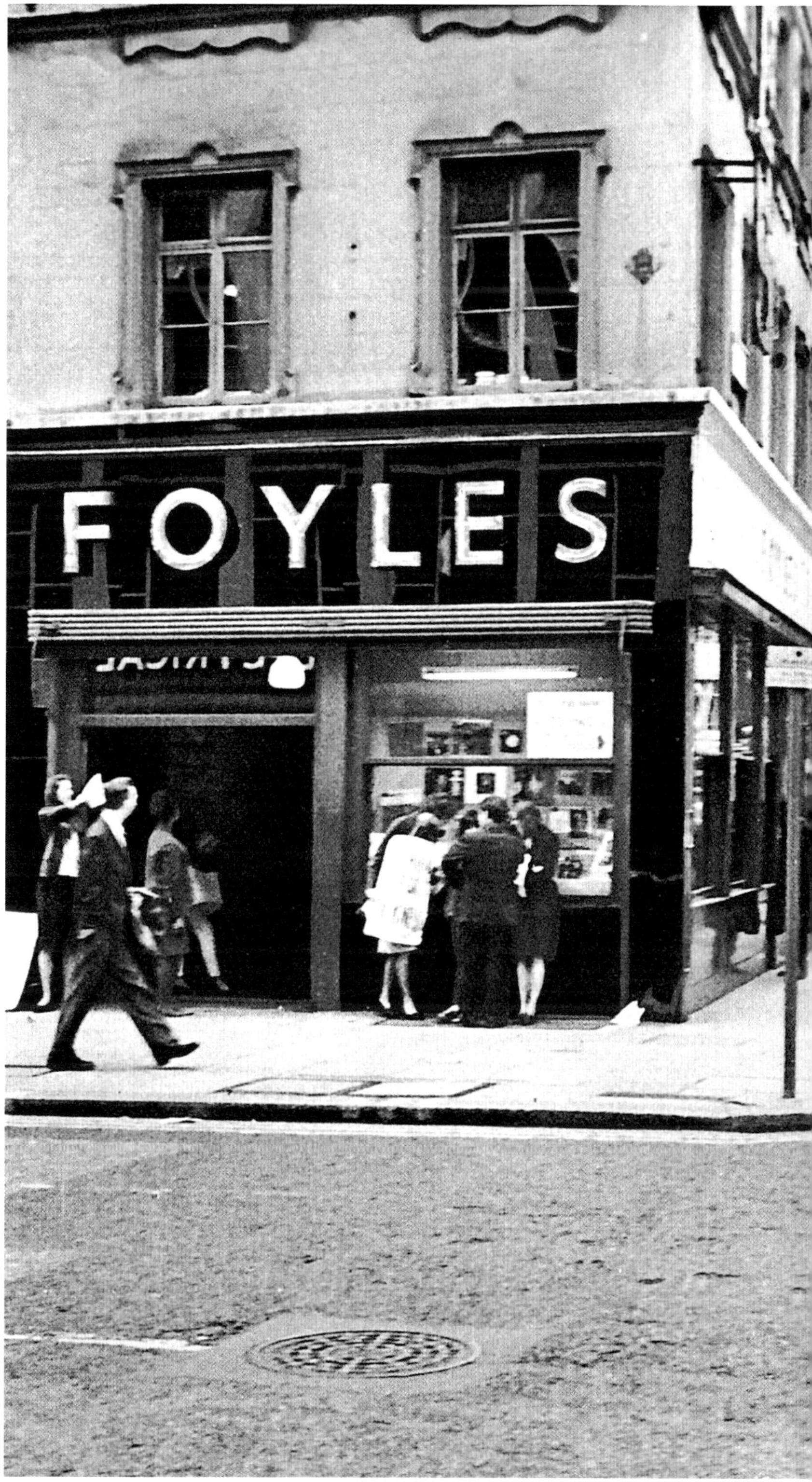

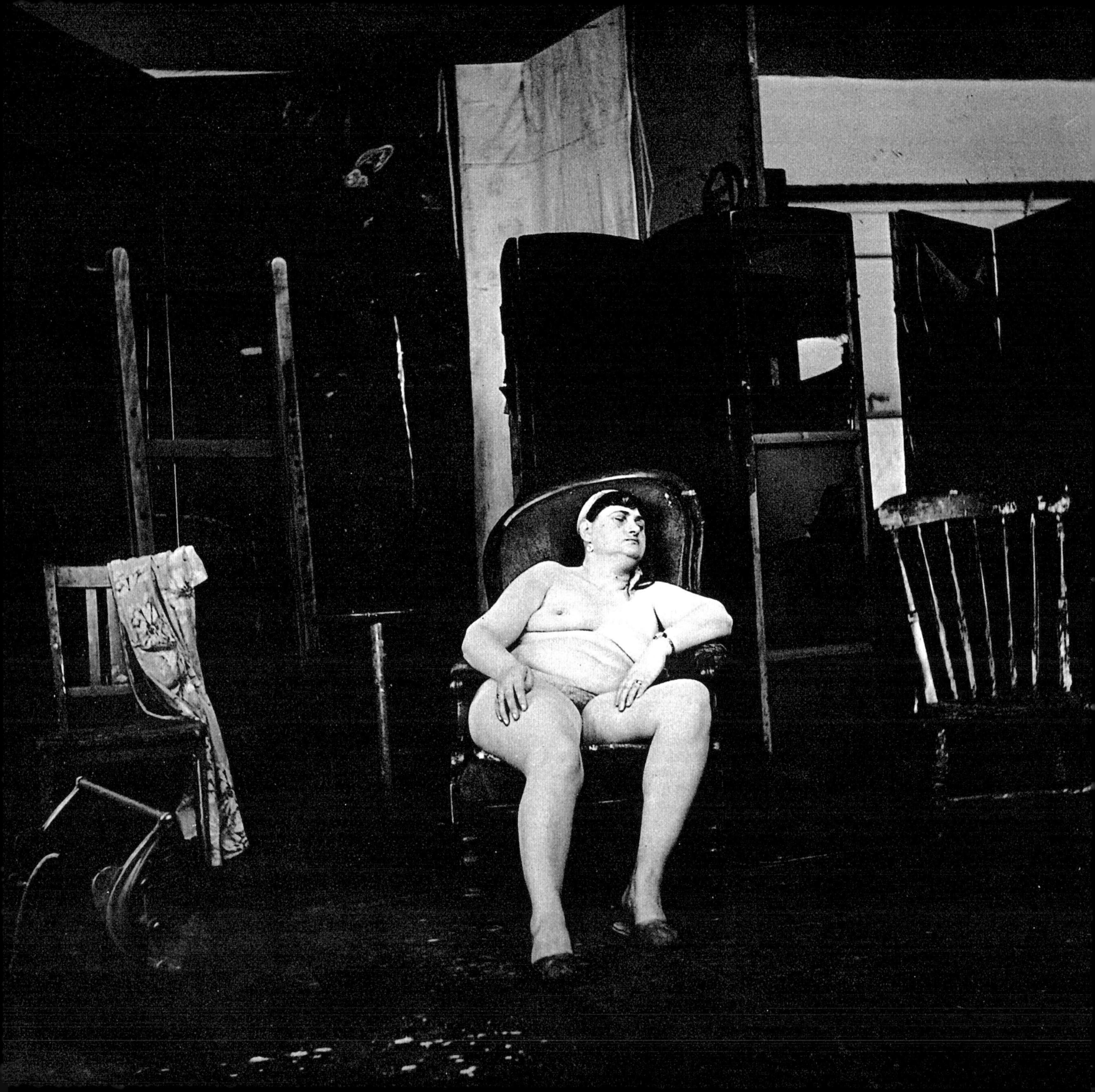

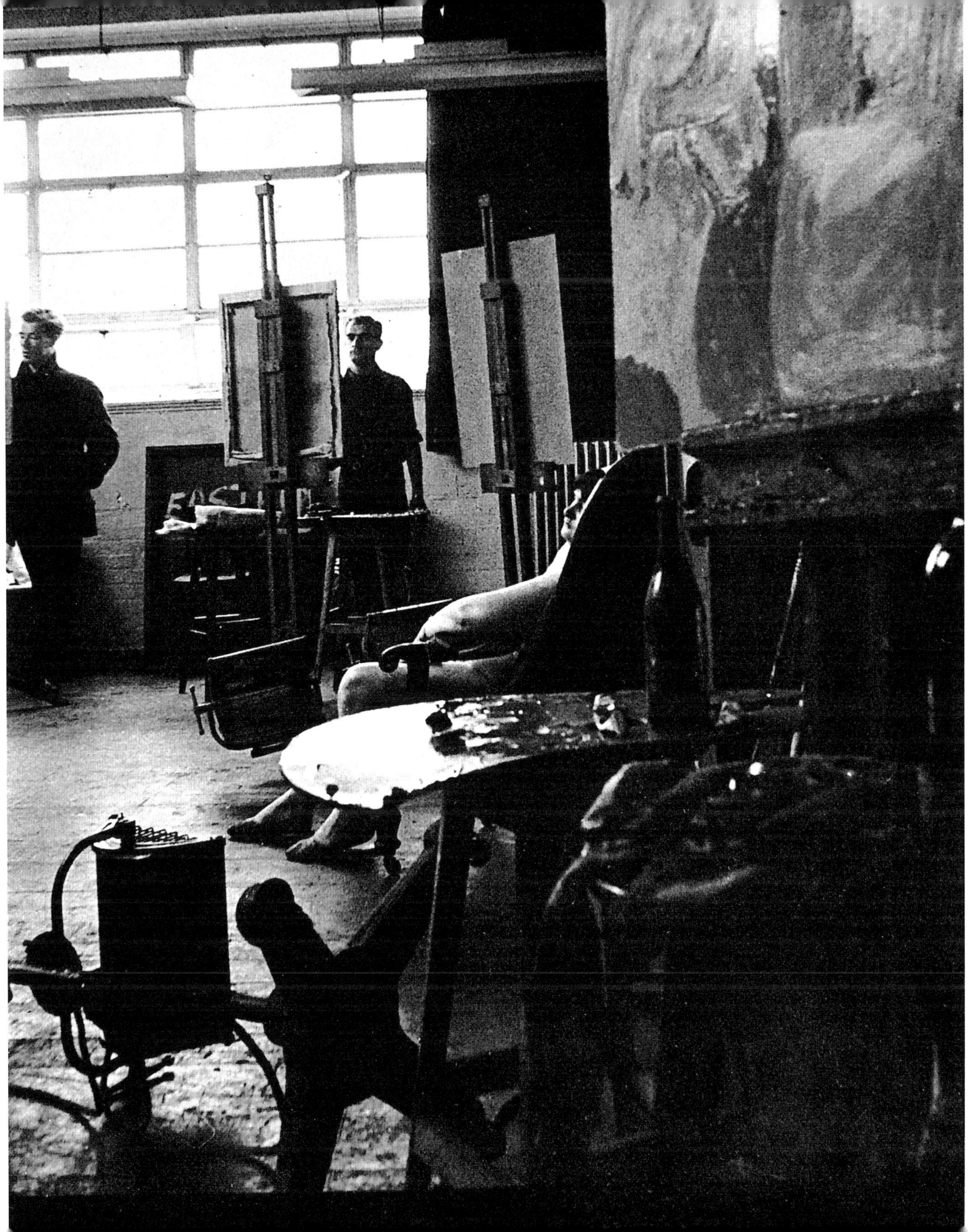

THE HAUNT OF MUSICIANS

Wandering around Soho you will pass many different kinds of businesses. Up near the Oxford Street end you will find the gown trade, and at the Shaftesbury Avenue end the musical shops. One of the things which used to confuse me over the years was seeing several hundred men standing on the corner of Archer Street and Windmill Street. Some time ago I found out that they were musicians. But why did they stand there every Monday afternoon? For a time I thought that they were something to do with the nearby Orchestra Association, but upon making enquiries I found out that this was by no means the case. The truth is they come looking for work or to get paid for work already done over the weekend. What happens is, the musicians arrive in their hundreds and wait around for the band leaders who hire them for gigs that are coming up during the coming week, and also pay them off for the gigs they did the week before. There is no office and all the transactions are done in shop doorways or the local cafes. I find this a very strange answer to the mystery because, although I believe it, I have never actually seen anything of the kind going on. All I have ever seen them do is stand around waiting for nothing whatever. Still it must be remembered that musicians are notorious for playing it cool.

While hanging about on the corner of Archer Street myself I thought I might just as well pop into the Orchestra Association and find out what they were all about. I spoke to Mr George Orrell who has worked there for forty years and has been secretary for ten of them. He told me that the boys hanging about on the corner outside were nothing to do with him, for his Association is a far more elevated affair. His members are all classical musicians, and when a musician applies for membership, he must first do an audition before he can be considered, and must prove himself to be a master of the instrument that he plays. If he can do this he can become a member for a subscription fee of ten shillings and sixpence per year.

The Association was founded in 1912, the year that the *Titanic* went down. There were eight musicians aboard, all of whom lost their lives. It so happened that Mr Orrell was bandmaster aboard the *Carpathia* (playing the violin). His ship picked up 712 survivors from the *Titanic* and he was given a medal on which is inscribed these words: 'In Recognition of Gallant & Heroic Service'. Though the eight musicians who perished on the *Titanic* were not in fact members of the Association, it was decided that something should be done to help their families. So it was that the Association organized the greatest gathering of musicians ever to be seen in one place in this country. It took place at the Albert Hall, there were 500 musicians assembled, and they were conducted by such great men as Sir Edward Elgar, Sir Thomas Beecham and Sir Henry Wood. It was a glittering occasion, the Albert Hall was packed to the ceiling, and the whole affair was a fantastic success. Not only did the Association organize this moving tribute, they also commissioned a sculptor to design a large memorial plaque to the eight musicians. It was cast in bronze and is still hanging on a wall in one of the upstairs rooms of the building.

It does however look as though the Association may soon have to look for a new home, for it would appear that they are standing in the way of progress or redevelopment or some such. Anyway the whole of Archer Street with the exception of their building has been bought up by a property company who are I gather much angered by the Association for not selling out. They hold a long lease on the property and are not keen on moving an inch. I can only wish them the best of British luck, *for British they certainly are*.

A stone's throw from the Orchestra Association there is a little mews, where stands a little drum maker's shop run by Mr Len Hunt, better known perhaps as the Drum Doc. Mr Hunt is an ex-jazz drummer and an ex-copper and he was most suspicious of my sudden arrival and asked me for my credentials, but as I am a person who never carries anything whatever in my pockets to prove who I am, I was not able to satisfy him of my good intentions. He then suggested that I write to him for an appointment giving him full details of who I was, what I wanted, etc. Somewhat disappointed I left the shop, but as I got to the door his secretary recognized me and I was dragged back inside like a long lost friend. I found Mr Hunt something of a character, for when introducing me to members of his staff he either got my name completely wrong, or else forgot it altogether. At one point I remember him introducing me to someone as John Harvey, author of *Things are not what they are*. Doc Hunt is probably the best known drum maker in England and he repairs and makes drums for the BBC, Jack Parnell, Ray Ellington and Eric Delaney. Sammy Davis Jr hired a set from him on his last visit here, and he also makes drums for the army.

The Doc's oldest employee is 74-year-old Mr Ernest Home, who has been making drums for sixty years. In spite of his age he told me that he is emigrating to Australia where he hopes to work as a drum maker, and is also going to meet his grand-daughter for the first time. After I had been talking to Doc Hunt for some time he asked us if we would care to join him in a drink in the club room of the Orchestra Association. I was slightly surprised at this for I hardly associated him with the Proms. However I could have not been more wrong for he is in fact one of the trustees of the Association—a remarkable man by any account.

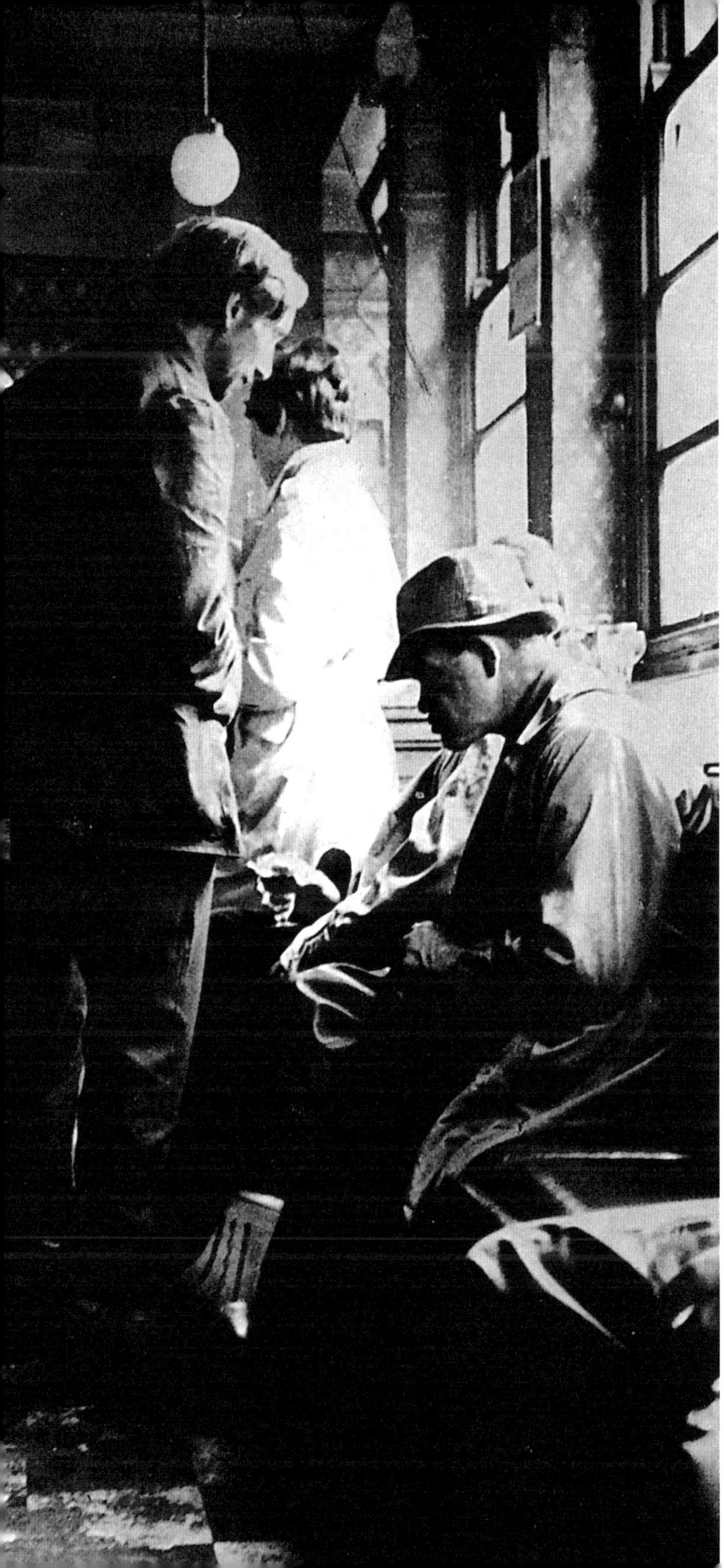

THE YORK MINSTER AND OTHERS

Without doubt the most famous and most publicized pub in Soho is The York Minster, known better by far as the French Pub. The pub was started by Monsieur Victor Berlemont in 1914, and since his death in 1951 has been continued by his son Gaston. Victor had the most famous moustache in Soho, measuring a foot from end to end. Gaston has clearly emulated his father for his fierce-looking moustache must measure just as much. Though the French Pub is still very popular it had its heyday during the war when its customers were almost entirely Free French forces stationed in England. In fact General de Gaulle was often to be seen drinking an aperitif at the bar. In those days cheerful young French sailors could be heard to chi-ike each other in the tangy accent of Toulon. The walls are covered with signed photographs of French vaudeville stars, French boxers, French bike-riders: there is Grock, the Fratellinis, Criqui, Siki, and Carpentier. It was the boast of M. Victor Berlemont that no celebrity had his picture hung on the wall until he had had a drink in The York Minster. Apart from running the pub Victor was second to many French fighters who visited this country: Ledoux, Criqui, Thil, Carpentier–and not another picture has been hung on the wall since his death. The days of 'Messieurs et mesdames; C'est passé

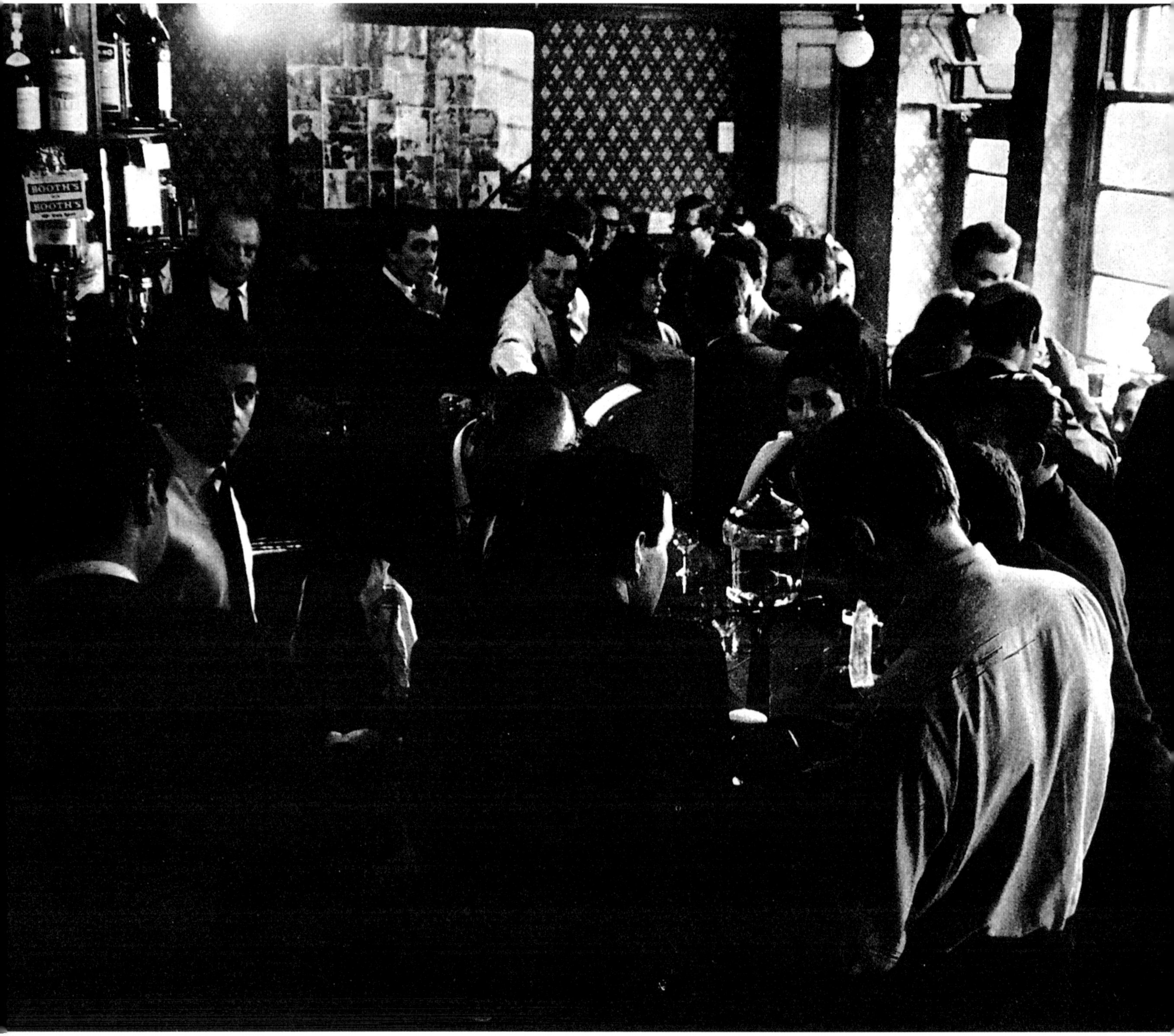
BOOTH'S
BOOTH'S

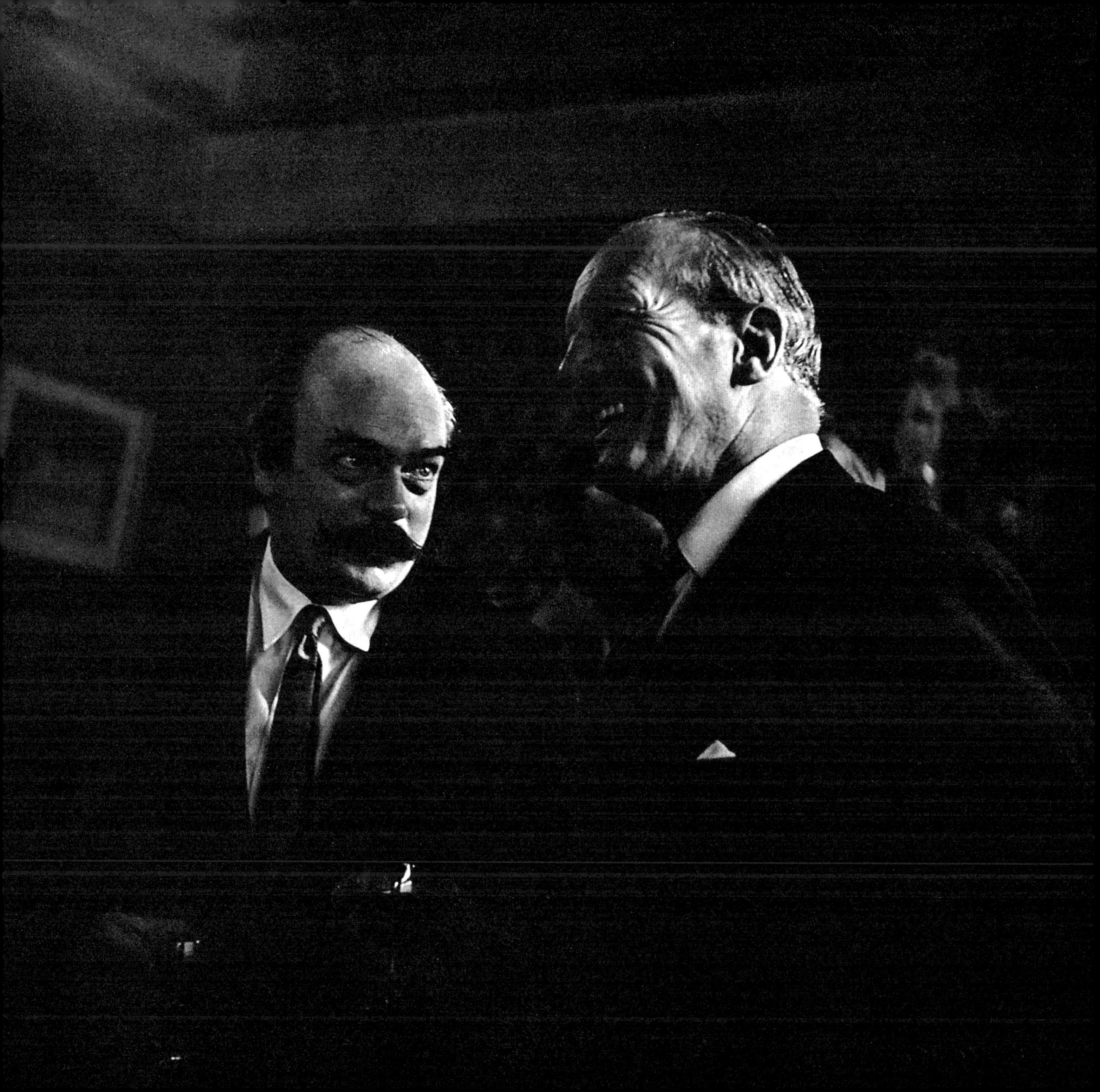

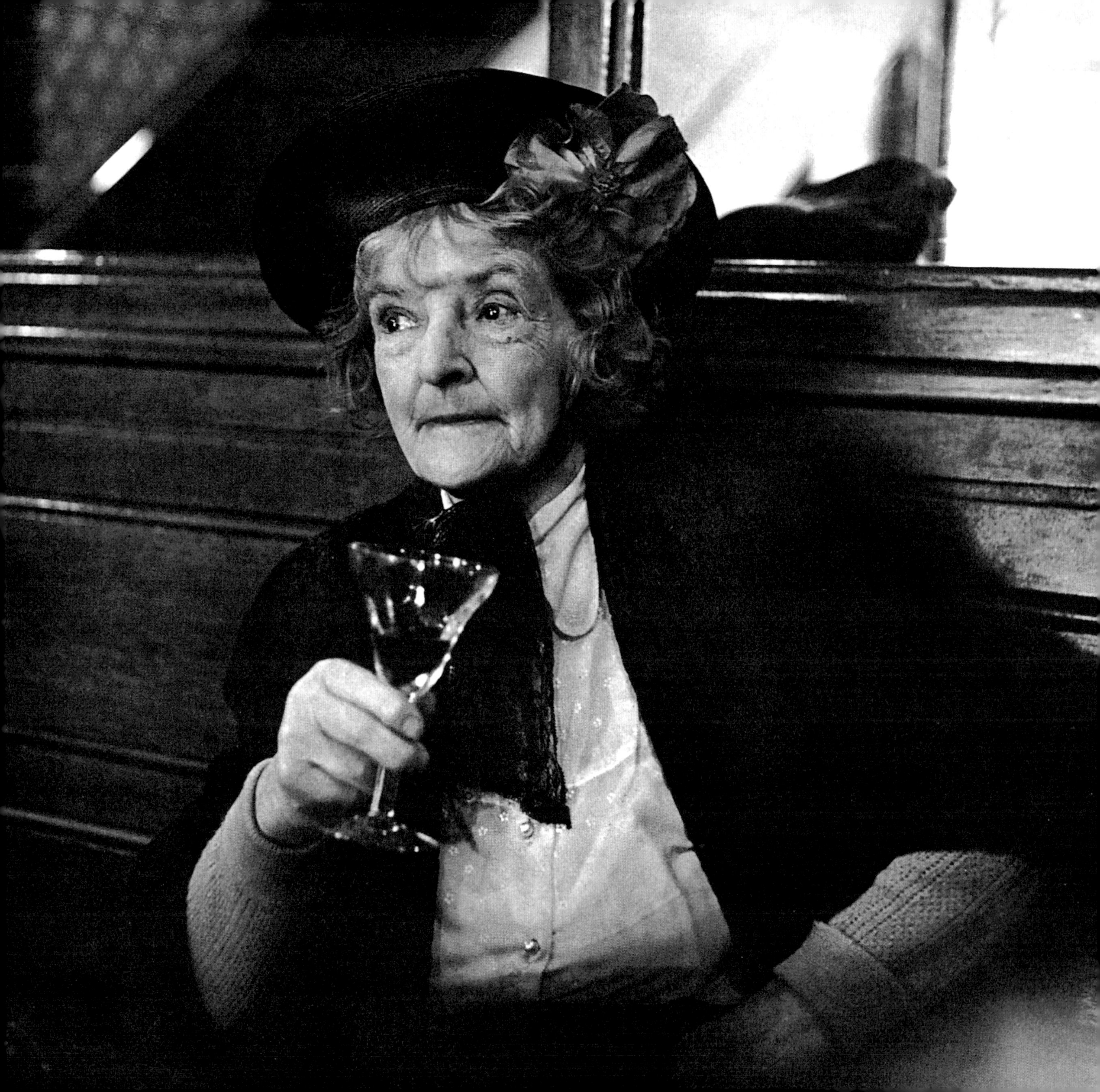

l'heure!' have long since passed and 'Time gentlemen please!' does the trick just as well. Though it is not unusual to see a Frenchman in The York Minster it is no longer a daily occurrance, with the exception of course of Gaston Berlemont.

There is a little dining-room above the French Pub where you can get good but plain French cooking served by French waiters. The restaurant was opened by Victor and in those days it was quite difficult to spend two bob: for eighteen pence you could have Hors d'oeuvre, fillet of plaice, beef steak and a rum pancake. Today sitting at the same table you would be lucky if you got the same meal for less than fifty bob.

One of the greatest assets of the French Pub is that it is almost impossible to get barred. If anyone gets a bit drunk and makes a lot of noise Gaston will come over and turf him out, but the following lunch time you are allowed back in again without a word being said about the activities of the night before, no matter how rowdy they may have been. Today the drinkers in the French Pub are a rather different bunch to those of long ago but it is still packed with advertising men, actors, a few writers, one or two bums, and a great many quite ordinary people, who have popped in for a glass of beer during their lunch hour, and there is never much elbow room. The strange thing is that although during the lunch time there is still some of the old spark left, with the evening trade it disappears completely, and gives way to a rather uncomfortable atmosphere. In spite of this it is still the best and most lively pub in Soho.

Of the others there is not much to say. There is The Intrepid Fox named after a politician called Charles James Fox who was said to be an 'intrepid fellow'. It has carpets on the floors, soft leather seats to sit on and a spotless bar to lean against—in fact for my money all the things that make life uncomfortable. The Round House on the corner of Wardour and Brewer Street I have never been in in my life and have no intention of starting now. The Swiss Pub too has changed out of all recognition: at one time it was a meeting place for artists of one kind and another, today it is full of whoever goes in there. There is however a very pleasant little pub on the corner of Archer Street called The White Horse, though it would not be true to say that the clientele are Soho people, mostly the customers are from the theatres nearby in Shaftesbury Avenue, such as The Globe, The Apollo and, of course, until recently The Windmill, which had been putting on nude shows for donkey's years. The girls came out of the theatre and into the pub wearing full stage make-up, and visitors from the North had to look twice, for they were not able to believe their eyes. Though it can hardly be said that it was a strip joint itself, The Windmill was the fore-runner of all the strip joints in London! In fact The Windmill was one of the most respectable places you could ever wish to find. True, the girls stood around six parts naked, but should they move so much as an eyelash the chances were they would get slung out on their ears, for it is laid down by the Lord Chamberlain that while it is all right for the girls to appear before the public naked they must not move a muscle. The shows at The Windmill were continuous from about lunch time, and many men wearing rather nasty raincoats used to line up outside the box office waiting for the first house, and sometimes did not leave until the end of the last!

During and after the War The Windmill's slogan was 'We never closed'. Alas, only a year ago it did close and now it is a cinema.

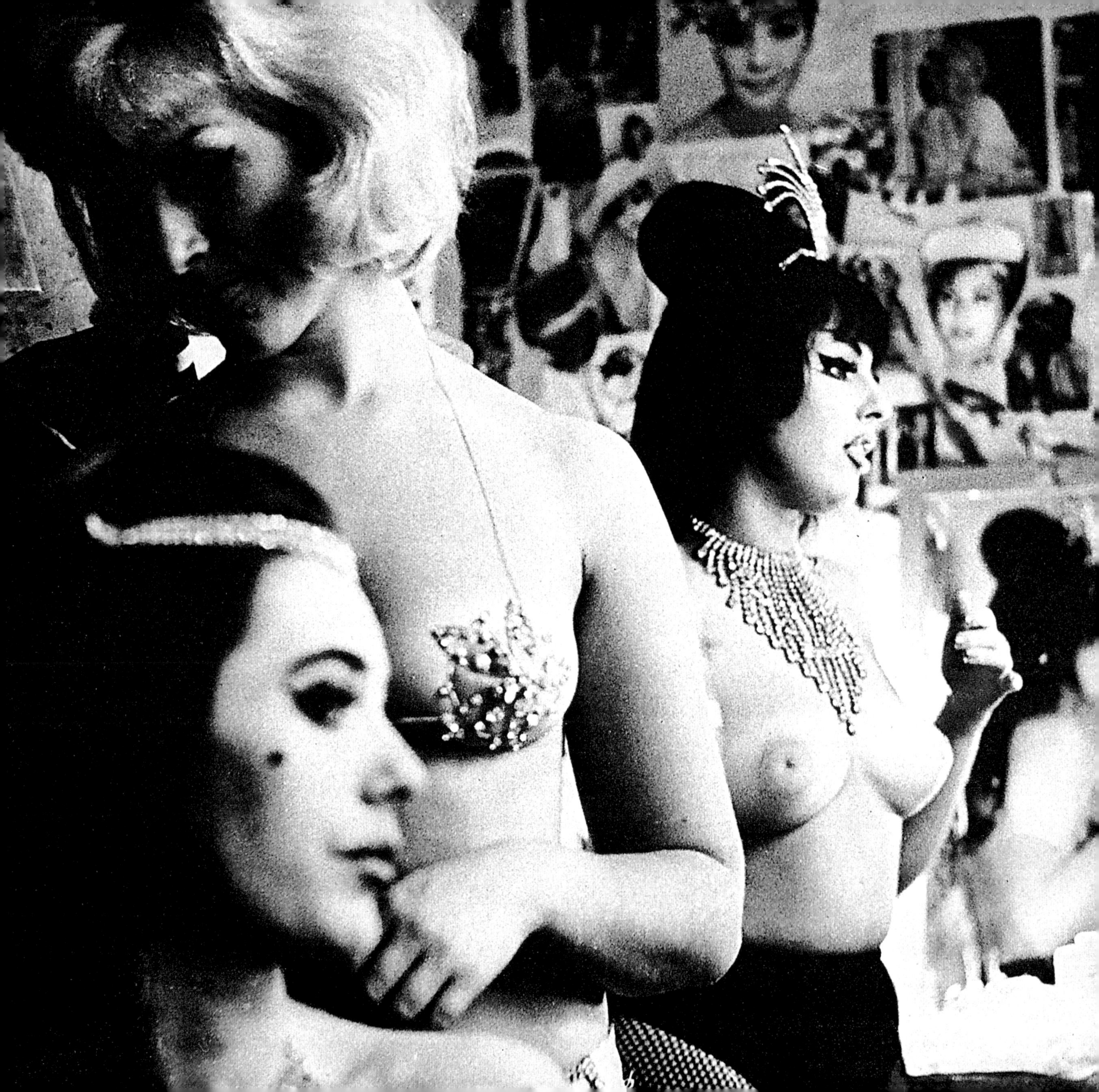

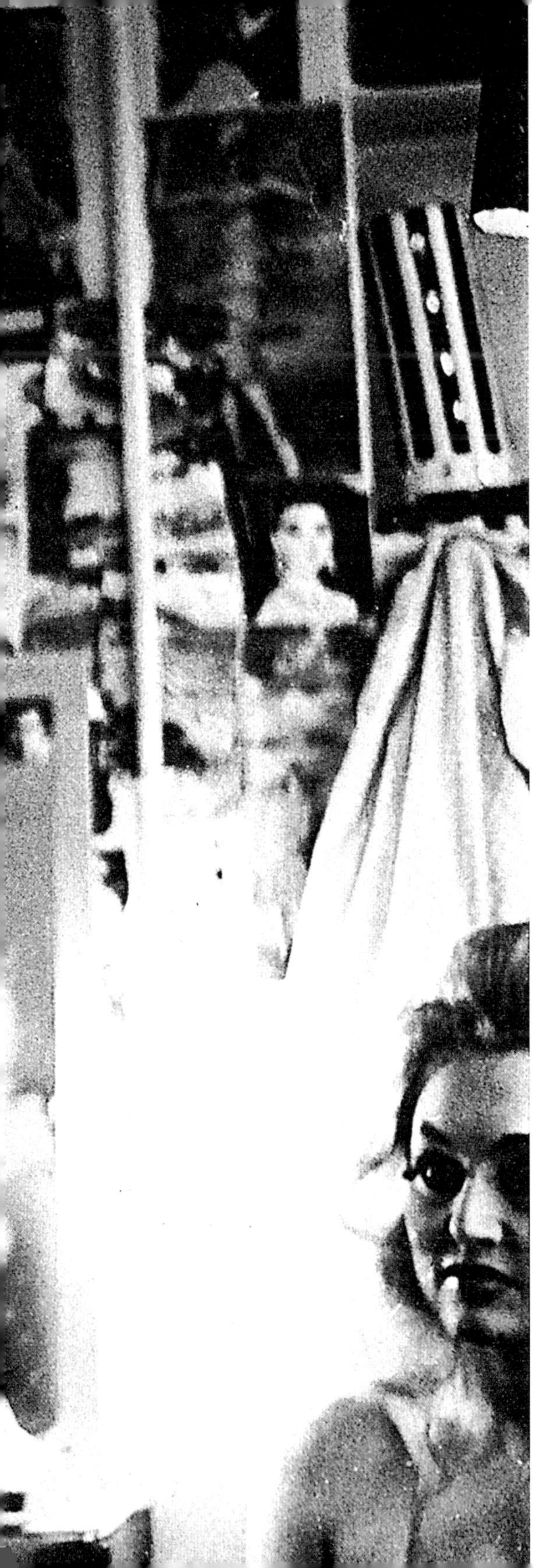

THE STRIP CLUBS

Since the girls have been driven off the streets and on to the telephone, the strip clubs in Soho have really come into their own. There is at least one in each street, and in some streets there are three or four, mostly they are nothing but holes in the ground where young and old girls peel off their clothes to the pulsating beat of a record on a Juke Box: the prices of admission are anything from seven and sixpence to twelve and sixpence depending on the class of the joint. On Saturday nights people come to Soho from all over the place, and if there is a North Country football team playing away at Chelsea or Fulham you cannot move for the crowds.

A man from Huddersfield who has come to London for the weekend to watch his team will, after the game, wander the streets of Soho looking for a whore. He may pause in St Anne's Court trying to make up his mind whether to go into the dirty bookshop or go into the strip joint next door or even climb the stairs and have a short time with the brass on the first floor above the cafe. He looks furtively up and down the street to see if anyone is watching him, and then he ducks into the strip joint, only to find that the girls are sexless and boring. They go through the business of taking their clothes off to the rhythm of an Eartha Kitt record—she is singing something about money and oil wells. The man watches the girl with his eyes on stalks: she has red hair with black roots, her figure is either falling apart or not yet developed, she is forty-two or seventeen. When he came in he had hoped to have his sex urges satisfied, now he finds himself with even greater sex urges. One act follows another, each one is worse than the last. He starts to hate the girls, they all hate him and all men like him. Eventually he rises to his feet and leaves the place

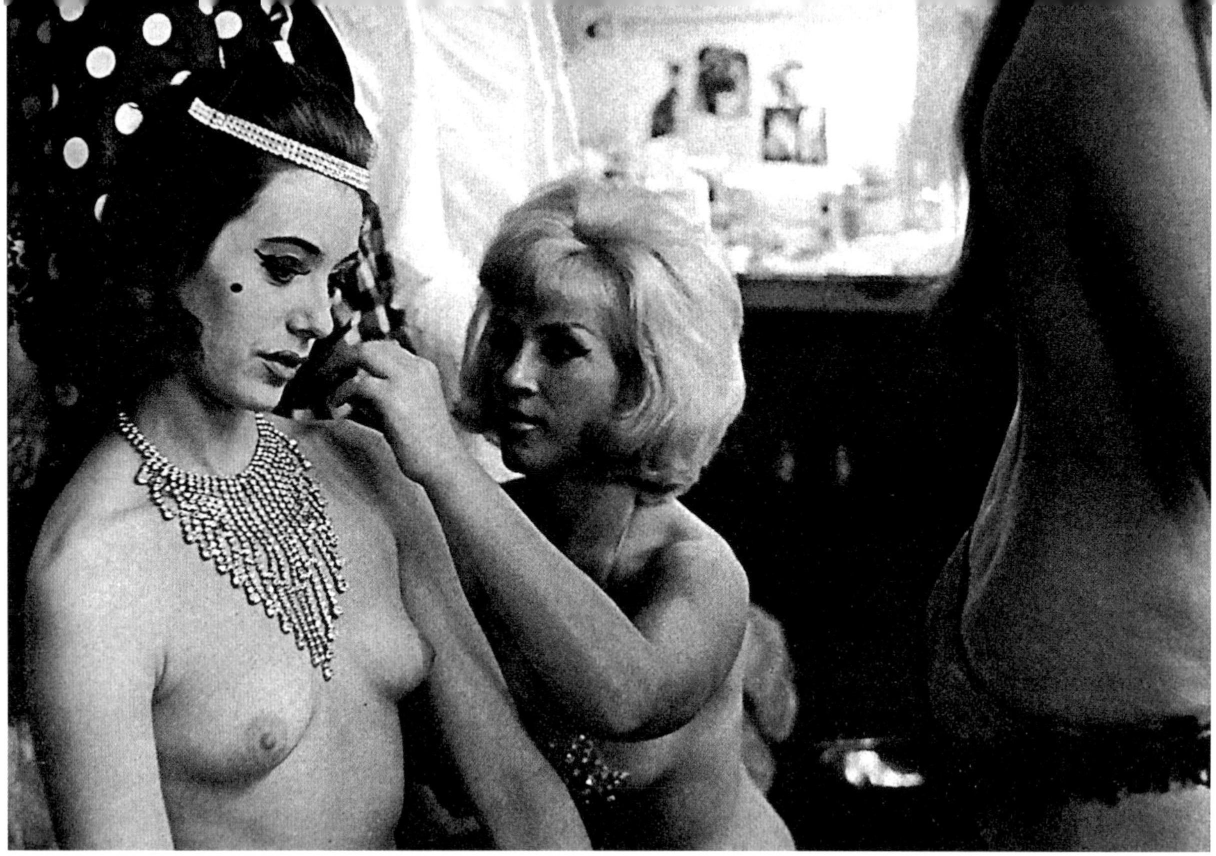

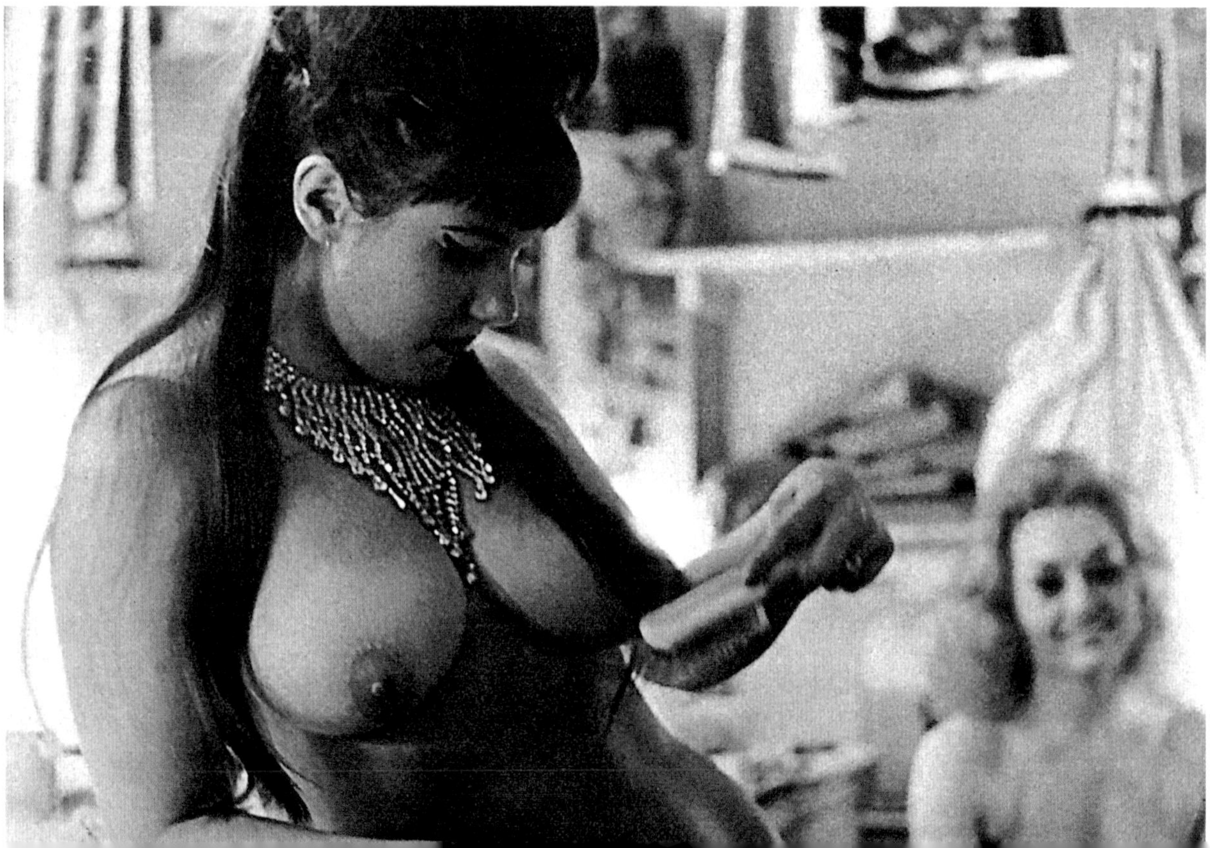

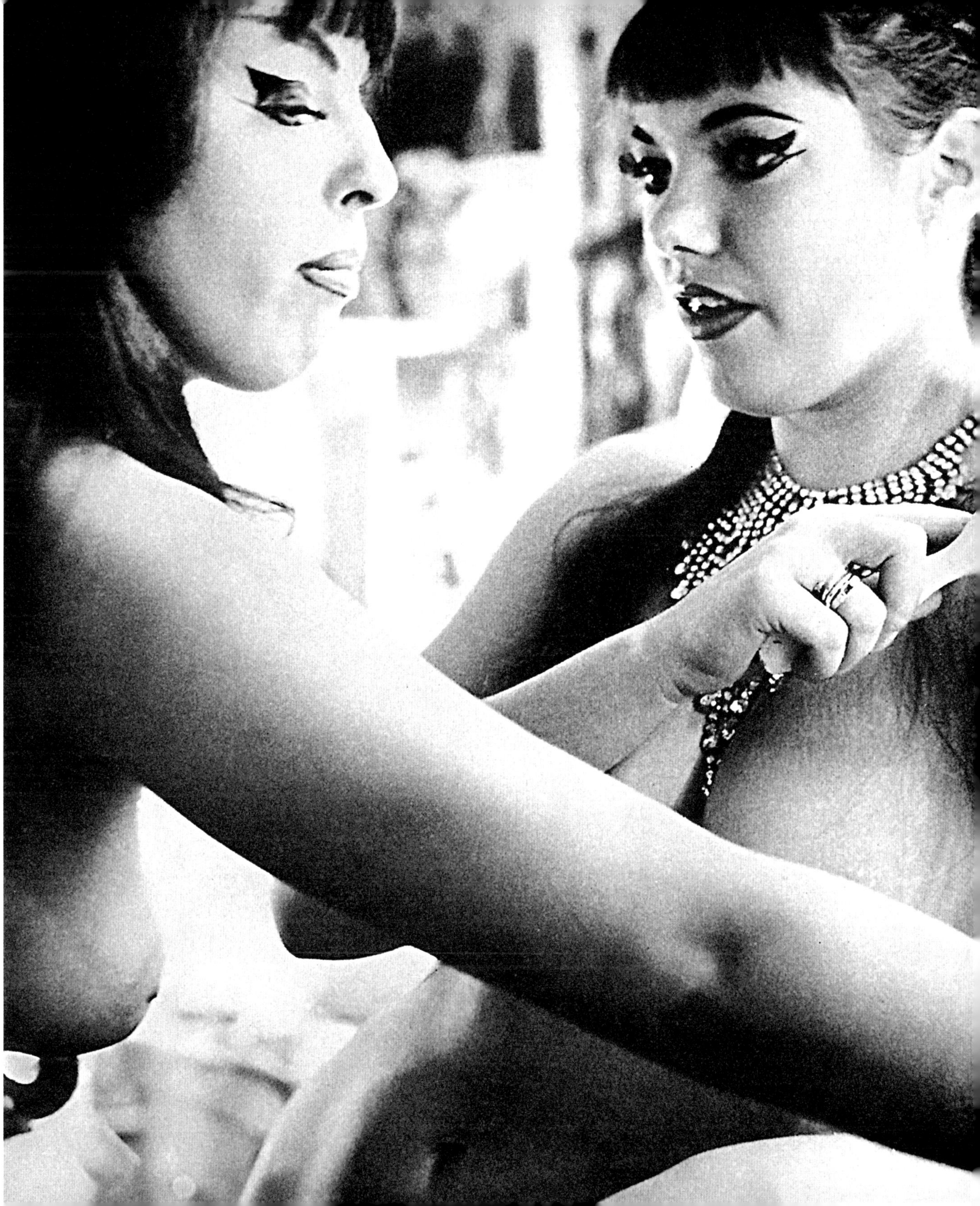

in disgust, and goes into the nearest pub and gets drunk. At closing time he returns to his little hotel in Paddington, broke, drunk and alone. The next morning he wakes up filled with alcoholic remorse, and swears that he will never do it again, but it is wishful thinking, for the next time his team are playing in London he will go on another search for excitement.

Not all strip joints are as crummy as those of which I have spoken. Some, in fact, are positively elegant, such as the Casino de Paris which is in Denman Street just off Piccadilly, and rejoices under the title of 'London's Leading Theatre Club'. It is run by two elegant young men called Ray Jackson and Eric Lindsay, and I must own that they have impeccable taste: even the air is purified by Fume-O-Dor, there are fitted carpets wall to wall an inch thick, and sparkling chandeliers hang from the ceilings. Unlike the sleazier Soho strip joints where during the course of a day the performers go from one place to the next in rotation, the girls at the Casino de Paris are more or less a permanent company. Many of the girls have been at the club for years: one of them, for instance has been there for over five years. The club opens at 2.30 p.m. each day, and the girls arrive at 2 o'clock, so as to have plenty of time to get their make-up on. They work eight hours a day, during which time they do four shows of about an hour and a half each. I found the show both artistic and tasteful, and the girls very pretty and some even beautiful. The shows are changed four times a year and are directed by the proprietors, and the productions are lavish and cost upwards of a thousand pounds each. The costumes too are expensive and are especially made for each production: they have to be well made, because of the wear and tear they get from being doffed so often. Prices here are of course much dearer.

The audiences often put in as many hours as the girls and in order to keep the regulars from being bored a bit of oo-lala is imported from time to time, a recent girl being Lydia Lova, who is said to be France's most decorated woman (for her bravery in the Resistance during the war). Personally I found her 'irresistible' and am not in the least surprised about the medals. She was at the time that I saw her the current star of the Folies Bergère in Paris and special permission had to be obtained so that she could come to London. And in 1960 Maxine Kessler was brought over from America to appear at the Casino de Paris: she was the first American striptease artist to appear in London since Gypsy Rose Lee. All the girls are trained dancers which gives the whole thing a very professional touch.

I think what amused me most at the Casino de Paris was the attitude of the girls towards the clients. The atmosphere back stage is sort of school-girlish with a touch of sophistication. In the dressing rooms I overheard such remarks as 'Old Footsy nearly caught me. He told me "You quayte stole the show m'dear". He had his mouth open so wide his teeth were hanging out.' Many of the regulars have been given nicknames by the girls, whom as far as I can make out are a happy jolly lot. I found it hard to believe that they were selling sex appeal or whatever it is they are supposed to be selling, and I got the impression that it did not occur to them either. The girls all get along together and a troublemaker does not last long, she is soon given the sack. For relaxation in between shows, the girls sit in the kitchen backstage scraping butter from the packet on to great wads of bread: it is a scene far removed from the glamour of the front of the house, where the gaping businessmen wait eagerly for the girls to appear on the mirrored stage. It is all a far cry from the sleazy holes of Greek, Old Compton and Frith Streets.

The strippers in the smarter clubs are highly paid, getting between £85 and £100 a week, and strangely enough there is nothing obscene in their acts. Even stranger is the fact that these girls are also extremely moral. After they have finished work they either go home and rest their sore feet or else go out to dinner with their boy friends. They seldom go home with any of the customers, and in some places it is a rule of the house that they should not do so.

It is not the same with the rough gaffs. I remember one day visiting a strip joint at the bottom end of Berwick Street. I was watching a pornographic-looking tart peeling her clothes off. On her face was an expression of absolute boredom, the strip joint was a tumble-down house and it stank, there was very little light, and the room was full of seedy-looking gents all with their hats on. I was leaning up against a rail at the back of the room, when a tearaway I know came in the door and sidled up to where I was standing. He was the governor of the club.

'Wotcha cock, how's tricks?' he asked with a cheery smile.

'Musn't grumble,' I replied, glancing at him sideways.

'I didn't know you went in for strippers,' said my friend with a leer.

'Just goes to show you,' I replied, 'you live and learn. As a matter of fact I am doing a bit of research.'

'Well you won't get much research around here son,' said my friend. 'All the birds who work here are scrubbers!!'

'Where do the girls come from who work here?' I asked.

'I dunno where they come from mate, I never ask 'em.' At that moment the old bag had finished taking her clothes off and disappeared into the wings. Her place was taken by another girl who was very young and she looked to me to be somewhat nervous. A record blared out and she slowly began to take her clothes off (they were obviously her ordinary street clothes). I heard a few geezers in the audience catch their breaths.

'Where did she come from for instance?' I asked.

'I dunno,' replied the tearaway, 'She arrived this morning and said she wanted a job, so I gave her a job . . . Not bad looking is she?'

'Not bad,' I said despondently.

'Listen, what's up with you anyway. If a bird comes and asks me for a job, I can't help it can I? If she is over twenty-one that's all I'm interested in.' I could tell that he was getting a little cross with me for some reason. 'Look' he went on, 'the Law won't let the girls earn any more. If they capture them hustling in the streets they sling them in the nick.' The little girl who was taking her street clothes off was down to her airtex panties and a fat sweating man in the front row let out a strangled sigh. 'Yes I guess you're right, they are better off earning a living indoors,' I replied, heading for the door.

I wonder where that little girl is now. I suppose she is still doffing her clobber in some flea pit, or maybe she has graduated to being on the game full time in Paddington. Of course there is a chance that she has seen the error of her ways and turned it all in, but I doubt it, because as I have already said, for some reason once a girl starts on the road to ruin there is little that will stop her continuing till the bitter end.

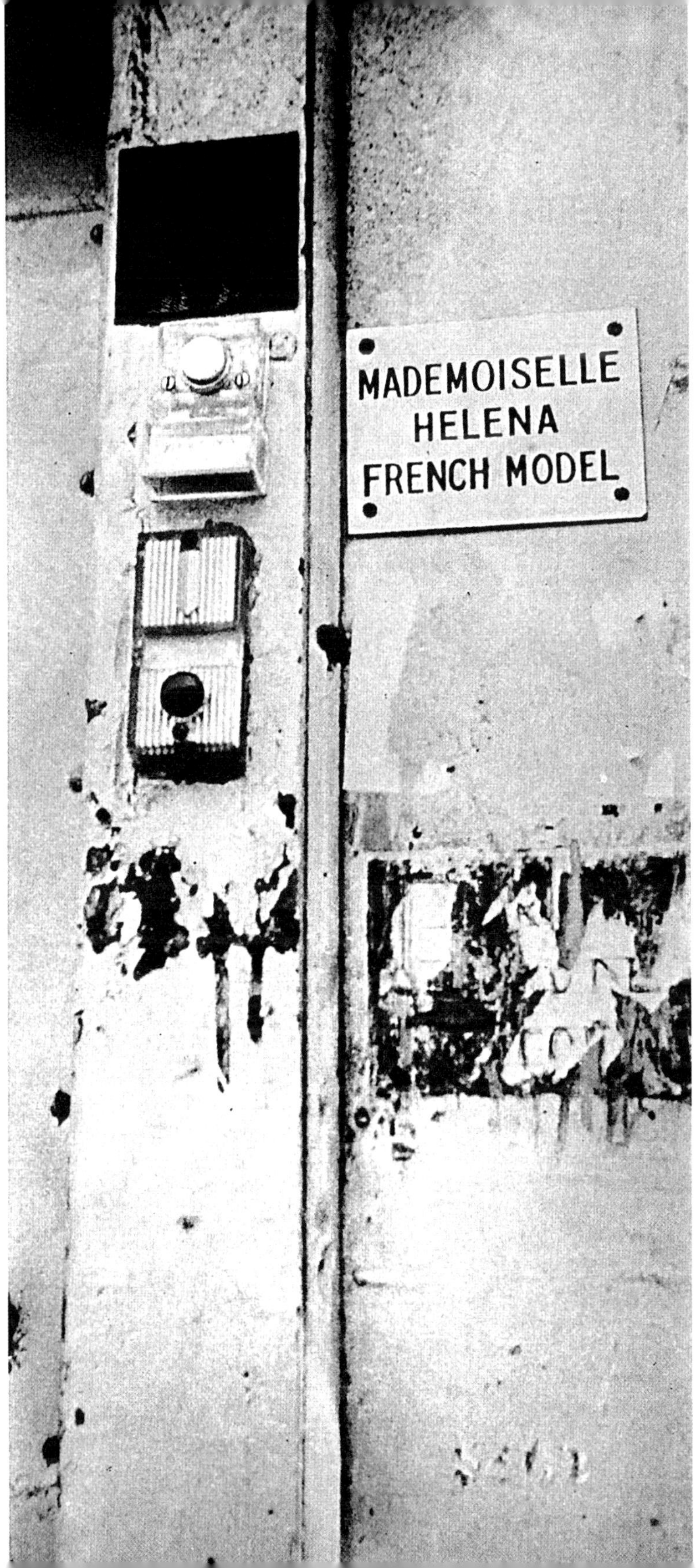

SOHO PROSTITUTES

There is no set 'type' of girl who becomes a prostitute. They come from every corner of society and there are as many girls from what are called 'good' homes who turn to prostitution as there are from 'bad'. Like everything else there are as many reasons as there are girls who are doing it. In point of fact since the Street Offences Act things have become much better for the girls, because almost the whole of their business is now done on the phone. I remember years ago when things were very hard they had to hustle clients on street corners, and although the fines were not very heavy there were other things for them to watch out for, such as encroaching on another girl's patch. A girl guilty of this used to find herself in dead bother with the other girls, and would often get beaten up by some tough brass, whose piece of pavement she had invaded. These were the days of the Messina brothers. Now the Messina brothers have gone, and the girls have disappeared underground. But there are disadvantages in this new state of affairs. Although it is less risky to do business by phone, the clients can't see the girls until they arrive at the address given them, therefore a man looking for a tall slim girl may get a short fat one and vice versa. This of course leads to frustration and dissatisfaction: where clients used to be able to pick and choose which girl he fancied, now he has to take pot luck.

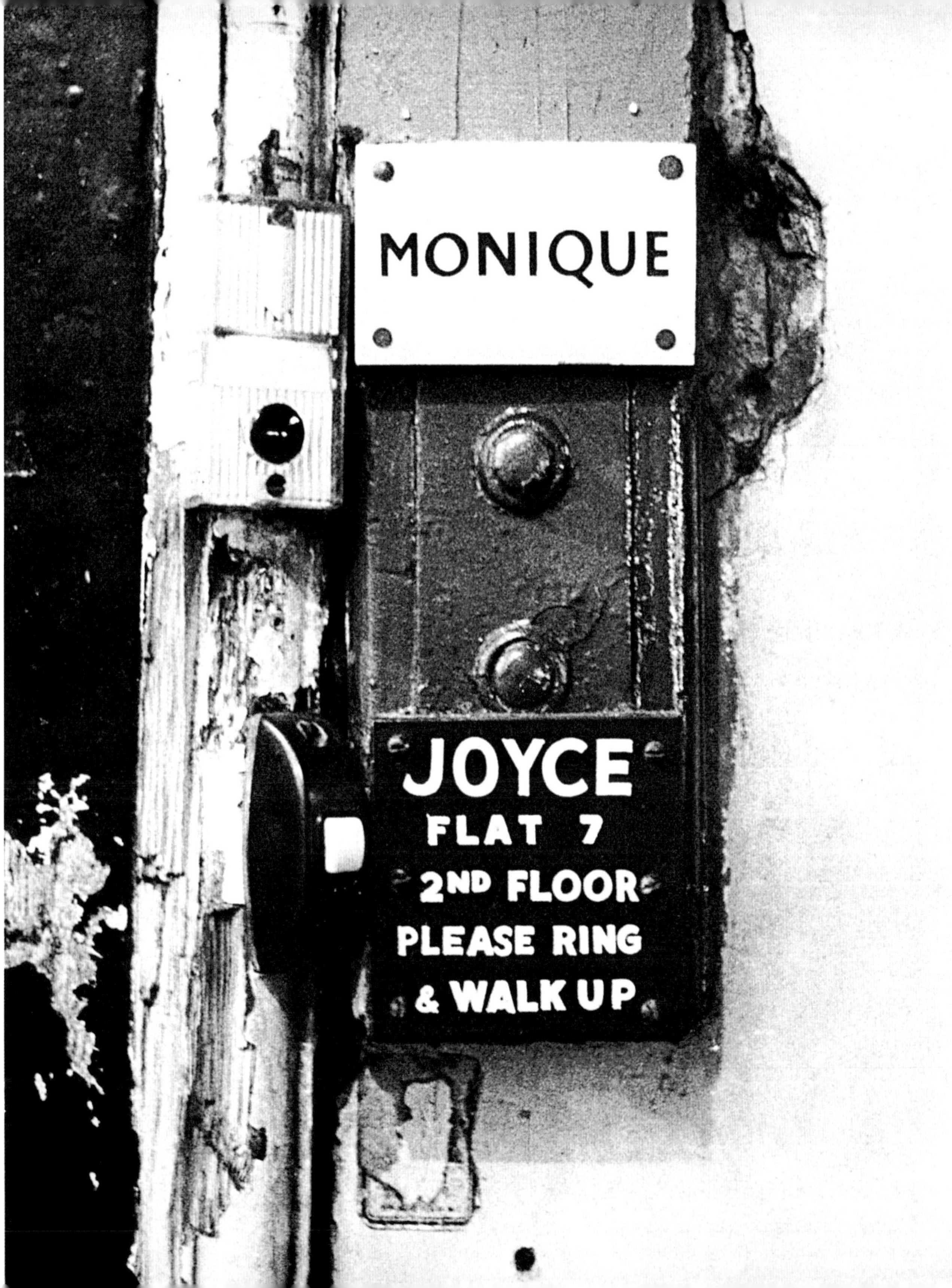
MONIQUE
JOYCE
FLAT 7
2ND FLOOR
PLEASE RING
& WALK UP

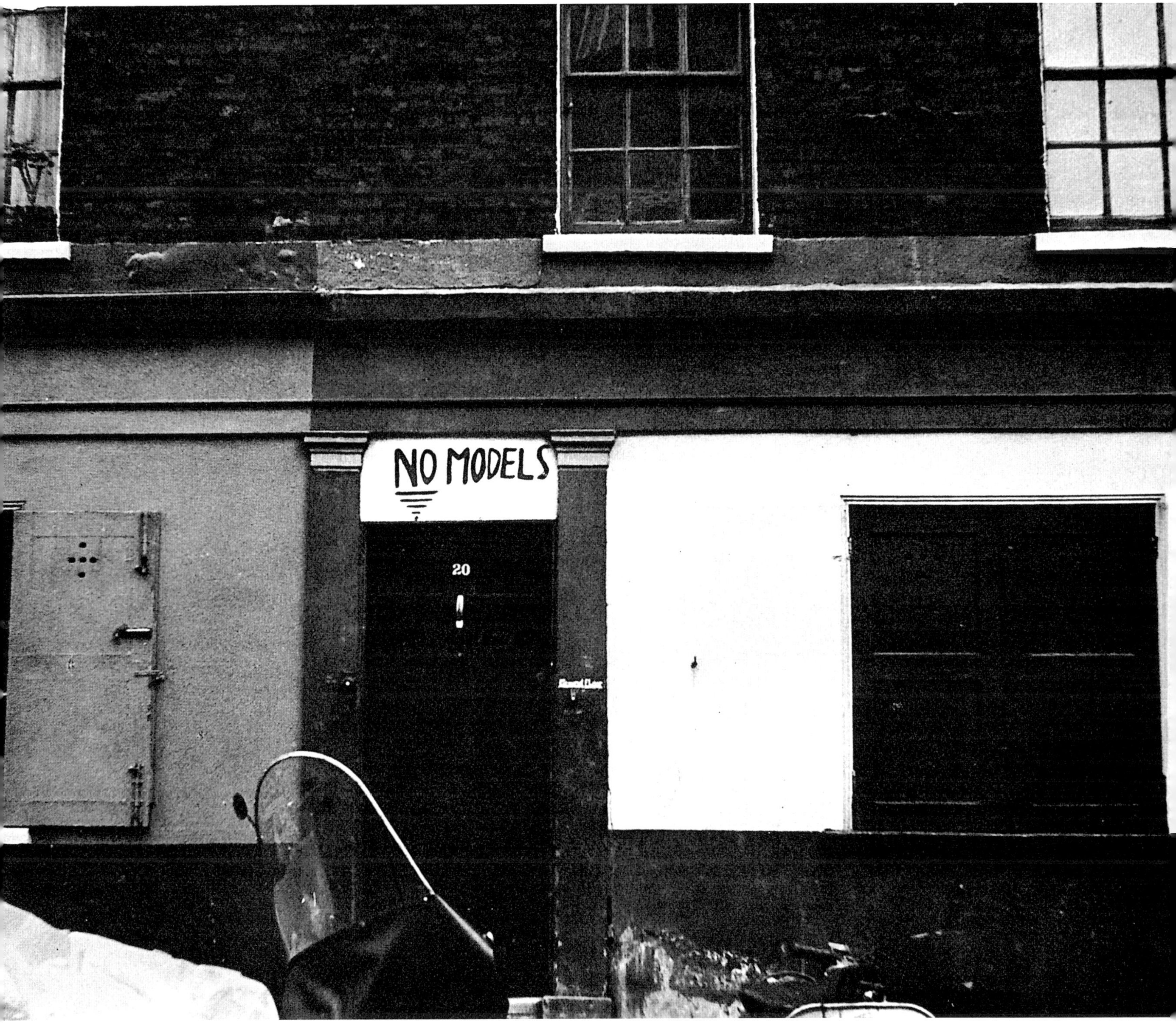
NO MODELS
20

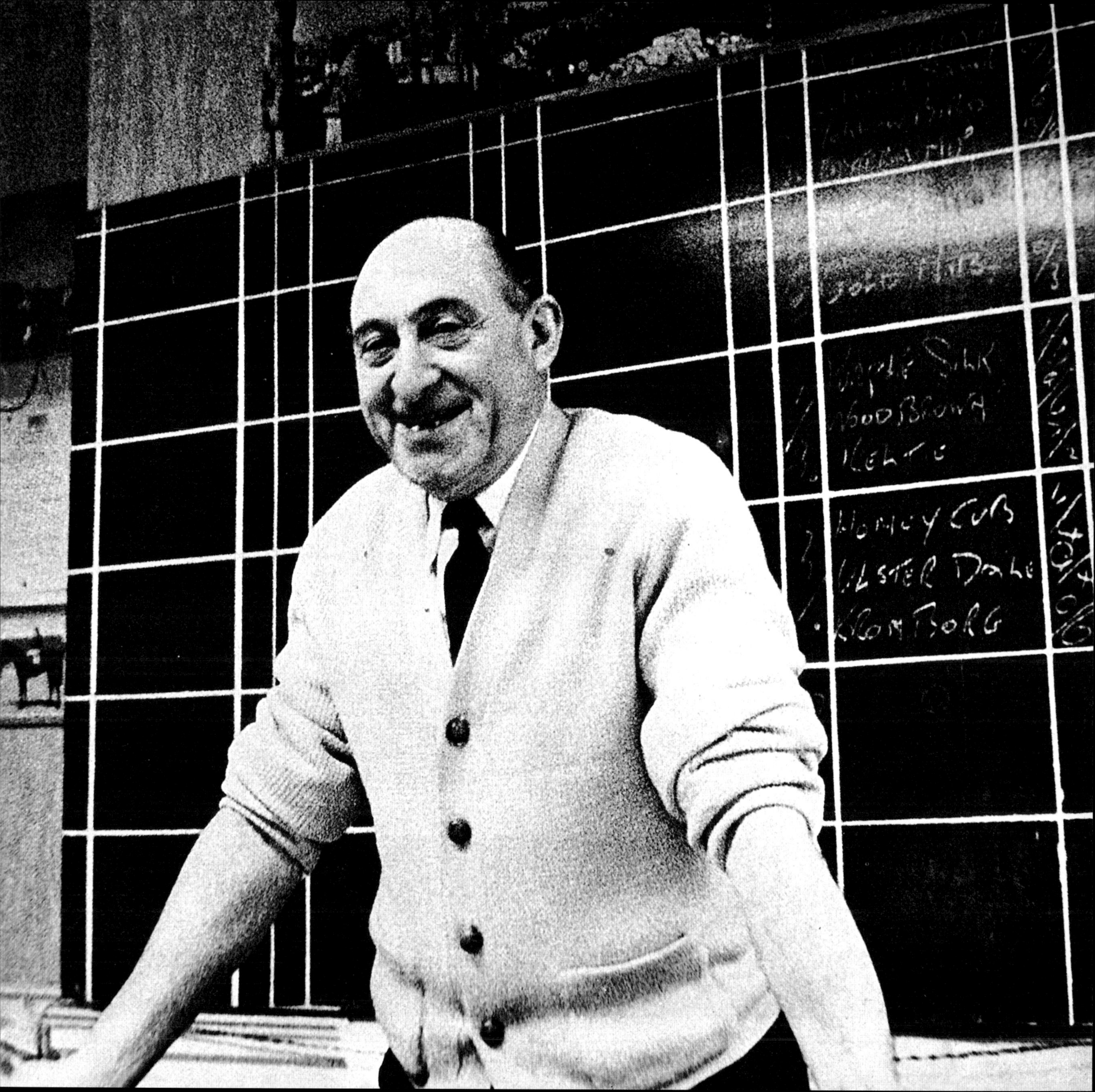

BETTING SHOPS AND GAMBLING CLUBS

A fairly new innovation in Soho is the betting shops. There is of course nothing new in gambling in Soho, or anywhere else. What is new however is the fact that it is now legal. There have always been schpielers in Soho, but until the gambling laws were changed they were for everlasting getting raided by the law, and persistent offenders often found themselves doing a bit of bird in Wandsworth. In the old days there were often differences of opinion between the tearaways who ran the schpielers, and these differences of opinion often resulted in punch-ups, carve-ups, and even the occasional shoot-up: it certainly was a tough old game. These days all is quiet, and what was once against the law now has the protection of it. The street bookies have now turned respectable and run licensed betting shops with such names as Major Collins, Joe Coral, and of course Terry Downes, the one-time middleweight champion of the world, who has a chain of betting shops stretching from Bermondsey to Wardour Street.

All the betting shops are run in a highly honest and professional manner by clerks who know the game well. Invariably they are most helpful to the punters, especially if they are novices who are not sure how to fill in a betting slip. It is indeed extraordinary the effect that the betting shops have had on the public. For old punters who have been playing the horses all their lives, the situation is easy. They can now place a bet and be sure of collecting their winnings (in the old days it was not completely unknown for a street bookie to do a scarper without paying out the punters). Apart from these old hands, quite ordinary people who have never had a bet in their lives will haunt betting shops daily during their lunch hours. Old ladies and young boys can be seen fighting their way to the front of the queue so as not to be too late to have a bet on the favourite in the two-thirty, or have two bob each way on a rank outsider.

But though the battles that used to go on years ago have now subsided there has been a little trouble with a few betting shops, such as the odd petrol bomb through the letter box in the dead of night, which is liable to distress the turf accountant who owns the shop somewhat. Whenever one of these bombings comes off, the police make vigorous enquiries which always without fail come to nothing at all. The owners of the betting shop say that they think it has been done by a punter who has lost a lot of money, and is not a very good sportsman. Personally I think that this is somewhat of a tall story, and that the truth of the matter is that there is some internal friction going on between rival betting shops. Anyway I hope this is the situation because I find the idea of an unlucky punter getting his own back a very great bore indeed, whereas if it is a bit of terrorism by rival mobs, it is all very exciting. Things have been very quiet for some time now, so maybe everyone has settled their differences, which, if true, is a great shame. For there is nothing like a bit of bother to keep

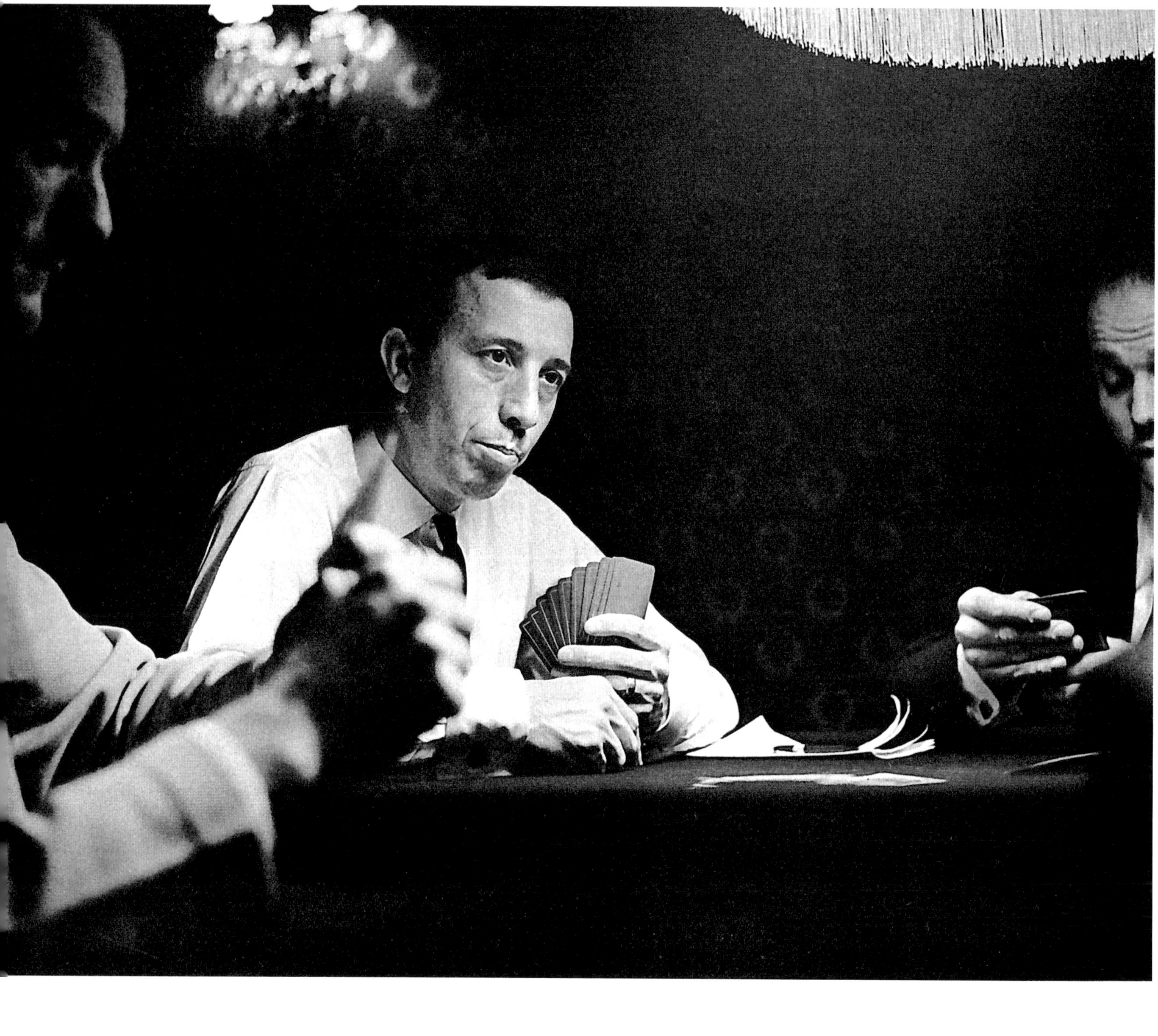

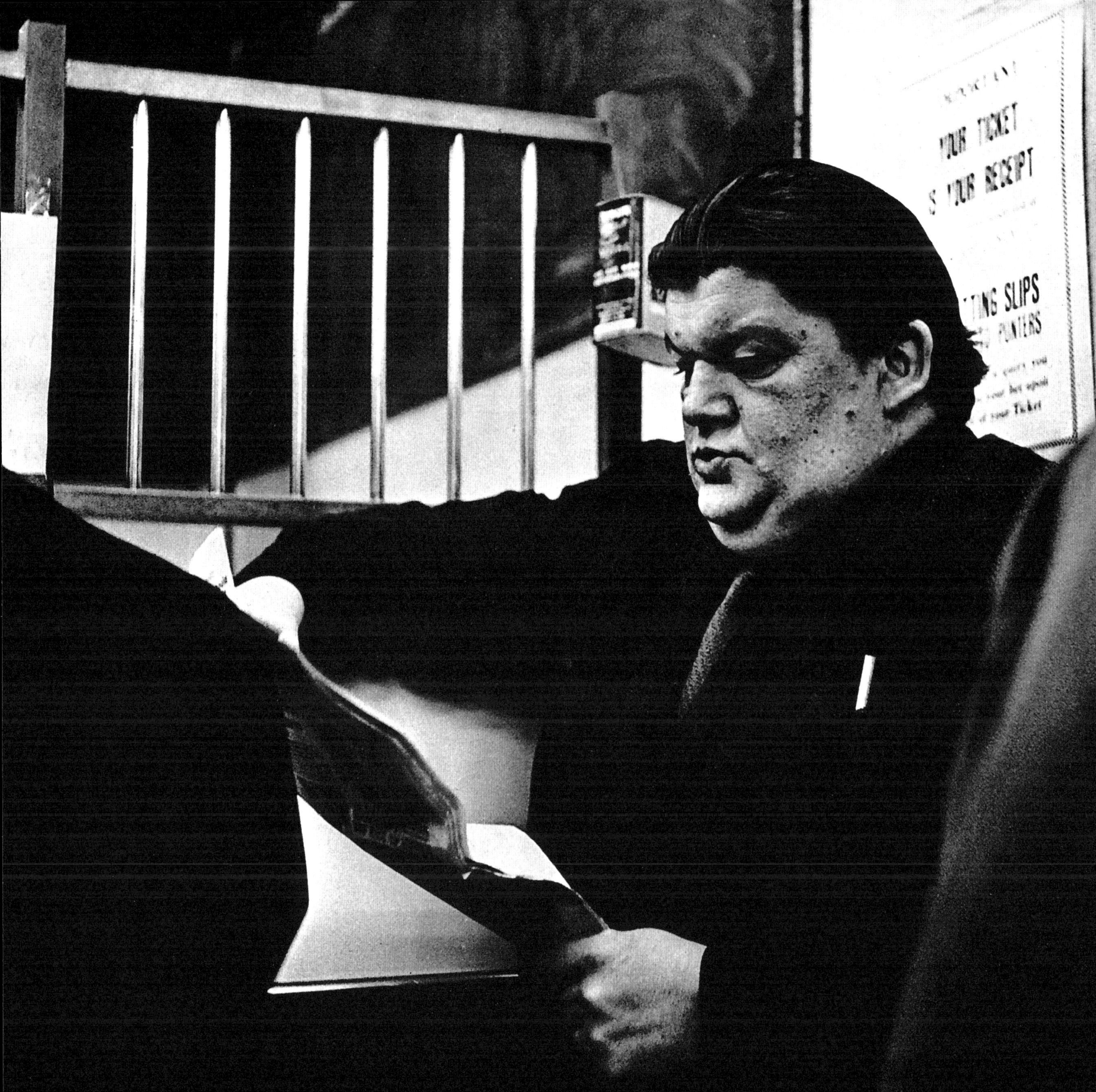
YOUR TICKET
IS YOUR RECEIPT

people on their toes.

The gambling clubs are also very popular these days. The public are of course a very gullible lot, and there is nothing they like better than getting rooked for all their money, and some people dearly love to be completely ruined. If you wish you can now play chemmy, poker, roulette, pontoon and faro all night long. Some games in fact have been known to go on for three days and nights, by the end of which so much money has changed hands that the house has got almost all of it. In some clubs the house money can be as much as half a crown in the pound, that is to say that of every pound that is bet half a crown of it goes to the house. This means that if four men play poker for ten hours and each one of them starts with a hundred pounds, the chances are the house will wind up with fifty or seventy-five of it. The house never loses even if everyone else goes skint.

Though most of these gambling clubs are run on the up and up, there are some that are as straight as a dog's hind leg. Such places are for me a great delight to visit. The governor is bent, so are the dealers, and even the barmaid leaves quite a lot to be desired in the honesty department. Most of these legal schpielers open at about nine, and keep open until everyone either loses all their money or are too tired to see the spots on the cards. The punters come from all walks of life except from the genuine working classes, for the workers would not last five minutes in a schpieler, they are far too poor. Some of the regular gamblers are very rich women who think they have infallible systems and who sit around the roulette wheel with diamonds resting on their flushed bosoms, all the while smoking Turkish cigarettes. They toss a five-pound chip on the red: it comes up so they follow it up: it comes up again: they go for double or nothing again and it comes up black and they lose their money and never learn, for the following night they will be back again for more punishment. Men arrive wearing dinner jackets, they have just been to a firm's dinner or a school reunion and have come to have a little flutter just to finish the evening off. They invariably wind up losing far more than they intend. Layabouts are also regular visitors to schpielers. I once saw a bum come into a room, put a tanner in a fruit machine, get the jackpot, which came to about seven quid, take his winnings over to the roulette table and walk away an hour later with two hundred quid, much to the annoyance of the rest of the punters. But needless to say he was back again the next night and lost the lot.

Gamblers are a funny lot. Some of them start one night just to show off in front of some girl and the next thing they know they are hooked, and before long they are compulsive gamblers and will do anything for a bet. They will sell all their belongings in order to pay off the gambling debts, and may eventually wind up stealing other people's property in order to gamble. Eventually they find themselves in so deep that they cannot get out no matter how much they try. The girl friend that they first tried to impress has long since left them, and nothing can cure them, the reason being that just when things are at their lowest ebb they will have a big win, and for a short time things may go well for them, so they jump back on the roundabout, thinking that they are always going to win. This of course is only wishful thinking because before they know what is happening they are in dead trouble again. It does not happen very often but occasionally girls can be just as bad as men when it comes to the gambling bug.

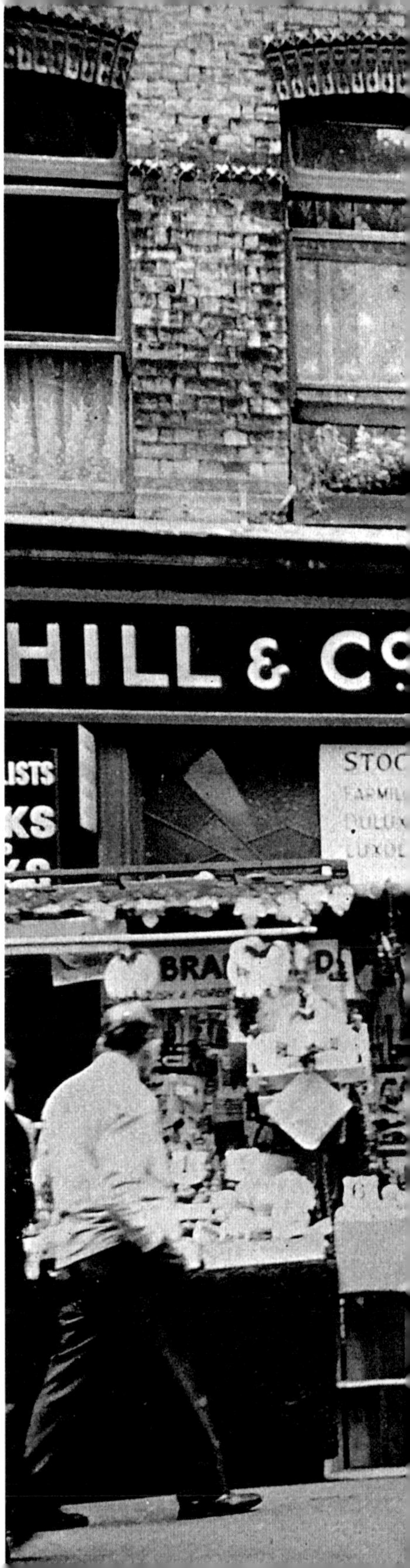

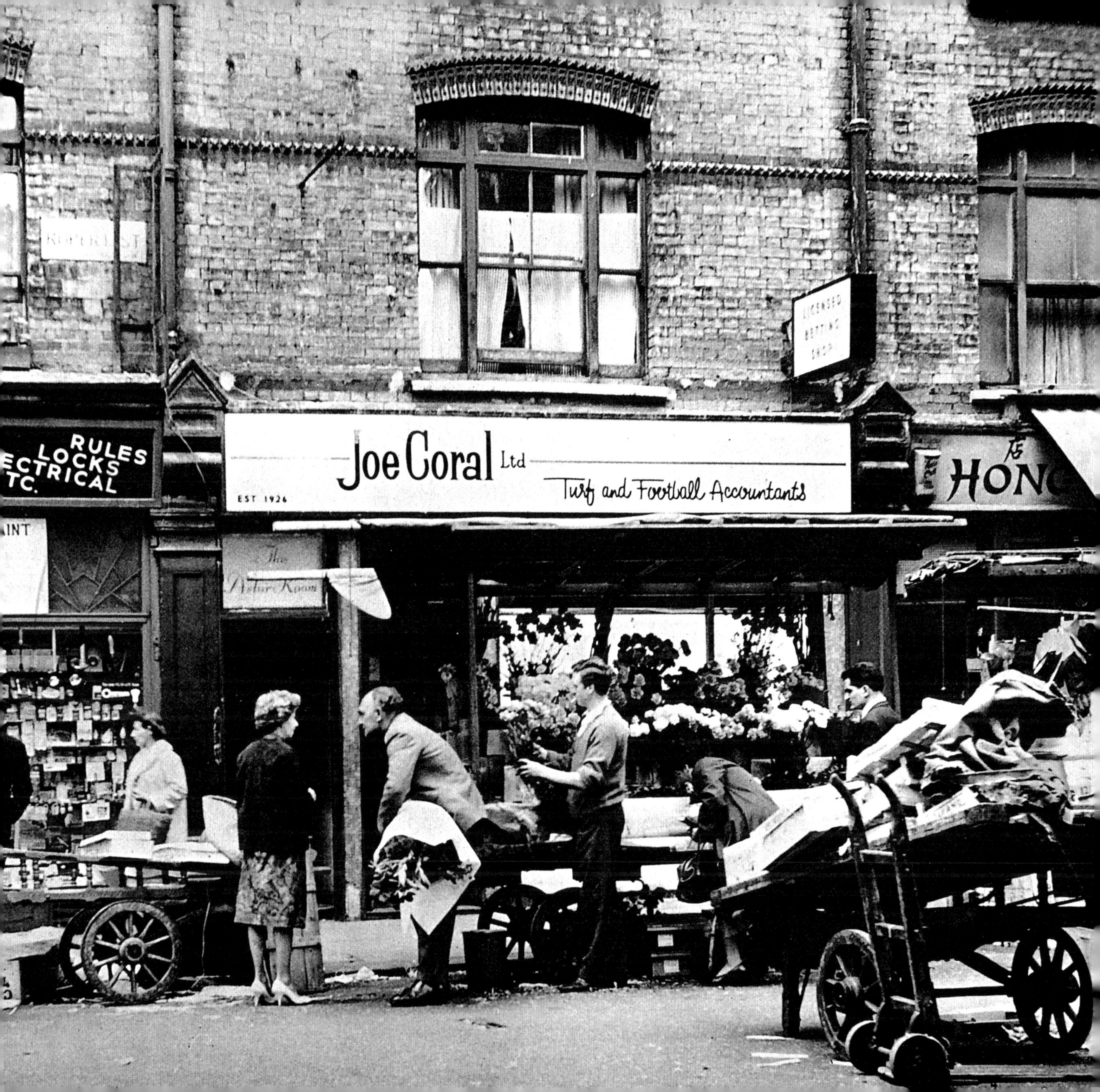
RULES
LOCKS
Joe Coral Ltd
EST 1926
Turf and Football Accountants
LICENSED BETTING SHOP

MURIEL'S, THE ROCKINGHAM, THE ESTABLISHMENT

In Soho there are many clubs, in fact the truth is there are literally hundreds. There are queer clubs, lesbian clubs, clubs where villains congregate to plot dastardly crimes, clubs where writers gather to talk things over, and clubs where nothing much whatever goes on except for a great deal of boozing. Boozing in fact the like of which I have never seen anywhere else in the world, not that I have been to many places. One of the strange things about club owners, and governors of pubs too, if it comes to that, is that if someone gets drunk and raises his voice somewhat, they become most indignant and are liable to turf one out on one's earhole. I consider it strange because they seem to forget that they are serving the where-with-all that makes people drunk, and they are well pleased that drinkers drink in their establishment, because this makes them rich. If you have a few over the top though, they do not like you any more and set about the business of slinging you out very lively indeed, saying such things as 'You are giving my place a bad name, go and never darken my door again'. Fortunately there are almost more places to drink than there are people to drink in them.

Up until recently the clubs used to open at three in the afternoon and not close until eleven o'clock at night. All that has now been changed, since some bright spark in the government introduced a bill which stated that drinking clubs should only be open to members during pub hours, that is to say from eleven-thirty to three and five-thirty till eleven at night. Who, I should like to know, wants to go to a club at eleven-thirty in the morning: only the daft politician who introduced the bill, no doubt. Needless to say this state of affairs has hurt the club owners considerably, in fact with many it has either halved their business or ruined it completely.

Before the clubs were closed down in the afternoons there was a daily procession from the French Pub and Wheelers to Miss Muriel Belcher's Colony Room in Dean Street. Muriel is without

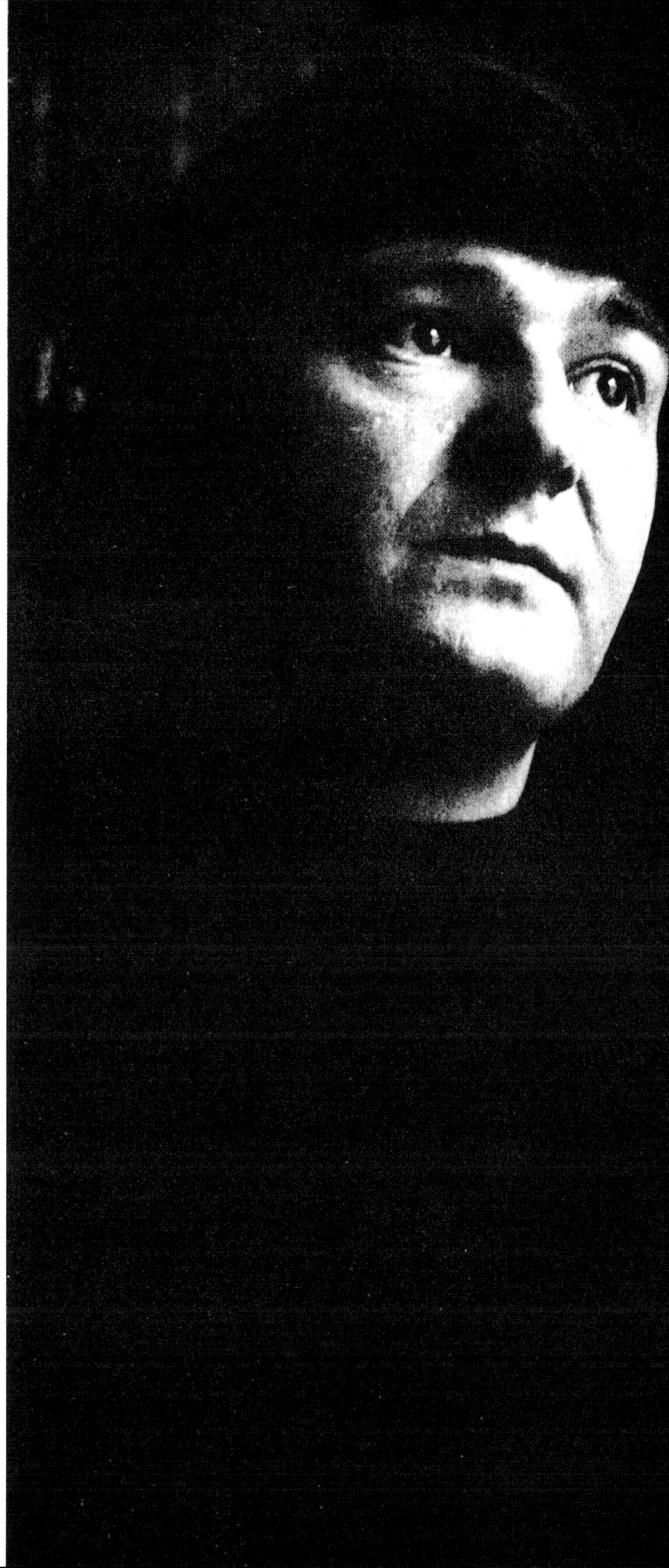

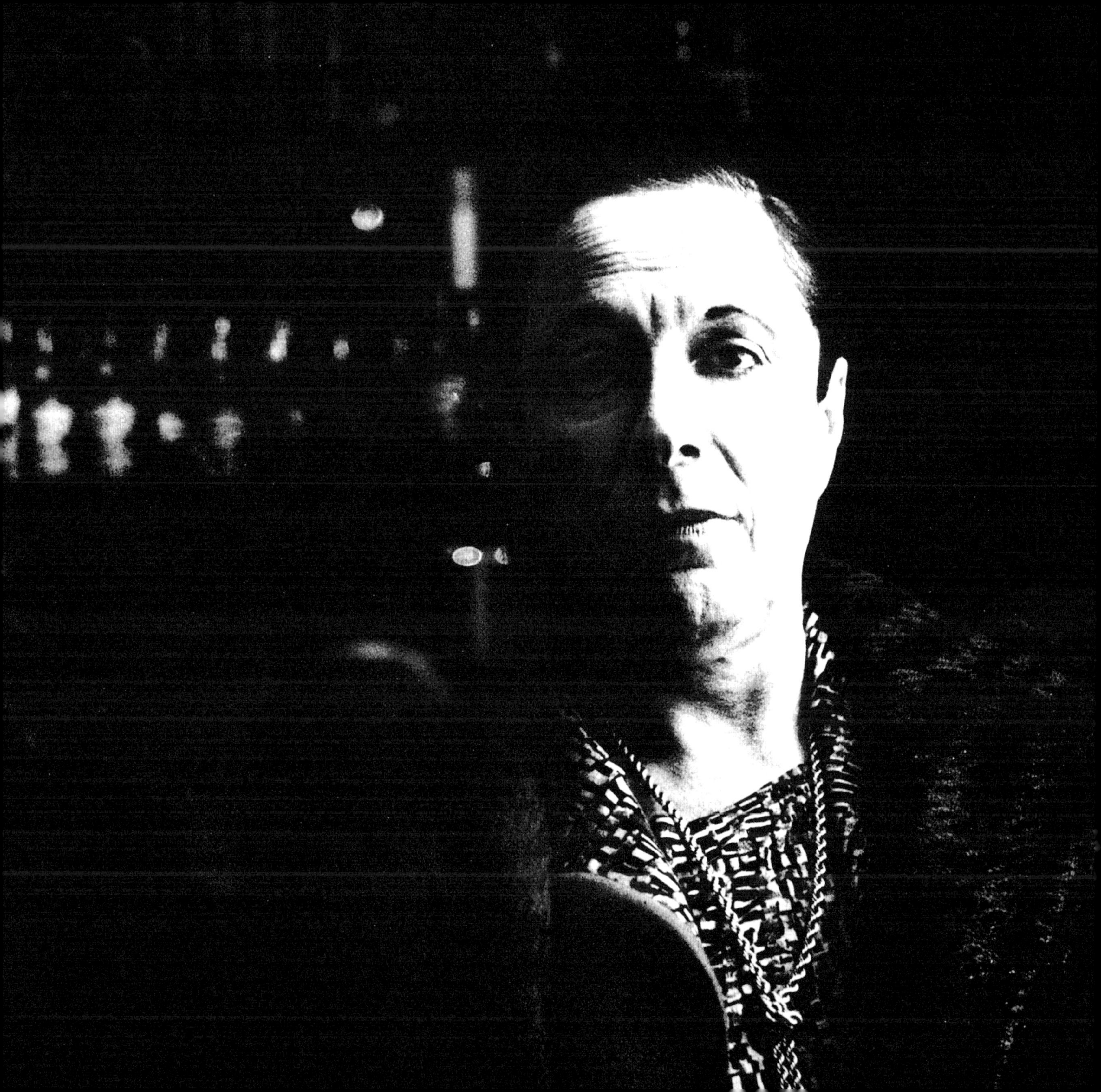

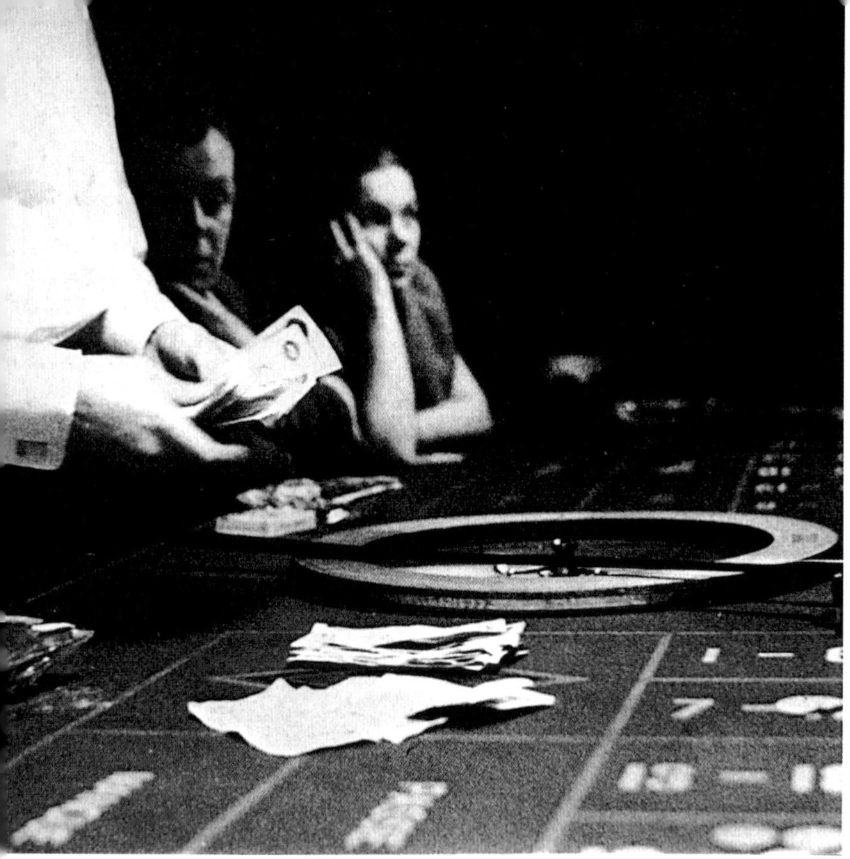

doubt the most famous and best loved of all the club proprietors in Soho. She has been in the club business all her life and has had the Colony Room for over fifteen years, and has never been known to complain no matter how much you drink, in fact the more you drink the better she likes it. Her clients come from every social stratum one could possibly imagine: stockbrokers, layabouts, advertising men, journalists—you name them, they go to Muriel's. She is good-natured but is very firm with liberty-takers, which I imagine accounts for her being so successful, for it is by no means an easy business running a club, in fact I would say that it is an art. You have to be sympathetic and tolerant when people are in trouble, and not get bored with hearing their troubles, and I must say that all of Muriel's customers have troubles at one time or another, and some of them seem to be in trouble the whole of the time, and never leave off moaning from morning till night. But Muriel never seems to get tired of listening to their troubles, and even if she does she never shows it. Occasionally Muriel manages to get an extension in order to give a party: this she dearly loves to do. A recent card that I had from her read 'We hope to see you at our re-opening party' (she had been on holiday and the club had been closed for a month). A little PS at the end of the card read 'Taking into consideration the visit paid on us by the gentleman from Savile Row accusing us of not supplying our members with sufficient supper, we re-open at five-thirty and at eleven you'll have to go . . . ' and that's the way it is around Soho these days.

Another popular and well established club is The Rockingham in Archer Street. It is run by Mr Toby Roe and like Muriel's has been running for fifteen years or so. When one meets Toby Roe for the first time it is unlikely that one would think he was a club proprietor, for the fact is he looks more like a stockbroker or a doctor. However after a short talk to him it becomes obvious from his charm and sparkle that he could only be a club proprietor. He is a man of impeccable taste. Before coming to London he lived in the country where there were no locks on the doors, or if there were any they were never used. When he came to Soho and opened his club he rather thoughtlessly did not change his ways, he never bothered to lock the club up at night, and friends dropped in whenever they felt like it to have a drink and a chat. For a time all went well. Then one night he was in bed asleep in his flat above the club when he was suddenly awakened by the sound of some people moving about downstairs. He listened and heard them talking, and it seems that they were looking for the light switch but could not find it—they had come to turn the place over but could not see what they were doing and eventually they left without taking anything. As soon as they had gone Toby searched around for the key so that he could lock the front door but it was nowhere to be found. After a time he gave up the search, took a hammer and some nails and began to nail up the front door. A copper who was passing became suspicious and asked him what he was up to, and though Toby explained the copper was not at all satisfied and was about to arrest him for breaking and entering. At the time Toby was dressed in a silk dressing gown, which did not help matters at all, but in the end he was luckily able to persuade the copper that all was well, and the following morning he found the keys and has not stopped using them from that day to this.

The thing that Toby misses most in Soho these days are his old customers, some of whom have died of drink and others of acute old age and then again there are some who have retired to the country. When he first opened the club he was patronized by what was then called the Princess Margaret 'set' who were very excited by Toby's club and made such remarks as: 'Toby darling you really are too brave . . . It really is the most divine little club but what a sordid district', or else: 'What a squalid little street: it's so quaint we really must bring all our friends'. Toby is only too delighted by the fact that they did not keep their promise. One of his early customers at The Rockingham was Hermione Baddeley—she arrived one afternoon and asked the barman for a pot of tea. She was greatly taken aback when she was told that they did not serve tea, and left, somewhat annoyed. But Toby ran after her, brought her back and soothed her with soft words and a pot of tea that he made for her himself in his flat. Toby Roe is absolutely devoted to Soho and hates all the changes that are going on. He feels that if improvements are necessary then the old buildings should remain standing and the improvements should be made inside them. Though this may prove an expensive proposition, the result, according to Toby, would be worth it because Soho would retain its character. I think he has a point.

The Rockingham has the most international membership list in the whole of Soho: there are Peruvians, Mexicans, Russians speaking impeccable English, and Arabs. It is amazing that such a mixed bunch can be in the same room together, let alone mix well, but Toby tells me that there is never any trouble, and I must own that I have never seen any. When Toby named the club he wanted to think up something distinctive and for some time he was stumped, but one day he was looking down a porcelain catalogue and came across the name Rockingham. Right away he went out and bought a Rockingham vase, and called the club after it. Unfortunately the vase got smashed but the club kept the name. Later on Toby discovered that there was a racehorse called Rockingham who won the St Leger in 1833. He bought a painting of the horse by Herring and it hangs on the wall to this day. Many people, including myself, were under the impression that the club was called after the horse, but the vase is the actual story, though I don't think it matters much either way. Not only has the club a comfortable air, and the staff a sympathetic nature, in addition Toby Roe is just about the most generous club man in the business. No sooner does one enter his club than a drink is forced into one's hand. Personally I think it is a crying shame that there are not more people like him, for if there is one thing that I like better than anything else, it is being bought drinks by people who own clubs, and even by people who do not own clubs as well.

In Greek Street stands the now somewhat defunct Establishment Club, opened some years ago by Nick Luard, and Peter Cook of the satirical revue 'Beyond The Fringe'. Their aims were high, for the original idea was to run it as a place that would become famous for way-out talent, and it must be said that they tried their best.

In the beginning things worked out well enough and the cabaret, written, directed and often starring Peter Cook, was a great success and got national coverage in the press. Lenny Bruce was imported from America and became a great draw, but unfortunately little by little the shows got as bad as the food always was until eventually the club went broke, changed hands, and is now a gambling club. They still have a cabaret but little notice is taken of it, because the fad for this kind of satire is over, the public are no longer interested in seeing the government lampooned, or the working classes taken the piss out of. Personally I am sorry to see the Establishment go, because I thought it a good thing for Soho, but as I have already suggested, a room does not automatically become a club simply by naming it one. A club without a personal touch will not last long in Soho or anywhere else if it comes to that. The members must be made to feel that they are wanted, and that the staff and management are pleased to see them whenever they visit the club. This was not so with the Establishment and I think that this contributed more than somewhat to its eventual failure. There were far too many members, and hardly any of them knew each other. For a club to be successful it is a good idea if the members know each other if only slightly, for then there is some kind of common bond. This is why clubs where villains congregate stay in business year after year. The governor of the club is often a tearaway of long standing, and most of the members have been in every nick in the country. For some strange reason the more time a chap has done inside the more respected he becomes and there are some clubs where every penny that passes across the bar has been nicked from somewhere or other. The law let such places stay in business because that way they know where everyone is: if they closed them down they might find it difficult to lay their hands on some law breaker whom they wish to arrest for a crime committed recently.

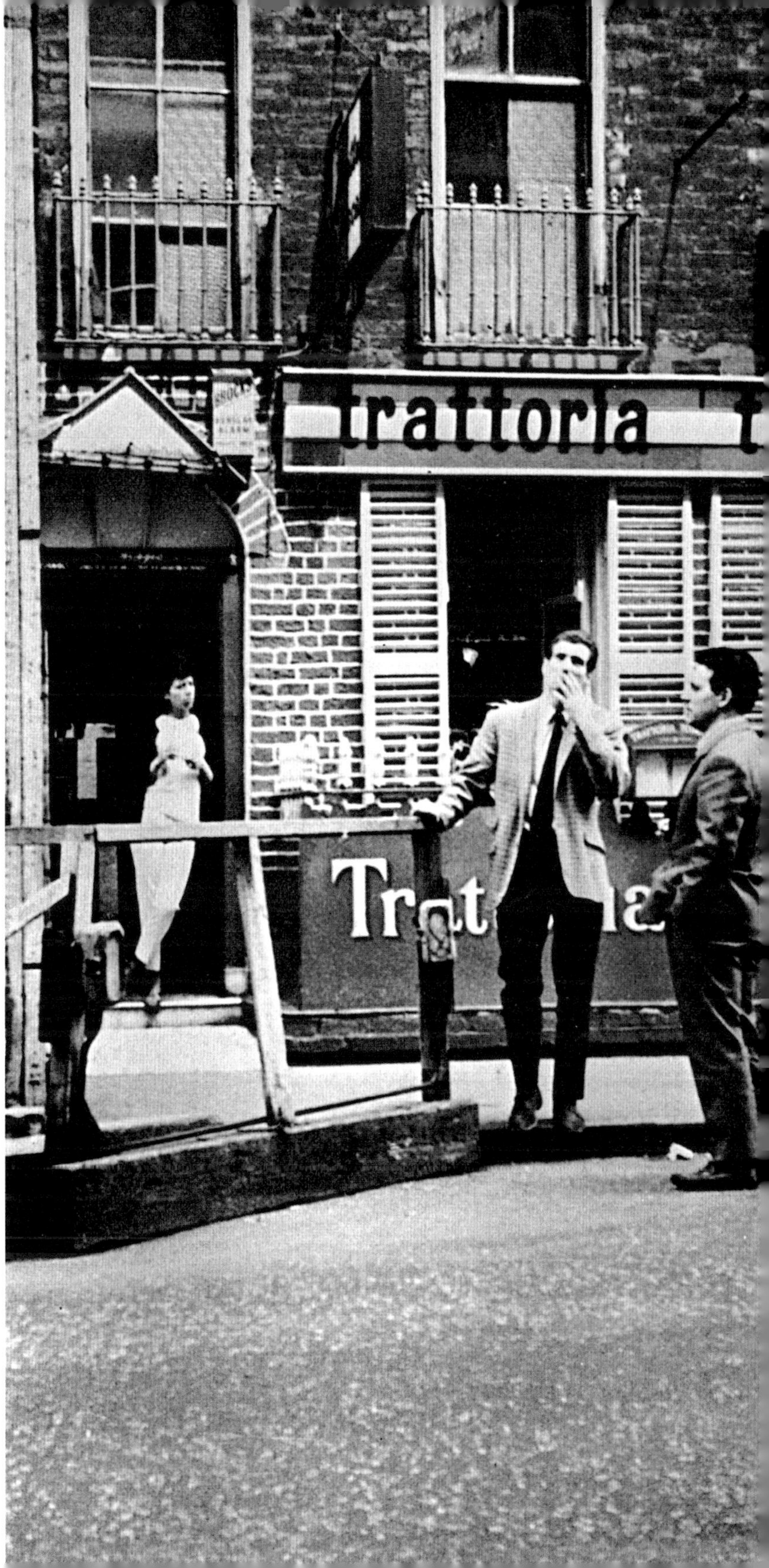

CLUBS AND THE LICENSING LAWS

The new licensing laws affecting clubs have caused many of the old ones to close down because the owners find that they no longer pay. Others are shut down by the police, for such reasons as not having a fire escape or not having enough ventilation or too much ventilation. Why the law should all of a sudden start worrying about fire escapes I simply can't understand, the offending buildings have been standing for over a hundred years without getting burnt down, so why the panic? In any case in nine cases out of ten it is not possible to build a fire escape at this late date, and even if it was there would be little point in doing so, for by the time the fire escape was built it would be time to knock the house down. As far as I can make out it is, as is usual these days, nothing but victimization, and as a result there is now a great deal of unrest in Soho club land, and things are not getting any better.

I was talking to a man who runs a club just off Old Compton Street, and he was bemoaning the fact that he had recently been raided by the law, and looked like losing his licence at worst or getting a heavy fine that he could ill afford at best. 'I can't understand it,' he said, shrugging his shoulders in a hopeless sort of a way. 'I have always been on very good terms with the law. In fact the CID often come up my place of a weekend for a drink. Then suddenly they turn me over. I just don't understand it . . . ' I could easily have told him the reason, except for the fact that he had already just told me it. Because it is well known all over the manor that it is a very dangerous business indeed to get too friendly with the law: in fact the friendlier you are with them the more chance you stand of getting nicked by them. The reason is simple enough: the friendlier you are the more they know about your business, and the more they know about your business the more they have against you. In the end they get to know you so well that they can find reasons for nicking you where you may think no reason exists. The best way to run a club is by not having anything to do with the law whatever.

Even if you are in some kind of trouble, it is not a good idea to call them in because once you do the chances are they will somehow or other twist the facts around in such a way as to make it appear that it is your own fault that you are in trouble.

In the old days when villains went in for protection rackets, clubs were easy prey for such mobs, and a club owner who resisted their demands would not stay in business for very long after doing so. One proprietor whose name I conveniently forget was approached by a protection mob, who demanded ten quid a week from him. He told them to go and get stuffed and other uncomplimentary remarks were hurled at the gang by the proprietor's wife. After the gang had left the wife got on the phone to the law, who came right around and interviewed them about this unhappy state of affairs. The CID took statements from all concerned and then went off on their merry way in search of people parking in places where they should not. Two days later as the proprietor and his wife were leaving their club half a dozen masked men rushed at them waving iron bars, the pair of them were smashed to the ground and the gang disappeared into the darkness of the night before anyone had really noticed that something amiss had taken place. The unfortunate couple were carted off to hospital where they remained for several weeks, during which time a further bunch of villains broke into their club and smashed the place to bits. Though the police went through the motions of investigating this turn of events no one was arrested, and within a week the incident was completely forgotten. That sort of thing is a rare occurrence in Soho these days, but the gangster's code still exists. If one villain does in another villain, it is a family affair and as far as the fraternity are concerned that is the end of that: they do not think that such internal problems are anything to do with the police or the public.

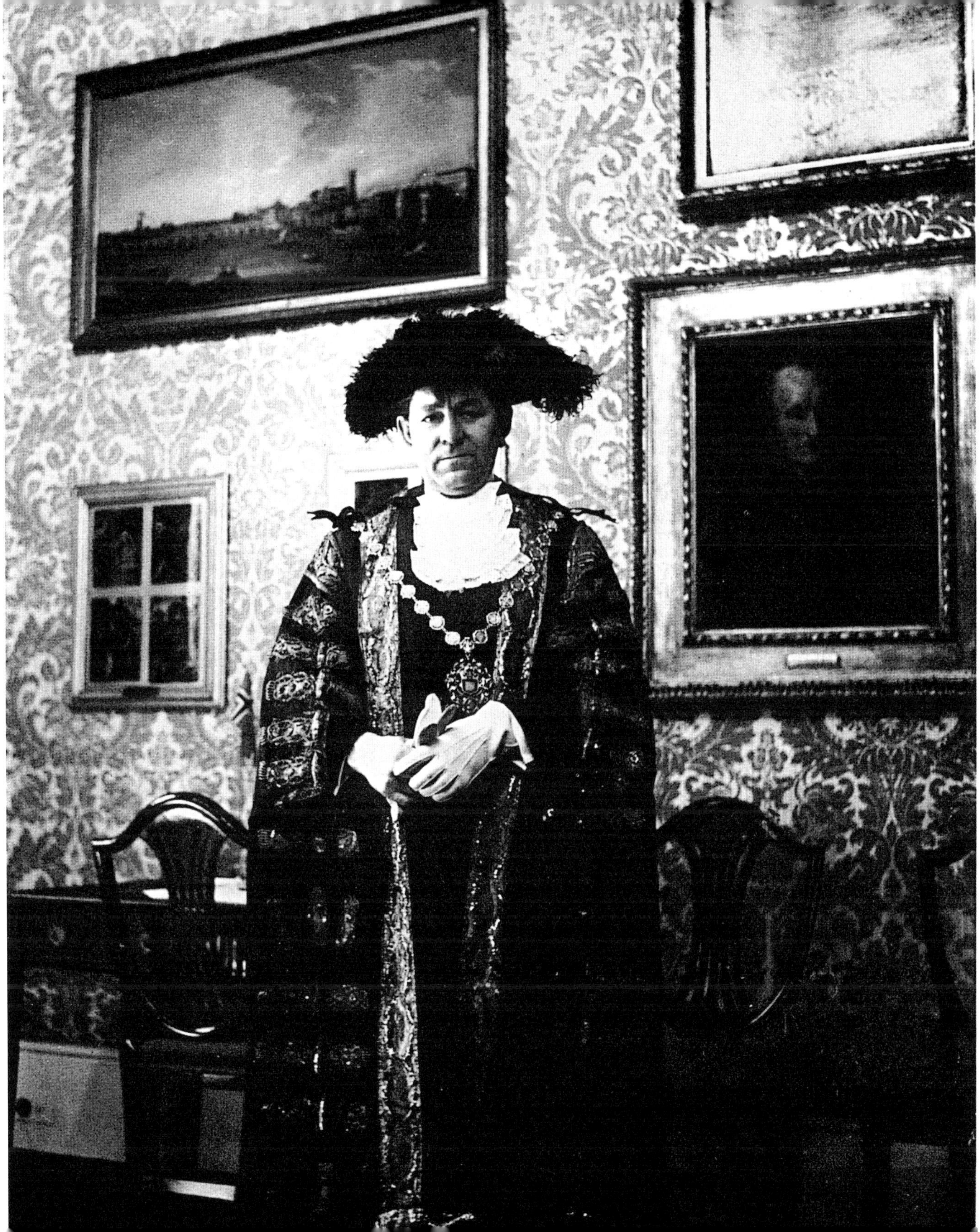

A SOHO MURDER

Of course when one of these bits of bother comes up the press make a great deal of it, especially if the bother has happened in Soho.

The most recent case that comes to mind is the shooting of Tony Mella which happened during the early part of 1963. Tony Mella had been around Soho for as long as I can remember, and had a reputation for being one of the hardest nuts in the entire world. In recent years he had been running a little clip joint next door to the bookshop in Dean Street. For many years business had been quiet and successful, the punters came and dutifully allowed themselves to be fleeced by the girls who worked for Tony. Now and then a little trouble might break out, caused by a dissatisfied customer who was under the impression that he was going to bed with one of the girls, and had become most disappointed when the girl had turned him down. But one light punch from Tony was enough to settle any argument of this kind, and the offender's lights would go out for maybe two hours or so. Most of the time, however, Tony never even found this kind of action necessary, for his reputation protected him from damaging his manicured finger nails any more than his cast iron muscles.

A story about Tony that will be handed down for many years to come is about the time he went around to saw one of the late Tommy Smithson's feet off, but was prevented from doing so in the nick of time by a fellow member of his mob. And there was another time when Tony hit a wrongdoer so hard that he took off and some say that the unfortunate chap came down fifty yards away, but I don't really believe this.

It seems that Tony Mella had been having some trouble with his right-hand man over a matter of some money, this not being a very unusual thing to have troubles about in some quarters. It seems that Tony had owed his right-hand man this money for a very long time, and had put off paying him, time and time again. For a long time the right-hand man brooded over the matter until in the end he got a gun and took it to the clip joint with him. The shooting was no accident because later it was found that the right-hand man had written a letter to his wife telling her what he was going to do. No one knows exactly what happened that night: it may have been that the two of them had a final showdown, or else something else sparked off the final action. But one thing is sure, Tony Mella was shot twice. He came crashing down the stairs of his clip joint and out into the street. He staggered to the corner of Romilly Street where he collapsed and a passer-by rushed to his aid and heard him whisper 'I've been shot' and these were the last words he uttered; seconds later he was dead. Meanwhile back at the club the right-hand man raised the same gun again, this time to his own temple. He squeezed the trigger, the gun went off, and he too crashed down the stairs, dying instantly. This terrifying story is not from an American detective novel, it happened in Dean Street not many years ago. The police arrived in force, but there was little for them to investigate; a crime had been committed and the guilty party had paid the price by his own hand and as far as the underworld was concerned justice had been done. This might be thought a somewhat anti-social point of view by society, but according to the people who live this sort of life it is a perfectly reasonable code.

The press however had a field day over this case and made as much of it as they possibly could. There were pictures of Tony immaculately dressed and extracts from the letter that the right-hand man left for his wife and it is therefore not very surprising that tourists are frightened to walk the streets of Soho by night. Yet in spite of this isolated case, Soho's reputation for villainy of one kind and another does not really stand up, for if you wander around the streets you will not see any open signs of it. True there are clip joints, and you may be asked if you would care to come in for a drink as you pass by, but all you have to do is keep on going. Now and then you may spy a suspicious-looking man in a black overcoat lurking in a doorway, but you can be assured that he is more worried about his own troubles than he is about yours. I really don't know why everyone worries so much about everything, for one thing is certain, you can't get out of life alive.

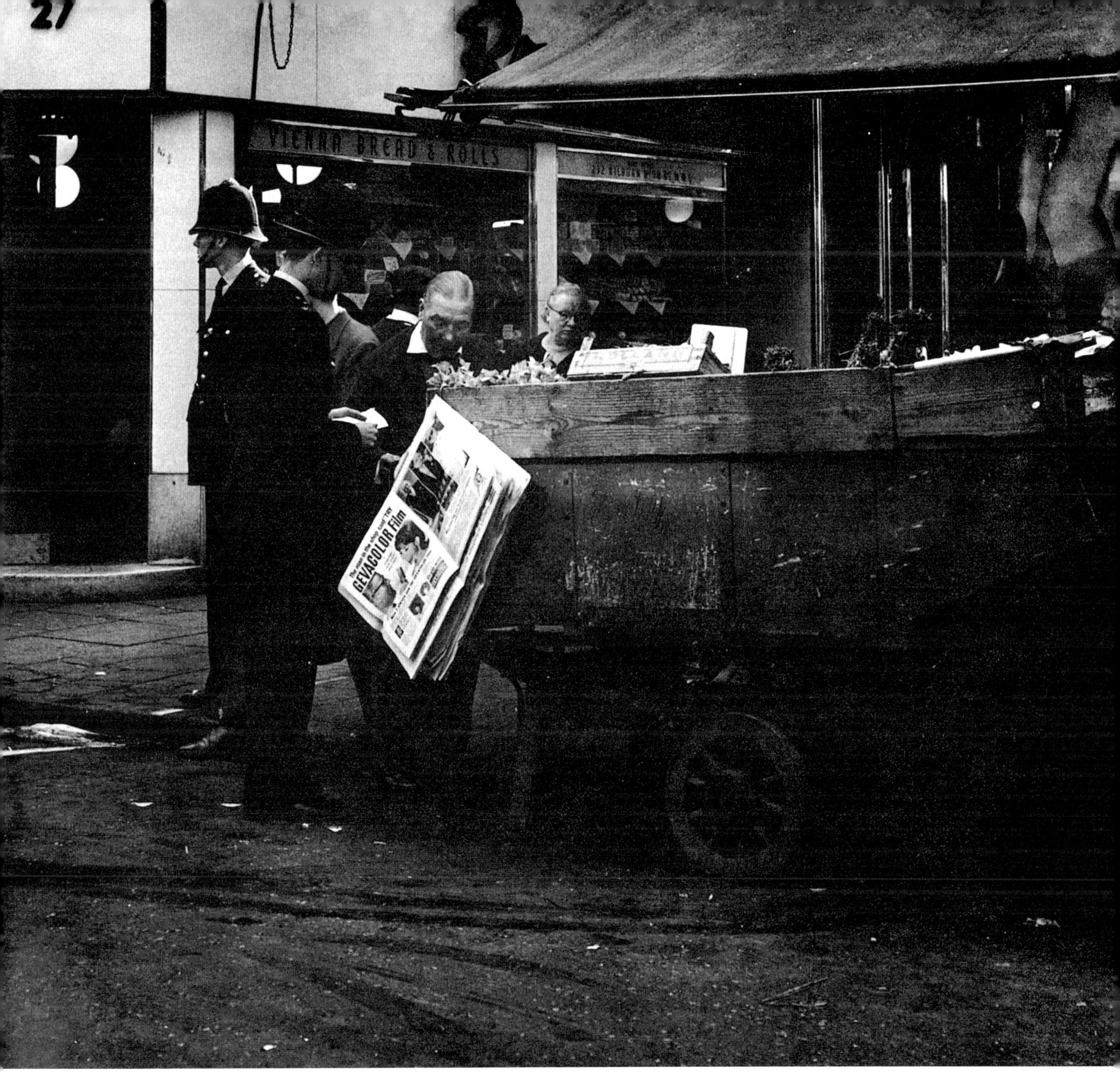
27
VIENNA BREAD & ROLLS
GEVACOLOR Film

THE SOHO ROUNDABOUT

I once ran into an American tourist who asked me hopefully if he would be beaten up and robbed if he wandered around Soho's streets on his own in the dead of night. I got the impression that he was very disappointed when I assured him that this was by no means the case and that he would be as safe as houses.

'But what about the gangs that roam the streets in search of victims?' he asked.

'There aren't any,' I replied.

'Come on tell me the truth,' he said with a laugh, 'you are just saying that so that I will not worry.'

'I am not,' I said flatly. 'I promise you, you will be perfectly safe.' I bought the tourist a drink and after a while he told me that he had been given to understand that Soho was a most dangerous place and that it was not safe to walk about on one's own and also that he had read the *News of the World*. Now of course as soon as he told me the *News of the World* bit I understood why he might be a bit frightened, for there is no doubt about it, journalists dearly love to put the fear of Christ up people with such headlines as 'WHITE SLAVE TRAP', followed by a smashing article about young girls coming to London from the North and being preyed upon by ruthless madames, who export them to Basra on the Persian Gulf where they are sold like cattle in the infamous Bull Ring to the highest bidder. Once sold they wind up either in brothels or else the personal slave of a wealthy Arab. It's all good stuff and the readers lap it up: there is however little truth in these stories. It is true that there are a few drug addicts, and that pushers flourish in back streets, but– there are just as many junkies in Chelsea or Hampstead as there are in Soho: it is just that the Soho ones get more publicity. Teenage purple heart bandits hang about on street corners all over England, but to hear people talk you would think that these kids can only be found in what is hilariously known as 'Soho's square mile of vice'. I did my best to allay my tourist friend's fears, but once a seed has been planted in someone's mind it is often very hard to kill it. Before you know it they have invented the most unlikely stories, and the stories that people think up about Soho are enough to make your blood run cold. The more fantastic the story the more likely you are to get people to believe it: personally I think it is all great fun. In the end I parted company with my tourist friend, and I must say I got the distinct impression that he was more than somewhat disappointed in me for smashing up his dreams of violence and dens of iniquity. I must say I felt a bit sorry for him because he really did want to be waylaid by a bandit. Because as everyone knows it is very easy to get beaten up and robbed in America, so I suppose he must have been feeling more than a little homesick for it.

Soho is a roundabout, which sometimes spins around so fast that it is impossible to jump off. Some people can keep their balance no matter how fast it goes around, whilst others become giddy, lose their balance and hit rock bottom, together with their wives, children and self-respect. To a large extent the roundabout runs on alcohol. To get on it all you have to be is a little dissatisfied with the way you are living or maybe if you are lonely or have just arrived in London from somewhere or other, and do not know your way around yet. You go into a Soho pub for a quiet lunchtime drink; you meet a Soho-ite; you buy him a drink; he may or may not buy you one back. At closing time he invites you to join him for another drink in some hole in the ground; you go; later you are pissed, and it is nice. The next day you do the same thing, and the next. The roundabout starts to move slowly at first, so slowly in fact that you do not notice it. But before you know it you are in the pub every day, in the hole in the ground every afternoon, and back in the pub again every night. Within two weeks you know everyone, and everyone knows you, you fall in love with them, but they cannot really stand the sight of you, you are spinning around so fast that you do not notice what is going on. Every morning you wake up feeling rotten and full of alcoholic remorse. You hate your own guts, and promise yourself that you will jump off the roundabout before it is too late, but you never do it. Now and then someone will kill himself, or else die from alcoholic poisoning. For a day the roundabout will pause for a second from fear, but not in sorrow—'Dear friends, look at each other and wonder who is going to be the next to go'—but by three o'clock closing time it is going again at full speed. People will keep telling you how well you look when inside you have gone rotten, and the only thing that makes you look alive is your whisky flush, which sometimes looks like a sun tan. 'Tell me darling have you been away?' asks someone with a ruined face.

'No,' you reply.

'I thought you had been to the South of France, you look so well.'

'Well I haven't.'

'Is that a fact, well you look as though you have. Could you lend me ten bob?' You give them the ten bob just so that they will go away.

Many a row breaks out on the roundabout. Some old dyke will throw a glass of gin and water into the face of a screaming old queer after they have had a bitchy argument over a guardsman or the price of a drink, and everyone on the roundabout bursts out laughing. The old queer won't talk to the dyke for a week but after that they will be the best of friends again. Every bit of scandal like this is grist to the mill on the roundabout, and the story is told over and over again, and with each telling becomes more and more elaborated upon until no one is really sure what actually happened, including the dyke and the queer. The love lives of these people are hateful and they thrive on it. The men go from one woman to another, rather than the women going from one man to another. No one knows who they are going to find themselves in bed with from one night to the next, a situation that becomes somewhat confusing from time to time. One might find oneself with a girl when she is eighteen and fall madly in love with her; eventually the affair is over. Ten years later you might find yourself having another affair with her. Since she was last with you she has been married twice and had four children, and her tummy is covered with stretch marks. It is an unloving roundabout, and people seem to thrive on bitterness and booze, yet somehow it is a very sophisticated whirl, full of good taste, disillusionment and disgraceful behaviour, whose motto is something like 'We all have to die sometime'. It is a world of drinking and dieting in the best restaurants, and you can wish you were dead till you are blue in the face, no one will give a f . . . one way or the other, for the louder you scream the softer you sound.

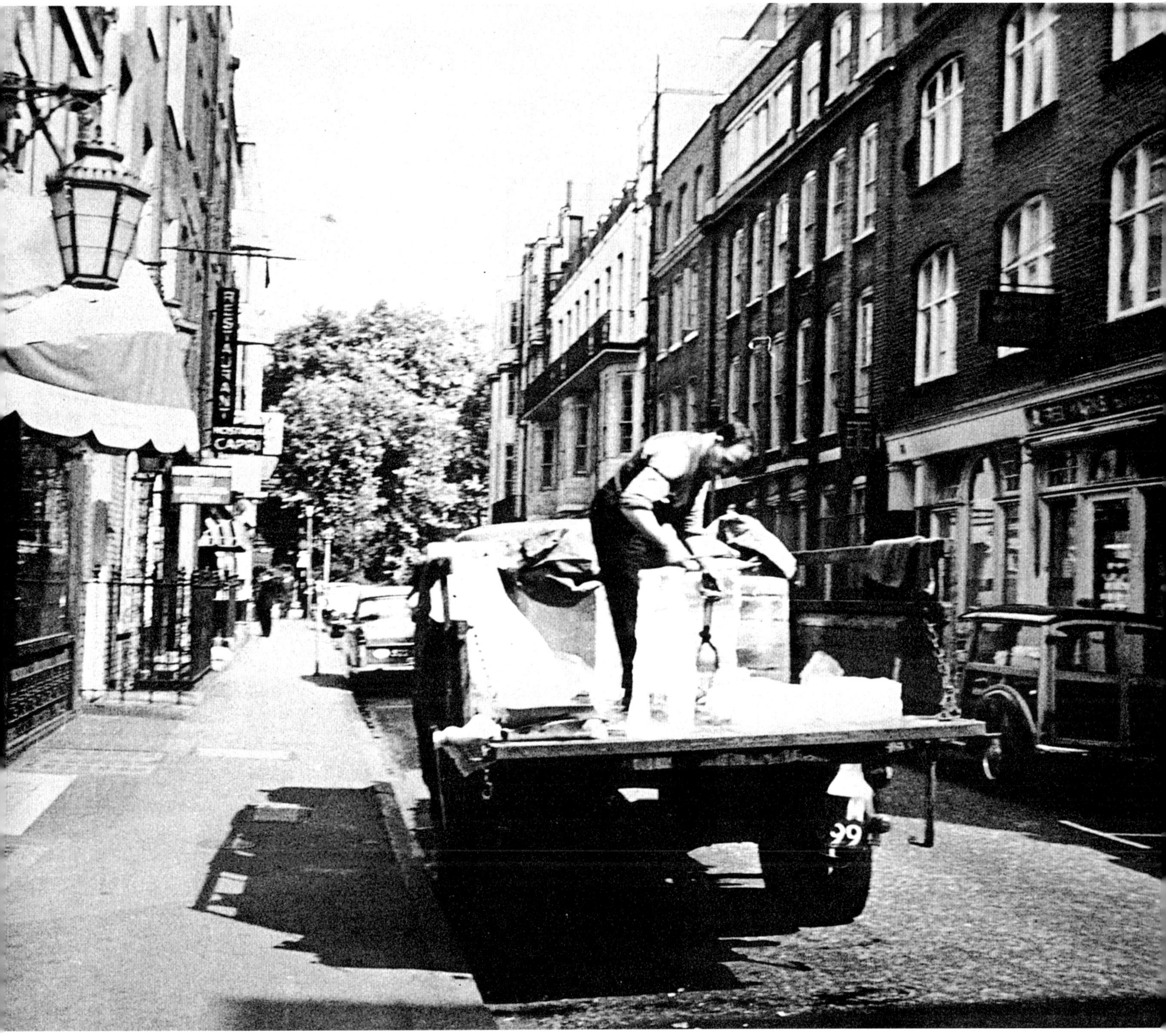
RESTAURANT
CAPRI

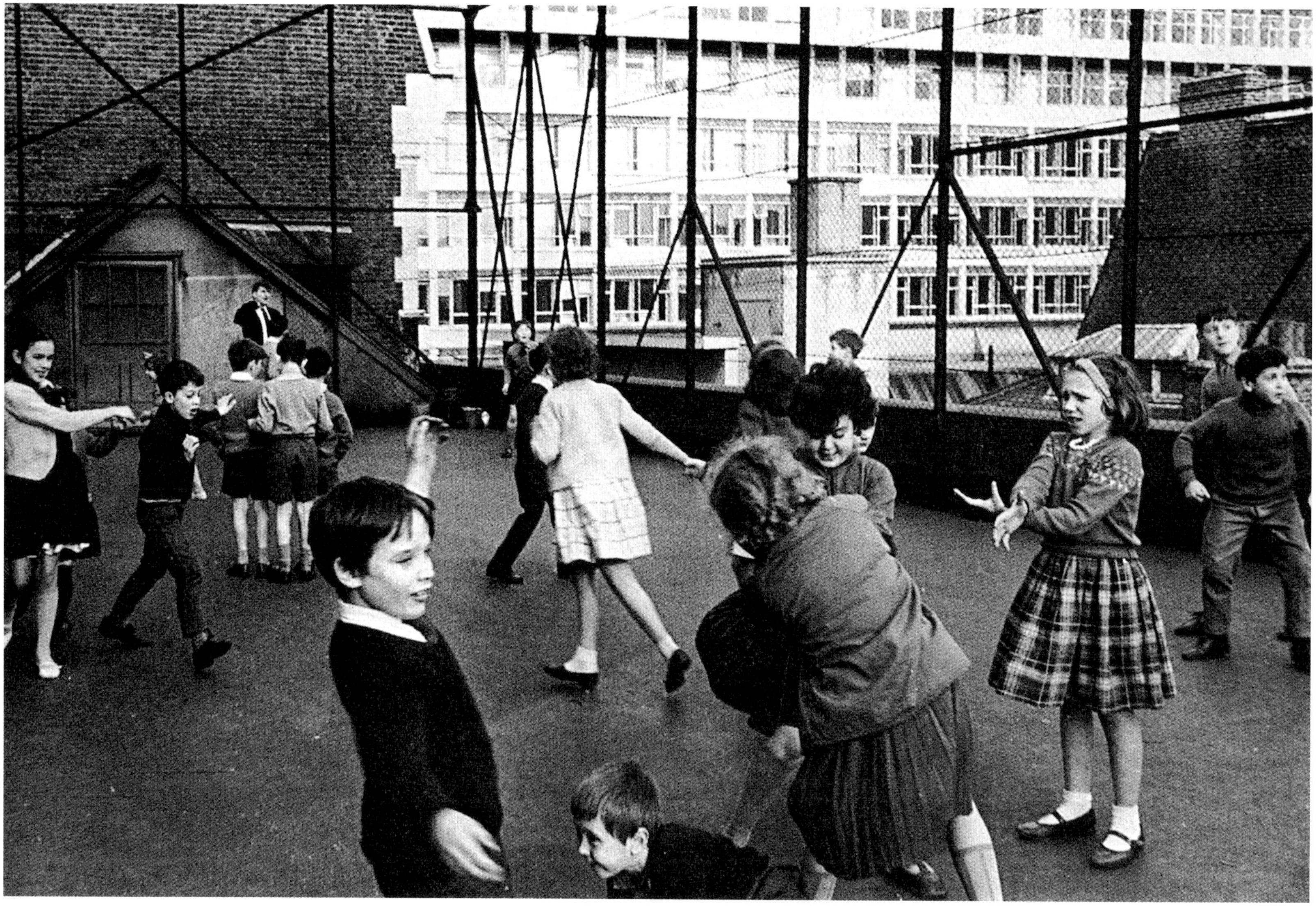

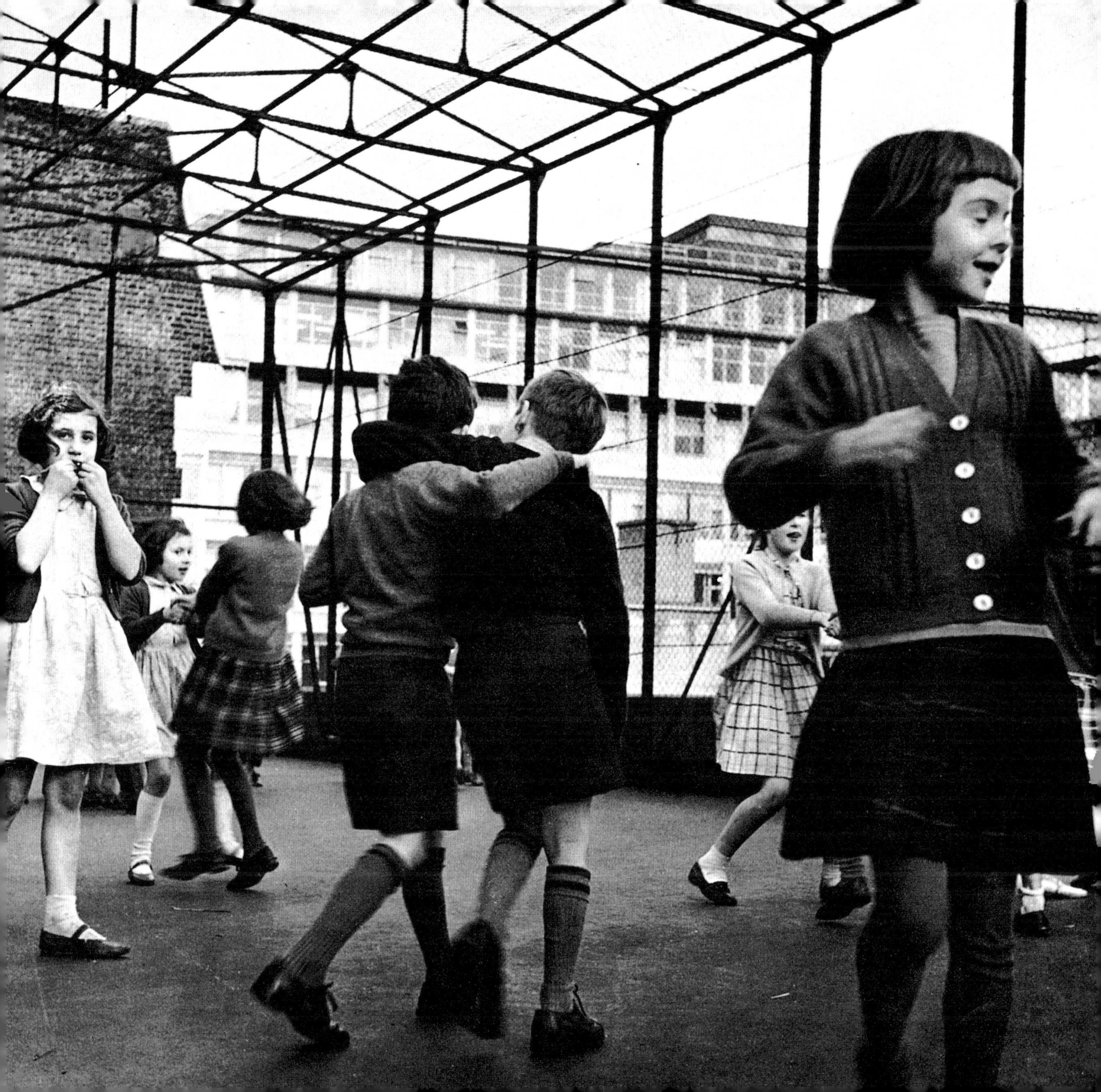

SOME SOHO PROBLEMS

One morning I went and visited the Mayor of Westminster, Councillor Leslie Farmiloe, in his parlour in Westminster City Hall. He greeted me warmly and wasted no time in giving me a drink. Councillor Farmiloe has lived in Westminster for forty years, and in Dean Street for the last few. He dearly loves Soho and its people and has always found them very kind and cheerful. He told me that when he was ill recently he sent across the street for a Chinese meal. The headwaiter sent over the menu and the meal was brought over, one course at a time, just as though he was in the restaurant. Eventually he asked for the bill and was told that it was on the house. We spoke of crime in Soho and he agreed that far too much was made of it. There is no more crime in Soho than there is anywhere else, he told me, 'It is just that it gets so much more publicity.'

I also asked him about the changing face of Soho. He told me that the Council are most careful not to upset any of the Soho people, but on the other hand it is simply impossible to please everyone. The old houses must come down and new ones must go up in their place and that is all there is to it. He was very sympathetic about old Soho folk who had lived there all their lives, but Soho had now become a place for go-ahead people, and he felt that the old would really be better off in the country, or if not better off, far more comfortable. Some of the old tailors whose shops have had to be demolished to make way for office blocks had been offered new flats in Soho with work rooms attached but they did not like the idea very much and many of them have chosen to move away rather than live in them. Old people are liable to be set in their ways and Soho's old people are even more set in their ways than others. Councillor Farmiloe is genuinely interested in the future of Soho, and is more than willing to listen to any complaints that Soho's residents and business people may have: if there are more like him on the Westminster City Council there is hope for us yet.

Another problem in Soho is the education of its children. There is a Catholic school, which is quite small, and consists mainly of classrooms, all of which seem to be on different floors, with the playground on the roof, for there is no space for it elsewhere. It is caged in so that the children cannot tumble over the edge but even so it is far from ideal. When a new school will be built no one knows, for the price of land in this square mile comes very high indeed, and is bought up by the big property investors as quick as a flash. However the kids at the school seem very happy, and will lark about on street corners and in the market for hours on end, until they are driven off by an irate barrow boy. These are the children of the poorer Soho families, for as mentioned earlier, the rich tradesmen send their kids to private schools just as soon as they are old enough.

The children in Soho take as much notice of strip joints and clip joints as country children do of an apple orchard, for they have grown up with them. The neon lights, drunks falling out of pubs and the odd punch up are as much of the Soho kid's life as the vicarage and the bun fight is part of the country child's. The difference of course is that the Soho kids grow up very fast. At ten they know as much about life as another kid of fifteen, if not more. They are quick-witted and fearless; the arse may be out of their trousers, but they are proud of themselves and the streets that are their hunting grounds. They are considered lawless by the less hardy but that is more because their faces are dirty than for the things they do, which only amount to high spirits anyway. It is true that from time to time one or two of them come up in front of the beak, but only for minor offences that in the old days would not be thought worth bringing a case about; in those days a cuff around the ear with a copper's white glove would have been enough to deter them in the future, but things have changed. One is arrested for the slightest infringement of the law these days, and that goes for kids as well.

And that is the strength of the situation as far as almost all aspects of Soho life are concerned. The parking problem for instance is absolutely impossible. The whole place is swarming with parking meters and the slightest infringement of the time limits will cost you two pounds. This kind of thing has in the last few years caused a great deal of hardship amongst Soho tradesmen, and also a deal of animosity. For a Soho ratepayer can no longer park his car outside his own home, for if he does he will get a parking ticket as quick as a flash, and that is no exaggeration. One restaurant owner parked his car outside the door of his restaurant in order to unload some vegetables from the boot of his car and he had been parked for less than a minute when a Warden pounced on him and handed him a ticket. The poor man became so angry that he could not contain himself, and he did no more but fetched the Warden off a right-hander that set him down on his backside. The police were called and a great fracas broke out. The restaurant owner was carted off to the nick, where he was charged with striking the Warden while carrying out his duty, or whatever the term might be, and was later fined rather heavily. This kind of thing is virtually a daily occurrence in Soho these days. The traffic Wardens are looked upon as the enemy by every motorist who comes to Soho for his lunch, or to go to the theatre. The Wardens in fact have become mad with power, and carry out their unpleasant task with great relish.

Because of the recent parking laws many Soho tradesmen have lost an enormous amount of business, for people will not risk stopping for a second to buy a loaf of French bread or a piece of garlic, for if they do the chances are they will return to find a ticket stuck under their windscreen wiper. Of course one realizes that the traffic in the West End is getting absolutely impossible, but I cannot see why the motorist should be penalized because of it. As is well known every single motorist pays a small fortune for the privilege of driving his car on the Queen's highway, only a small percentage of which is used for improving the roads and for

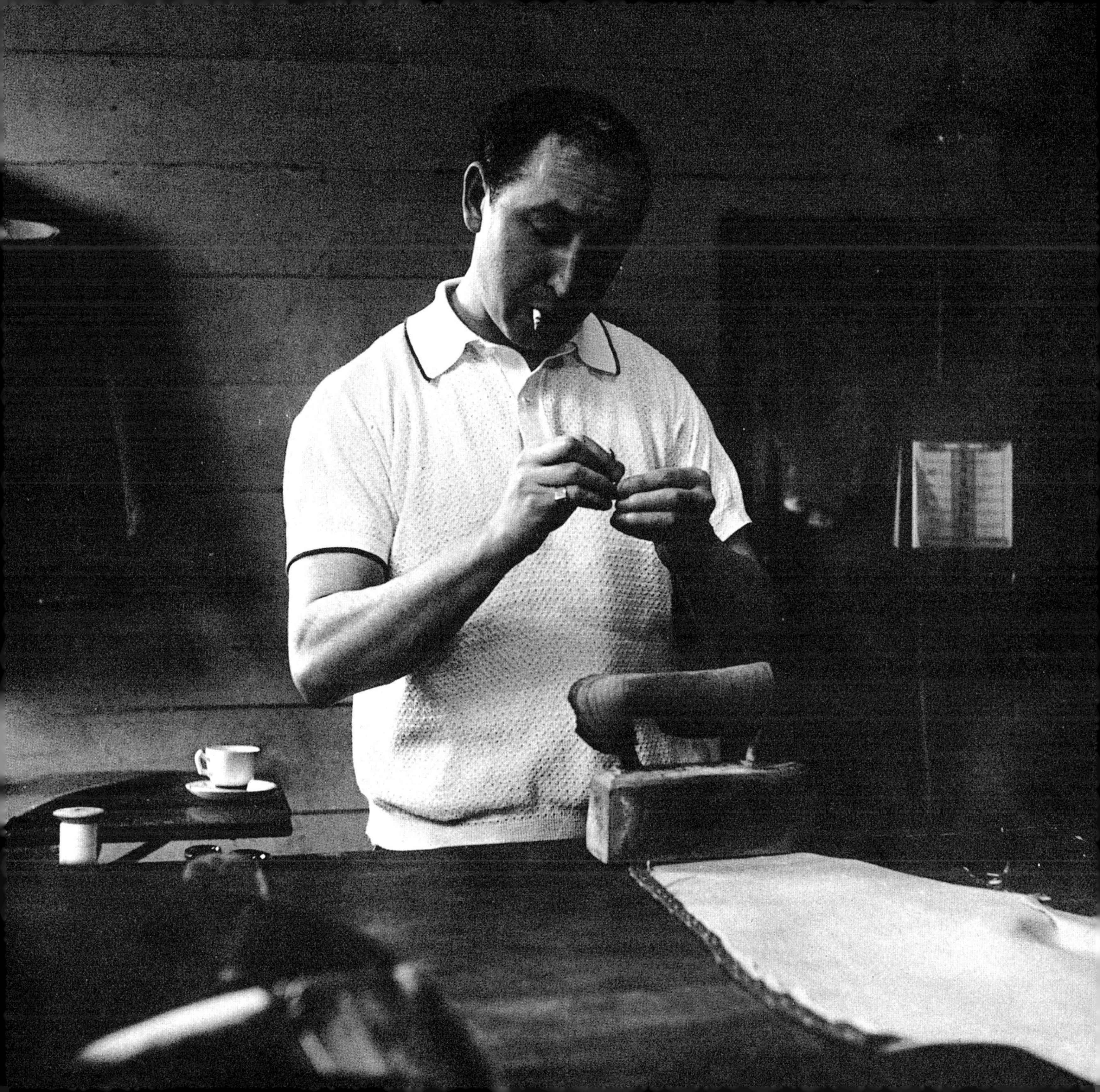

opening off-street car parks. In my opinion this is a state of affairs that cannot be allowed to go on any longer. The government have the money, and they must be made to do something about the motorists' plight, instead of telling us that everything that can be done is being done, for such reassurances do nothing to help anyone. In the meantime everyone loses patience with everyone else, hooters sound, people shout and curse and nobody gets anywhere fast. What with the parking and other restrictions the Soho people are not having too good a time of it at the moment.

A friend of mine who has a restaurant in Soho was recently summoned by the police for serving drinks after hours. He has had a restaurant on the same site since the end of the First World War, and had up until this time never had the slightest trouble of any kind. Then one day the law came charging in shouting 'This is a raid, nobody move!' or words to that effect. Everyone was aghast and just sat there with their mouths hanging open. Names and addresses were taken, and the law left saying that further action would be taken in this matter. My friend was terribly upset, for he is very sensitive and unaccustomed to this kind of treatment. Within a week or two papers were served on him and he had to appear in court. Luckily the case was dismissed, but of course he still had to pay his own legal fees. All this came about because they had found half a glass of brandy on one of the customer's tables. This is the kind of thing that is getting the Soho people down. The law seem to have a licence to do exactly what they like and how they like. For the onus is not on them to prove their allegations, it is upon the defendant to disprove them. And as the word of the police is without question taken as the gospel truth, the defendant has his work cut out to prove his innocence. Very often someone will be found guilty on cooked-up evidence or will, out of desperation, plead guilty when he is innocent, simply to avoid expense and trouble, for if a defendant elects to go to trial in the high court he will have to pay his own costs even if he is found not guilty. This state of affairs is diabolical, and something should be done about it immediately. Strangely (or not strangely) enough these devious practices are far more prone to happen in Soho than in other parts of London, for there are many people whose lives could not stand to be looked at too closely, and for these few everyone else has to take the can back. The police in Soho strut around like peacocks, moving people along and generally bullying one and all, none of which gives for a very quiet life.

The strange thing about the West End police is that very few of them come from London. For the main part they come from places in the North such as Newcastle or Liverpool. I have never been able to find out exactly why this is, but my theory is that the Home Office feel that London policemen are too sympathetic when they are given a beat on their own 'manor'. On my occasional visits to the City where almost all of the police are Londoners, I have found them to be most polite and helpful. They do not arrest people if they can help it; on the other hand it could simply be that Londoners don't fancy being policemen all that much, including those who are. Whatever the fact of the matter is, one thing is for certain: the relationship between the police and the Soho people has reached an all-time low and is getting even worse as time goes on. I don't suppose anyone will do anything about it until there is a great flare up of some sort. That is the way things usually happen around this town.

A SOHO MISCELLANY

Comparative newcomers to Soho are the staff of *Private Eye* who have their office at 22 Greek Street. The magazine is run by a crowd of public school boys of the satirical variety, the big difference between the staff of *Private Eye* and other public school boys who try to be funny is that the former *are*. In fact this magazine has become as important as any national newspaper, for the staff are fearless to a man. They will take the rise out of anyone no matter how powerful or lowly and they are not afraid to attack nor are they afraid to defend. It is these qualities that have made them such a success. The most famous of the group is the rotund William Rushton, who rose to fame through the TV programme 'That Was The Week That Was'. The magazine was started in the beginning of the 'satirical boom', if it can be called that. To begin with it was thought of as rather comical and the thing to read. But after a few issues it began to be sued by important and famous people, Randolph Churchill being one of them. Though all the cases were settled out of court they were widely publicized, thus making the magazine a household name. I think their best piece of work was when they brought the Hal Woolf case to light. It was a case that no one else would dare to touch. Hal Woolf was knocked over by a car, taken to hospital, and later the same night he was released but was later arrested by the police because they suspected that he was carrying drugs. What happened after that no one really knows, except that he died while he was in custody. The whole thing was hushed up until *Private Eye* brought the case to light. The Police Commissioner apologized to Mrs Woolf and said that there had been 'an administrative failure' and that he deplored it. Sydney Silverman MP was moved to action and demanded a new inquest: eventually there was an enquiry at which it was more or less decided that no one was to blame, but if any one was no one knew who it was. This was of course a most unsatisfactory result, but this kind of thing is liable to happen when the truth might be too unsavoury for words. The point is however that this case would never have been heard of at all if *Private Eye*

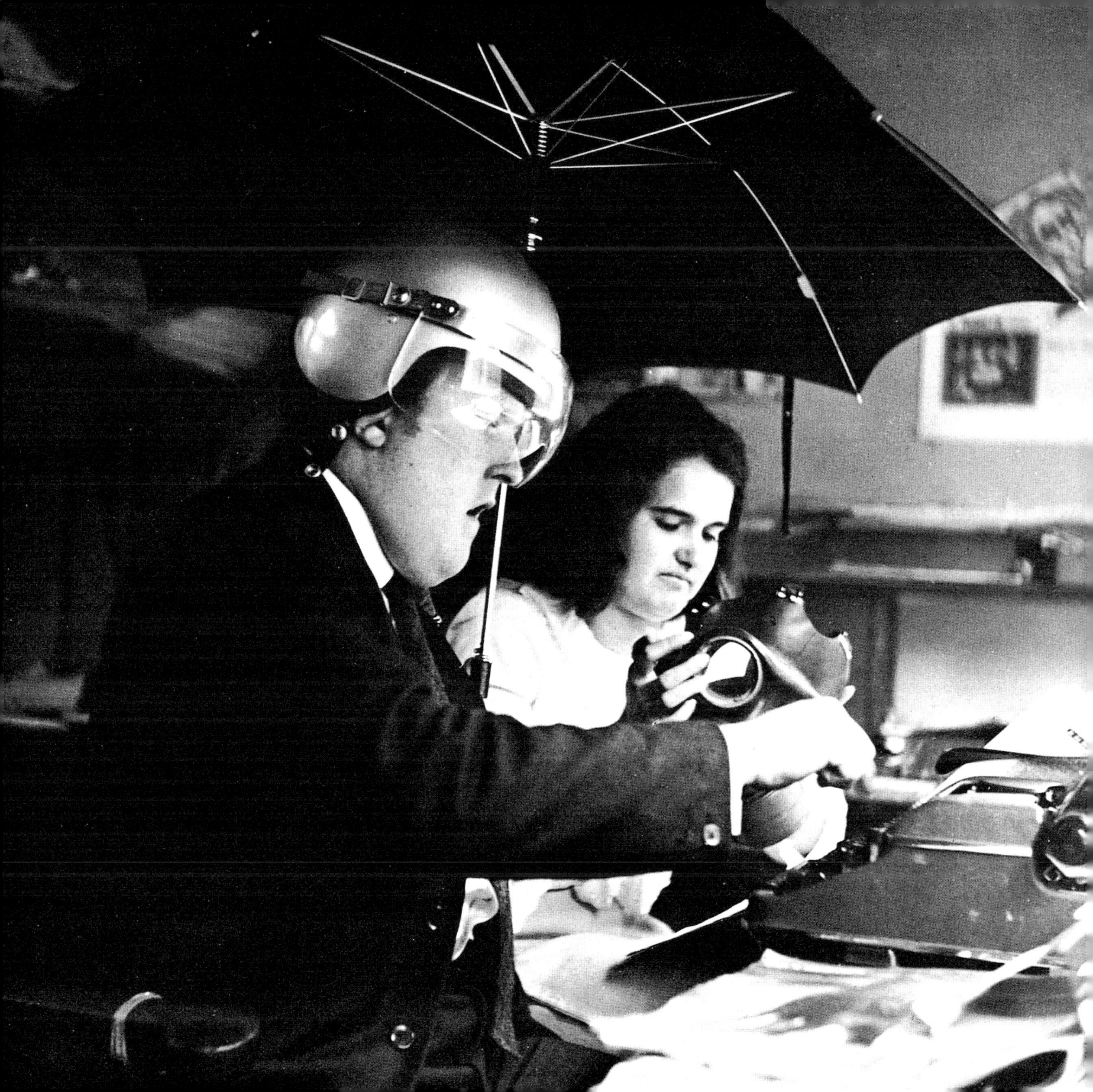

had not taken up the case: for this alone they are to be highly complimented.

A man who knows Soho as well as anyone is Tom Driberg MP. We recently had dinner together at the Au Jardin des Gourmets, which is just about the most expensive restaurant in Soho and also one of the oldest. Among his memories of Soho, of which he has many, is the time that he had a grim 'maigre' meal with Dorothy Sayers at the Moulin D'or restaurant after going to church one Good Friday. Of the changing face he told me that great harm is being done to the charm and character of Soho, for Soho is quite a tourist attraction, but will not be for very much longer if the demolishing continues. Every city is getting to look like every other city. Tom Driberg told me that when he was recently in Samarkand which is in Uzbekistan, fairytale domes are being pulled down and great concrete slabs are being erected in their place.

Driberg came to Soho after leaving Oxford. He wanted to write, but felt that he could not do so in the country, so he came to London to be in the centre of things. To begin with he worked as a film extra, for which he was paid a guinea a day. He lived for a time at 66 Frith Street where he had a room the rent of which was twelve and sixpence a week. Eventually he ran out of money and had to move out of the room: this was in the winter of 1927–28. He then landed himself a job in a slimy kitchen in a cafe in Church Street, now called Romilly Street. He was given a bed on the premises, his food, and five bob a week pocket money. The cafe was open all night and some of Soho's roughest characters were regular customers: they teased him endlessly because of his Oxford accent and rather refined ways.

Over the top of the cafe there was a brothel which was run by an Irish lady by the name of Mother Corry. All the girls were fat and in fact the word was put in front of their names as though it were a title, i.e. Fat Pat, Fat Rosy or Fat Hilda. Without exception the men who visited the brothel were as skinny as rakes. One of the fat girls took a shine to young Tom and gave him the works of Colonel Ingersoll who was a great Victorian rationalist. Each morning when he had finished work the owner of the restaurant would take both Tom and the cook to Lyons Corner House for breakfast: sometimes they would have eggs and other times porridge and cream. He remembers one day when the brothel upstairs was raided by the police. Mother Corry gave them a volley of Irish abuse that would have put even Brendan Behan in the shade.

Eventually some of Tom's smart friends found out where he was and came to save him, much to his embarrassment, for the rough customers and the fat girls upstairs laughed in their faces. Eventually Osbert and Edith Sitwell came and rescued him, and got him a job on the *Daily Express* where he wrote the Hickey column for a time. Tom Driberg was most insistent when we talked that I should not give the impression that he started life in the gutter for this was by no means the case. It is interesting however that so many upper class people spend a period of their life on the bum around Soho. I have never thought of Soho as a slum nor have I thought of the hungry artist as poor, for most of the poverty is self-inflicted. An artist can get inspiration from washing dishes, but cannot get any from working in an office. This may be why so many people who are now successful started off by bumming around Soho without a bed to sleep in or food in their stomachs. To starve in Soho is an education, for though it may not appear very nice at the time, in later years one looks back on it with a certain amount of pleasure, and will come back again and again, just to see what is going on.

It would not be right to say that a layabout's life is easy; writers, painters, musicians and poets have to work very hard at not working, and only the hardy can survive: weaklings fall by the wayside. That is to say they give in, get jobs and settle down. This kind of thing is thought to be admirable by society, but is frowned upon by the hard-bitten Soho bums. For although the majority of Soho layabouts give it up after a while, there is a minority who stay with it until the bitter end. There are some people still around who were around when I was sixteen years old: their hair has gone grey and their faces are lined, they have not progressed an inch in eighteen years and do not intend to do so during the next eighteen either. Personally I think this is rather sad, because a young bum has his health and strength, but one's youth does not last long when one is living the rough life. Some people seem to get old almost overnight. You see them one day, and it seems as though their hair has turned to silver by the following morning. They do not have days and nights, all they have is time: there are no weekends when you are on the bum, nor are there any Christmases or Bank Holidays.

I remember once it came around to Christmas and absolutely nobody in Soho had any money whatever, the layabouts were either sleeping on park benches or walking the streets. I was comparatively lucky for I had a roof over my head. I was sleeping on the floor in a bombed house with a bunch of characters who had escaped from a Hogarth drawing. I awoke on Christmas morning to find myself without any money whatever, and no prospect whatever of eating that day. I wandered around the streets wondering what to do when suddenly I remembered a friend of mine who had a small room in Berwick Street so, nothing ventured nothing gained, I went around to visit him and wish him a Merry Christmas. I arrived at the house and pushed the bell. After a time he opened the door a fraction of an inch, saw who it was and was about to shut it again but this being the season of goodwill towards all men, even me, he opened the door a little wider and asked me to come in for a cup of tea. The room in which he was living was nothing but a cupboard with a bed and a gas ring in it. On the gas ring there was a frying pan, in which a very small piece of steak was frying. This being the season of good cheer he offered me half of it. I thanked him profusely, but the truth of the matter was that there was hardly a mouthful altogether, and half of it came to half a half a mouthful. In fact nothing but a taste, but sometimes even a taste can be better than nothing. As mentioned earlier there are not very many people living like this any more in Soho, but there are a few.

Soho is a ramshackle place, like a jigsaw puzzle that will not fit together because the pieces come from every puzzle that has ever been made, and a piece from each has been put together in the same box. Soho Square looks like any other well kept village square, while Frith Street looks as though it should be in France or Italy instead of the heart of London's West End. In many cafes you cannot hear a word of English spoken, yet one or two pubs are as English as cricket. It is loving, violent, charming, and in fact a drug: in other words alive. It will be a crying shame when it is rebuilt, for then it will be gone for ever.

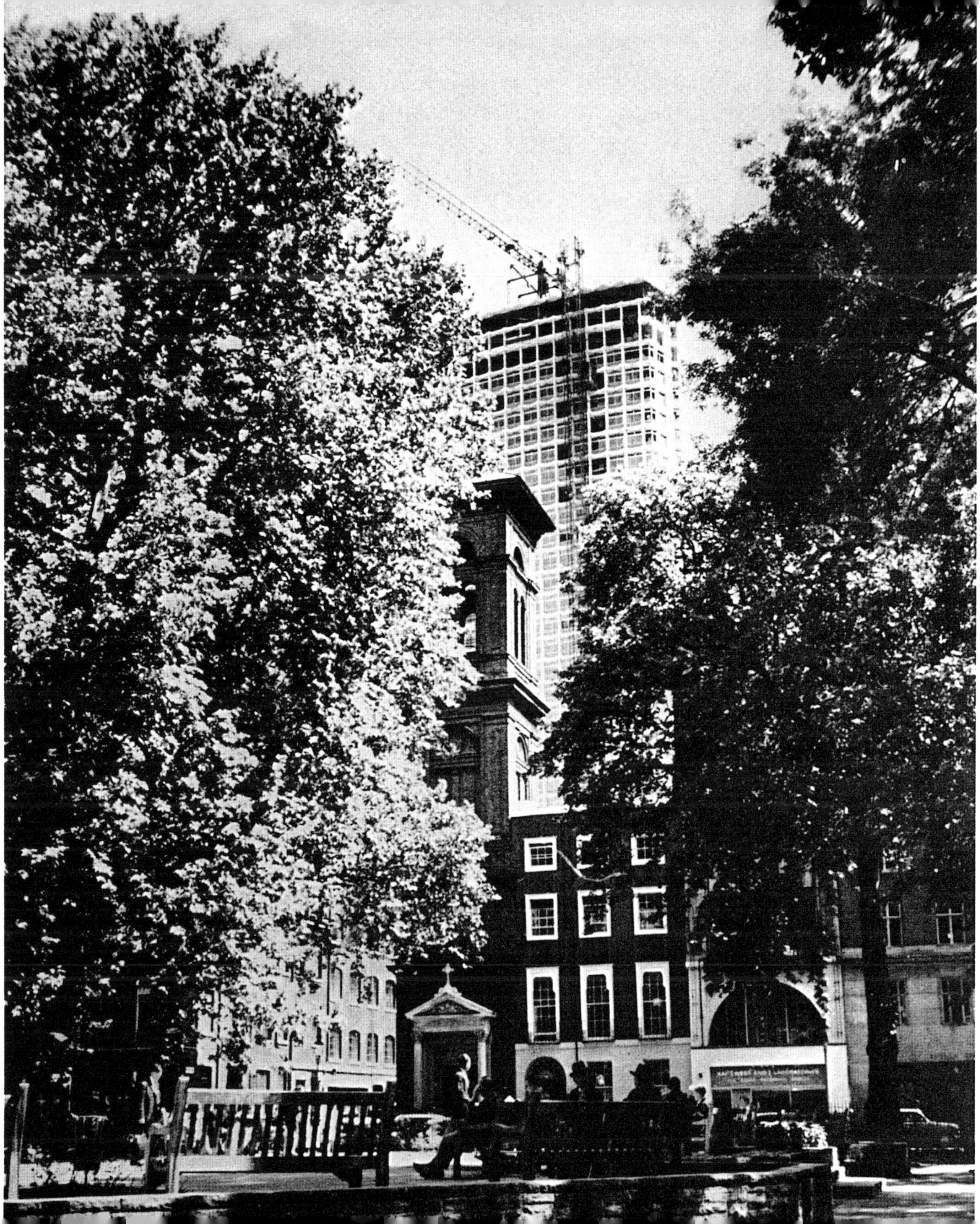

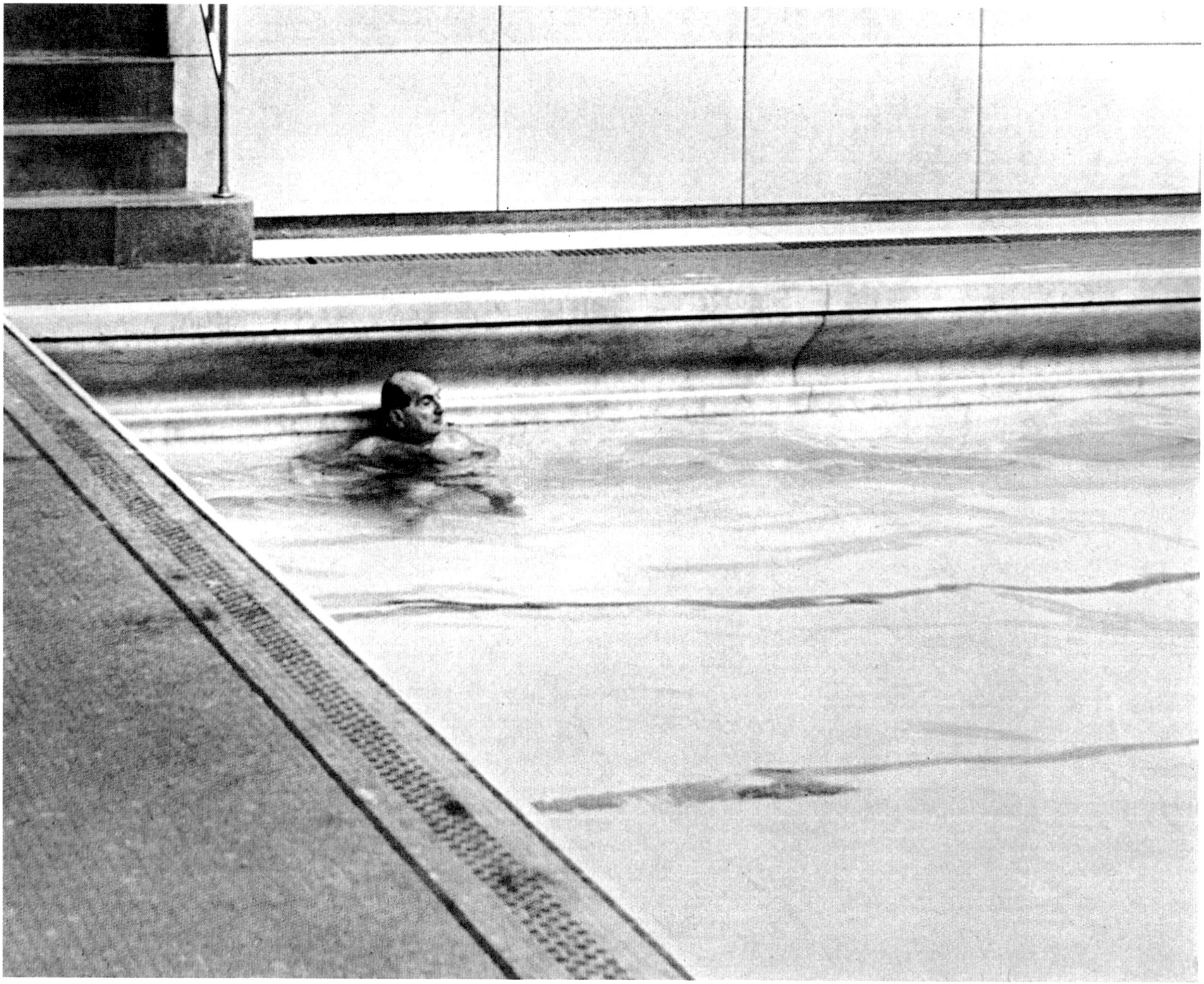

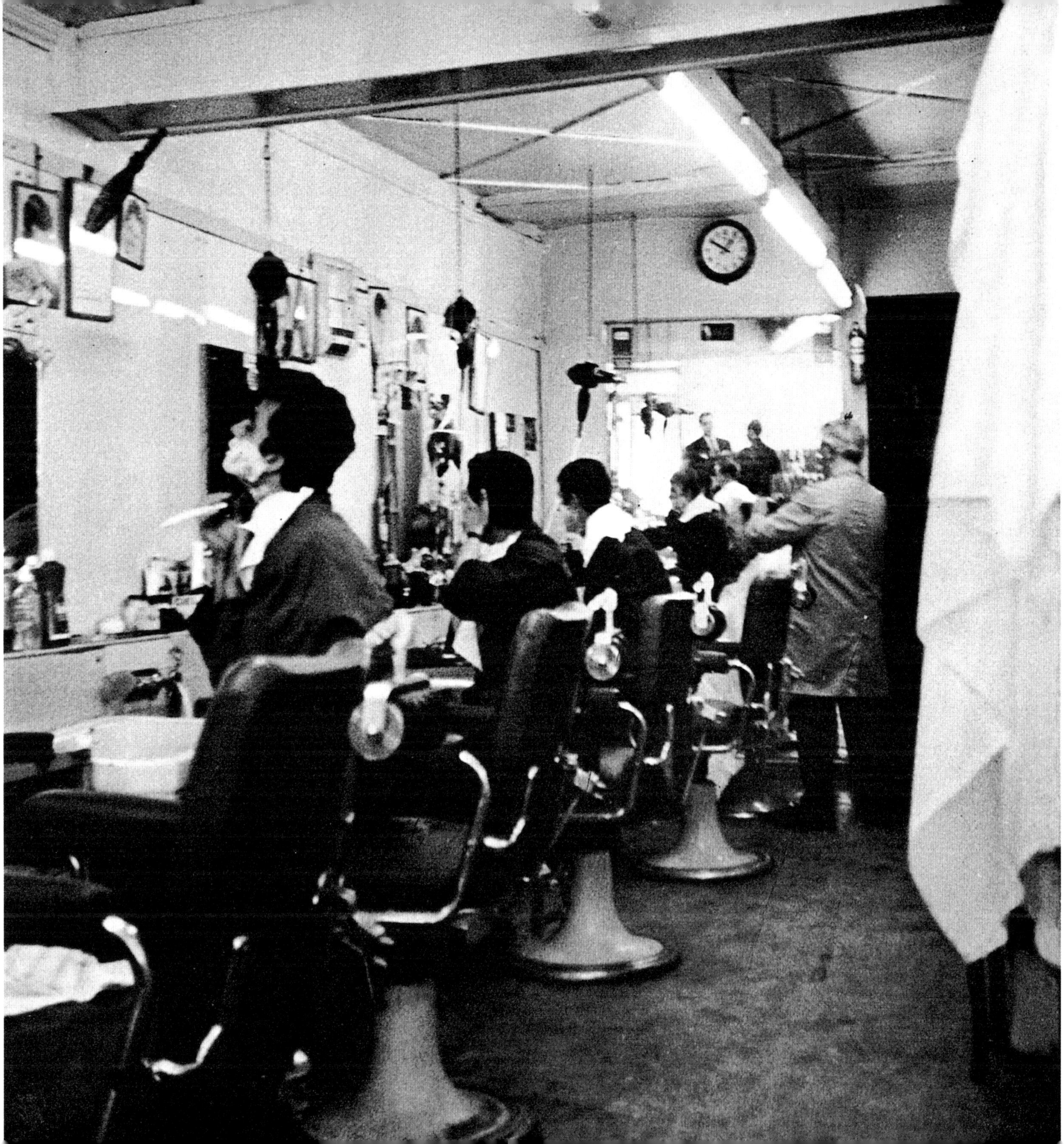

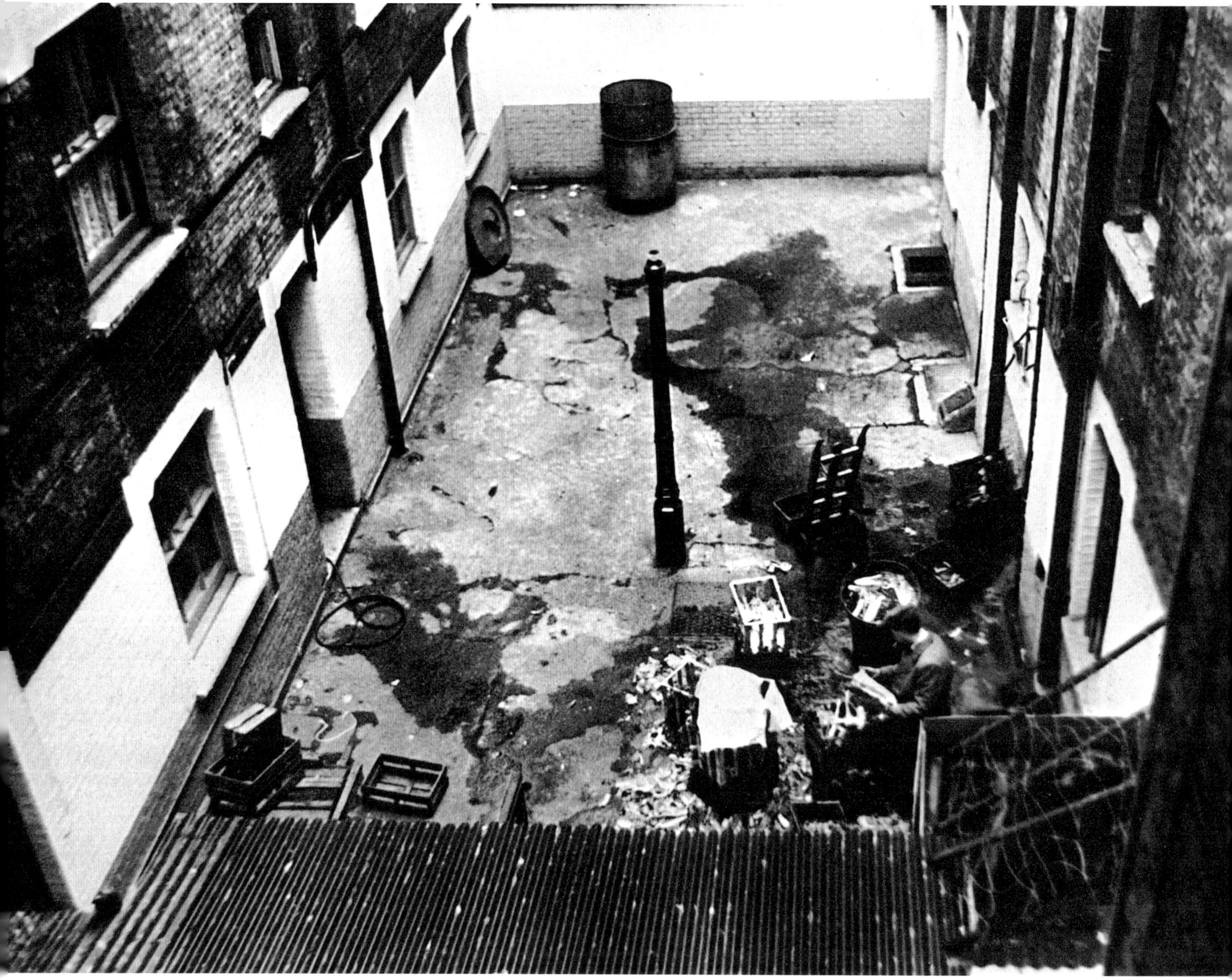

A DAY IN SOHO

Spending a day in Soho depends entirely on who you are. If you are rich you can spend a great deal of money in the course of a day without really realizing that you are doing it, and if you are poor you can usually manage to make out one way or another. But let me suppose that you have money, and wish to spend a day in Soho from say six o'clock in the morning until three the following morning (which I consider an absolutely mad thing to want to do). At six o'clock in the morning nothing whatever is going on except for the tail end of a poker school in a schpieler, and the girls in the clip joints have long since gone home with their ill-gotten gains, which they have conned off unsuspecting lonely businessmen. The clubs and restaurants are also closed, but you might see a hard-working restaurant owner arriving to make an early start with his buying at the market. The borough council dust cart will be slowly cruising along Soho's streets collecting mountains of rubbish from outside the doors of the shops and offices. The dustmen may disturb an odd tramp here and there who is fast asleep behind a pile of cardboard boxes. He wakes up, blinks at the dustmen, and then shambles off down the street. The dustmen throw the boxes on to the dust cart and move further along the street. These days there are no cafes open at this hour of the morning but you may be able to buy a few freshly baked rolls from the bakery in Greek Street.

Soho does not really wake up until nine o'clock when the hordes of office workers begin to arrive for work. Mostly they are girls. Secretary birds flit along Wardour Street disappearing into office blocks and part-time waitresses arrive at coffee houses—they are paid five quid a week with tips on top and they only do it so that they won't have to rely on their fathers for pocket money while they are students at St Martin's. The shop girls, bank clerks, salesmen, strippers, car park attendants, barmen and shopkeepers come pouring out of the tube stations; it is like an invasion. At six in the morning there is little sound in Soho's streets: by nine-thirty the whole place is jumping with activity. Pop records blare out of the doorway of the Record Center, the drays arrive with barrels of beer and the traffic rushes around in all directions in search of a parking meter, all of which have been taken long before. Drivers begin to lose their tempers with each other and the inevitable rear-end collision happens on the corner of Frith Street. With a screeching of brakes and a loud metallic crash the day has really begun.

At eleven o'clock sharp the bolts are drawn on the doors of all pubs in Soho and there is a mad rush for the first drink of the day by the alcoholics who down the first one in one gulp in order to stop their hands from shaking. Film men drop in with a can of film under their arm en route for a cutting room in the next street and strippers come in for a gin and bitter lemon before starting the day's unfulfilled promises. If the sun is shining you can stand outside the French pub at lunch time sipping a glass of pernod and watch the pretty office girls mince by in their thin summer dresses: it is all a very pleasant scene. If you wish you can then spoil yourself by having a prolonged lunch at Wheeler's or if you cannot afford that you can get a cheap plate of bacon and eggs or spaghetti in one of the hundred coffee houses. Or else you could buy a loaf of French bread and a piece of cheese and sit eating it in Soho Square, though things being the way they are these days it is quite possible that there is a law against it.

The pubs close at three o'clock, and as the afternoon drinking clubs are now closed there is very little that you can do during the afternoon. There are of course the shops where you can buy expensive salami and bottles of red wine, but on the other hand it is quite pleasant to wander around window shopping. If there is any racing, which there always is, you can have a bet at one of the betting shops and listen to a commentary on the race over the blower system. In point of fact Soho does not have much in the way of entertainment to offer during the day, for it is essentially a night place. During the day the people are busy earning their money so that they can buy cars and washing machines. As you wander around you may be shouted at aggressively by a prostitute from a top floor window or sidled up to by a tout from a near-beer joint: if you are wise, you will ignore both, for given the chance they will fleece you of every penny you may be carrying in your pocket. You can get a game of snooker or a game of eleven to four rummy in the Windmill Street snooker hall, but I wouldn't advise it unless you are very good, for the opponents that you are likely to run into down there are experts. And if they think you are a bit of a mug punter the chances are you will find yourself hustled gutless before you can say knife. The ideal thing to do during the afternoon is leave Soho altogether and go to the pictures in Leicester Square or Coventry Street and not return until the neon lights are blazing.

At night the atmosphere of Soho changes, people rush around in evening dress to and from the theatres in Shaftesbury Avenue and Charing Cross Road, lovers have a quiet meal together in little Italian restaurants (all the time playing footsy under the the table) and it is very lonely to watch if you are on your own. The pubs become packed with boozers whose only thought is to get paralytic as quickly as possible. Young girls wearing high-heeled boots and tight short skirts hurry along the streets in groups on their way to jazz clubs where they will twist and shake until the early hours of the morning. As you drift from one place to another you may detect a sense of urgency in all this merrymaking. A bunch of kids hanging about outside a strip joint hoping for something, even they do not know what. A young girl walks past on her own and the boys whistle and shout at her. She looks to neither right nor left, as she passes by the boys block her passage. 'Hello darling, how's it all going on,' says one in a saucy tone of voice. 'My, but doesn't she look beautiful,' says another who is so young that his voice has not yet broken. 'I don't think she's sixteen,' he adds. The young girl pretends that she does not hear them. The insults begin to lack conviction and they become as bored with the girl as they are with wandering around looking for some action. The action they are looking for may be going on behind the very wall they are leaning up against, but they don't know and even if they did they would not know how to get inside. In the end they wander off to the 2i's in desperation. There are many things to see if you wander around Soho at night. An American sailor will come up to you and ask you where he can 'get a bit of ass'. He is half drunk and a long way from home and he has weaved his way into the distance before you can answer his question.

It seems that everyone in Soho has got troubles of one kind or another. If you go into a pub to order a drink and mind your own business, before you know it someone is telling you how bad things are with them just at the moment: their wife has left them, they are dead broke and out of work, everyone hates them, and will you buy them a drink and lend them a fiver, and talk to them for hours on end, take them to dinner and sympathize, especially sympathize. You will run into many such people during your day in Soho.

The drinking clubs are open. The letter of the law says you have to be a member but in many of them you can become a member right away. Club land is a place all on its own, and the people who live in it are not of this world. Its citizens have only one interest in life and that is booze, though some do have a few other minor interests such as sex and death and it will take you a lot longer than your day out in Soho to fathom it all out. In point of fact some of the people who use these clubs are to be admired, for they have completely given up the struggle for survival. Their only interest is in drinking, and laying people, sex optional. Many of them have been successes of one kind or another at sometime in their lives, and then after their meteoric rise to fame have crashed to the ground, some because they did not like

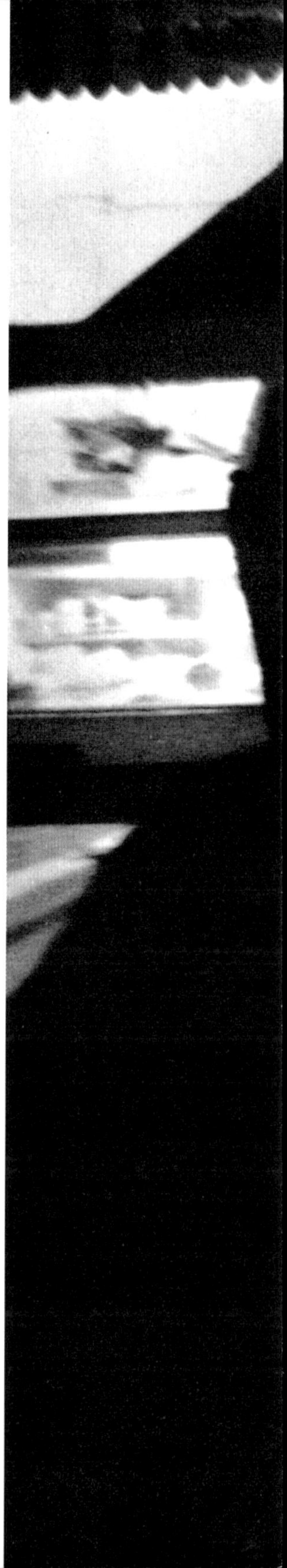

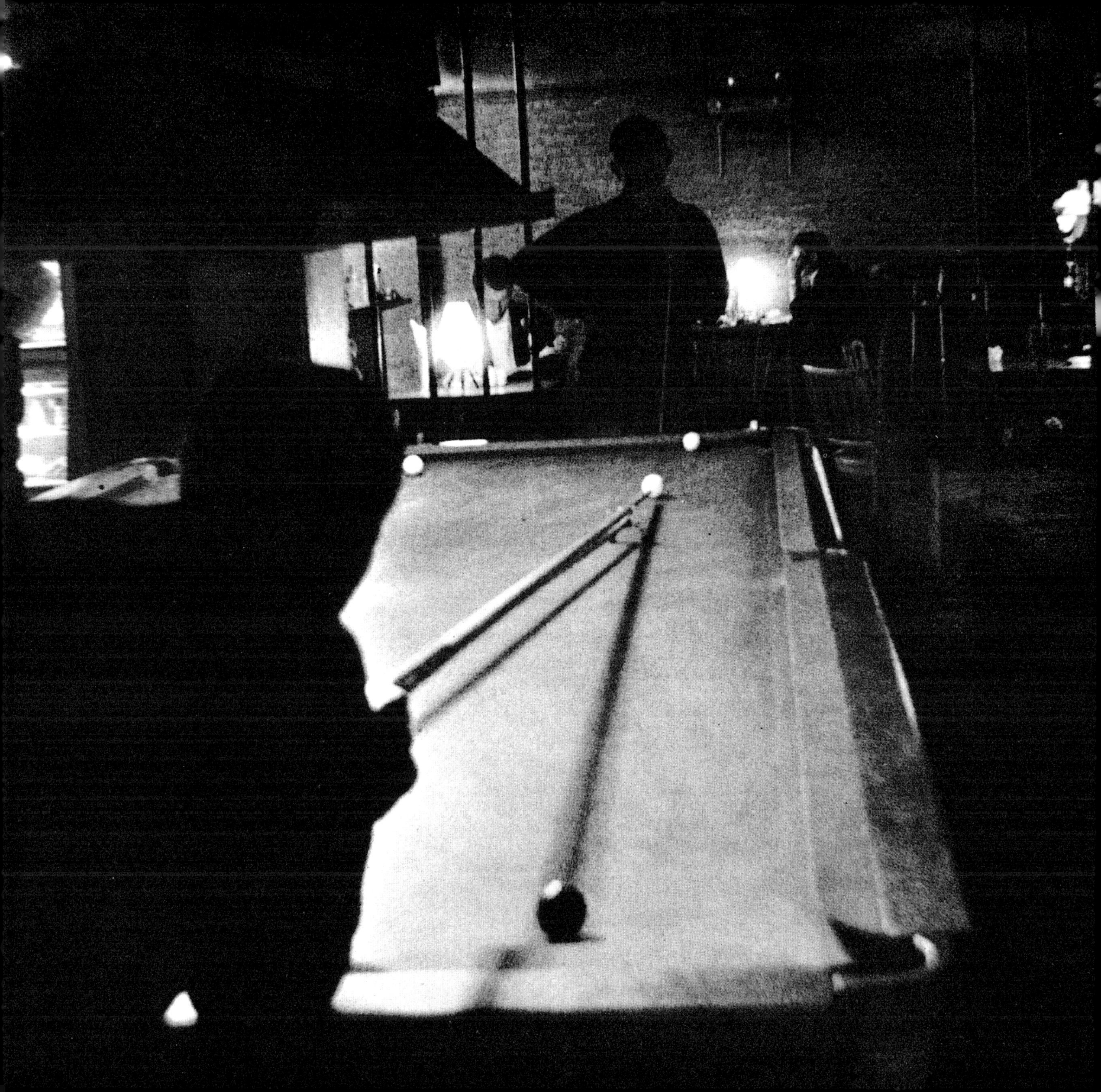

success and others because they ran out of whatever talent they had. They bitch at each other and about other people who make it until these others join their ranks, which often happens sooner than you may think, for the powers of evil are and always have been far stronger than the powers of good. I do not wish to sound like the first person who has ever said that line, but it could not be applied better than to the inhabitants of Soho's club land. They are creatures of the night, their habitat is dark rooms with worn carpets and faded wallpaper in basements in back alleys, their faces are pale and blotchy and their clothes are tawdry. The conversation is liable to be extravagant and camp, but in spite of all this there is something enchanting about these people. Such clubs are well worth a visit during your day in Soho.

If you feel like gambling, I strongly recommend that you do not do it in Soho, for the dealers are professionals and so are the people you are playing against, and although you may not be actually cheated out of your money, the odds against you winning are very high indeed. Many a mug has lost every penny in his pocket, and afterwards wondered how it happened. There are quite a few compulsive gamblers who visit Soho's gambling clubs every single night of their lives. They beg, borrow or steal the money only to lose it in a few minutes on a spin of the wheel or the turn of a card. The biggest gamblers of all are the Greeks. They will bet any amount of money on very nearly anything. I once knew a cafe proprietor who lost several hundred pounds in a poker school and then bet his business on a cut of the cards; he lost and had to go home and tell his wife and children that they would have to move out in the morning. A few days later he went back and won another cafe from another Greek and he then did a deal with the man to whom he lost the original cafe, so that he could stay in his own place. Fantastic as this may sound it is by no means an uncommon occurrence. There was another man who won £10,000 in one night and then lost most of it on the horses the following day. The next night he went back to the schpieler and lost £14,000 on top. That is the way it is with gamblers, one day they are up and the next day they are down, the money they win is only borrowed for a few hours and what they lose is only lent. There are few women who gamble, but those who do are liable to do so even more avidly than the men. They sit at the tables with diamonds sparkling on their chests and their scarlet lips set in a thin line. They ask for no quarter because of their sex, nor do they give any. They are fearless, and in a strange way rather sexy. To see a woman with glittering rings on her fingers push a stack of chips across a card table is quite an exciting sight. If they have a lover or a husband they will not let him gamble at all. It is a strange thing about gamblers that they are inclined to be very puritanical about other people getting the bug–it is a question of 'Do not do as I do but do as I say'. They will do everything in their power to prevent their nearest and dearest from becoming smitten. It is like some tearaways I have met, who will cut someone's ears off for no better reason than they don't like their faces, but on the other hand they are greatly shocked if they hear someone swear or see someone drunk, for they consider drink and swearing to be very immoral indeed, which just goes to show you something or other. You will not find it out in one day but the rather shady inhabitants of Soho have a morality all their own. They have their own commandments, such as 'Thou shalt not inform on your mates to the law', 'Thou shalt pay your gambling debts', 'Thou shalt not have it off with your mate's old woman while he is in the nick', 'Thou shalt not cheat at cards when playing with your mates (but it is all right to do so when playing a mug punter)', 'Thou shalt be extremely wary of all and sundry', etc. It will take you some time to get used to this set of rules, particularly if you are what is called a respectable member of society, but once you have accepted them your life in Soho will become easier. Much to the amazement of the villainy there are few ordinary people who will accept this set of rules as gospel.

Though there are always masses of people milling about in Soho, you can, if you are a stranger, feel very lonely and find your day in Soho a great bore. You wander around in an aimless fashion not knowing what to do or where to go. The blazing neon lights are no comfort to you, and you shy away from the girls who try their best to waylay you. 'Short time deary?' asks an old whore from a second-floor window. You ignore her and hurry along the street wishing you were at home watching the telly. For you lack the courage that it takes to mount the flight of stairs to her room, or else it is just possible that you do not have the inclination. You hope that you are going to run into someone beautiful who is going to fall madly in love with you for no better reason than that you need it. You walk past restaurants, but do not enter any of them for it is no fun having dinner by yourself. A tramp comes up to you and asks you for the price of a cup of tea and you are so delighted that someone has noticed you that you give him half a crown. 'Gawd bless ya guvnor', says the old tramp, and shambles off up the street in search of his next victim, and you are alone again. Your dream of meeting someone exciting is shattered, but still you do not give up and go home to your bed for you are a terror for punishment. You may wander into a coffee bar: the juke box is blaring, and the mods and rockers are having a ball, they give you a suspicious glance but that is all, you are still alone. A staggeringly beautiful young girl comes in with her boy friend and they put some money in the juke box and begin to dance together. You cannot take your eyes off the young girl's backside as it jerks wildly from one side to another. After a time she notices that you are watching her but pretends that she has not. She starts to get even more brazen in her movements and you get up and rush out wiping beads of sweat from your brow. You go as you came, only now a little more hopeless than you were before, thinking that this surely must be the night that you are going to put your head in the gas oven, but it never is because the next day is going to be better. Tomorrow you are going to meet someone beautiful and your life is going to be all new and exciting; but it never is for the battle is against yourself, and you cannot win. Many such people can be seen wandering around Soho during the course of a day or night.

The pubs shut at eleven o'clock and most people go home at this time, but if you wish you can continue your night out at a night club. These days Soho is not renowned for its night clubs. Years ago the Gargoyle was the most famous club in London, let alone Soho, but though it is still open the atmosphere is entirely different. It is now just a night club where, as in the late forties and early fifties, it was the meeting place of London's big spenders. As a matter of fact all the night clubs in the West End have now become extremely mercenary. On entering a night club you will be shown to a table by the head-waiter, who will ask you if you would like a hostess to join you. If you say that you would one

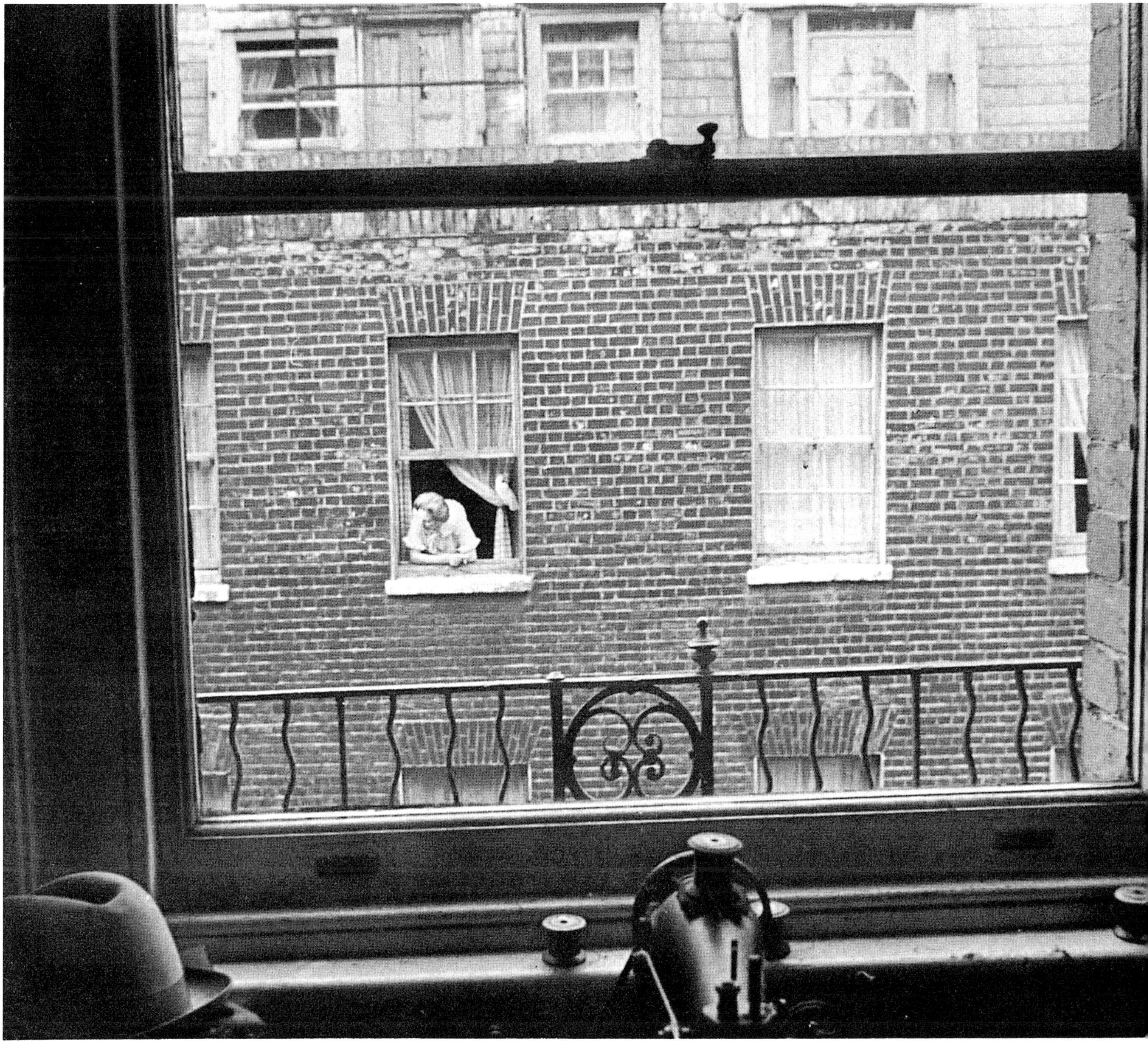

will be shown to your table. Her price is five pounds for sitting and talking to you, and that is likely to be only the beginning, for when you ask her what she would like to drink she will of course 'like' a bottle of champagne. Unfortunately she has also run out of cigarettes so you call over the cigarette girl: the cigarettes are in boxes of 200 so you buy the girl a box. After a while she will press her leg against yours and tell you how handsome you look. You ask her if she would like to dance. She dances very close to you but you don't find it very sexy. You sit down at the table again and she starts to tell you her life story, about how she came to London in search of a job as a singer and how she met this man who gave her a baby and then deserted her, so now she has to look after the child all by herself and how much everything costs. You sense that the speech has been rehearsed and has been told often before, and you are right. A girl with a camera comes over to your table and asks you if you would like to have your picture taken with the hostess, who giggles and says 'What fun'. She combs her hair and throws her arms around you, the flash goes off and nearly blinds you: 'That will be three pounds please sir,' says the girl with the camera. As the night progresses you find that you have bought the hostess a cuddly teddy bear, five pounds, a giant box of chocolates, five pounds, a baby doll nightie, five pounds, and a box of nylon stockings, five pounds, all of which the girl will give back to the management for a pound a piece. At about three in the morning the girl may suggest that you come home with her for a price, which might be twenty pounds. If you agree, you can say that this is not the cheapest night out you have ever had. The hostesses are very skilful in the art of getting money out of unsuspecting clients.

What does all this amount to? It amounts to the fact that Soho is a very dangerous place to wander around in on your own whether you are a man or woman, especially if you do not know the strength. Though you will not be knocked over the head and robbed you may well be robbed in these more subtle ways. The dangers for a girl are obvious. She may allow herself to be picked up by someone who will set her on a path that leads nowhere but to tears, heartbreak and the abortionist's couch.

The ideal suggestion about spending a day in Soho is—don't do it. Have lunch or dinner by all means, for there are no better restaurants in London than the ones in Soho, but hanging about all day is no fun. All you can expect to get is an overdose of frustration and boredom, added to which your feet will get sore. It is however the ideal place for seeking a little vice if that is your fancy, but more often than not you will find that you have bitten off a little more than you can chew, for the girls have far more meat than you've got gravy.

Mind you, for hundreds of people spending a day in Soho is a daily chore. Businessmen in bowler hats and carrying umbrellas rush up and down the narrow streets, waiters go to the restaurants where they work with a heavy step, shopkeepers open up their shutters, newspaper sellers shout 'All the latest', publicans sell drink and throw out any customers who get drunk, the copper on his beat tells people the way to wherever it is that they want to go and the tailor sits stitching in a back room. For all these people and many more Soho is just a place of work. They are accustomed to the colour and do not notice it. If you were to suggest to them that there was some romance about Soho they would likely as not laugh in your face.

A businessman will arrive for work at the office at about ten o'clock in the morning. His secretary has already opened his mail and he dictates some answers, signs some cheques, attends a board meeting, has lunch with a client from one till three. He goes back to his office in the afternoon and dictates a few more letters. From his window he can see the changing face of Soho as the new buildings go up all around him, but he does not really notice them for he is far too preoccupied with the business of making money.

In fact such a businessman is not really concerned with the goings on in Soho in the least, that is to say apart from what goes on in his own office, which might as well be in Thames Ditton for all it matters to him. At five o'clock sharp he will put on his bowler hat and leave the office and go home to his wife in the suburbs. He will do this same trip day in day out for years and never really have anything to do with any of the people of Soho. There is, of course, no reason why he should, but it seems rather strange just the same.

This also works in reverse, because there are people whose only connection with Soho is that they live there. Every morning they will leave Soho for their work, which might be as far afield as Kensington or Bishopsgate. In the evening they will return to their homes in Berwick or Brewer Streets tired and hungry and they will not have a night out on the town any more often than someone who lives in the suburbs. Strangely enough the publishers of this book* are situated in Soho, in Carlisle Street, just off Soho Square. Luckily they are men of the world and as such are very interested in Soho and its many aspects. They spend their days in Soho and are also not opposed to spending their nights as well, though only in a highly respectable way of course, for strange as it may seem this too it is possible to do in Soho.

So there you have it. Soho, like anywhere else, is a place you either love or hate; though I do not think it is possible to hate it entirely. It has great charm and loads of character, and one of its amenities is bound to appeal to you. It will be a crying shame when it has all gone for go it must. However so long as the restaurants continue to serve good food, the people will come. And until a law is passed banning sex, the clients will patronize the girls. And no matter how many headmasters give sixth-formers pep talks, boys will come to Soho in search of their fortunes.

* Publishers of the 1st edition, Martin Secker and Warburg Ltd.

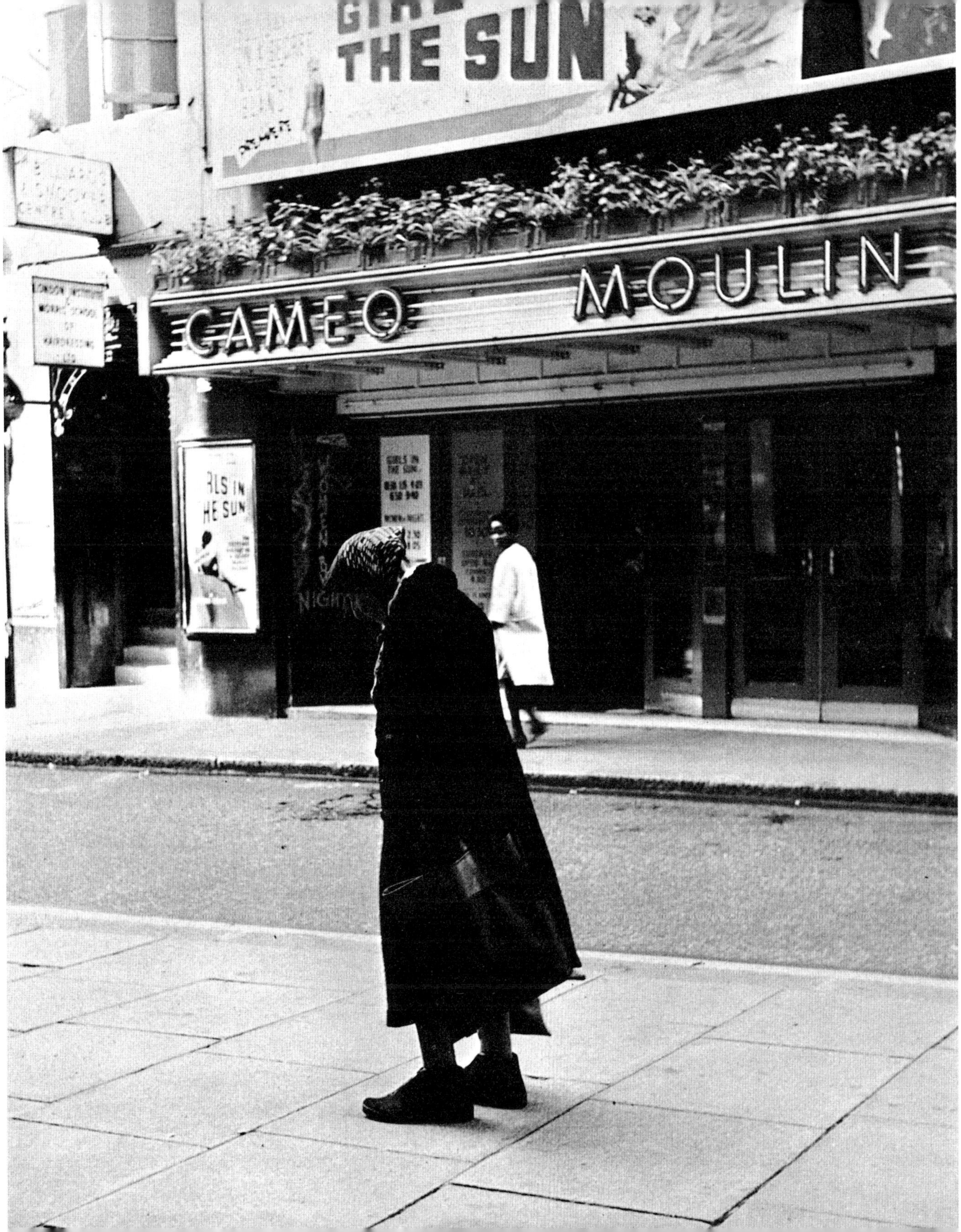
THE SUN
CAMEO
MOULIN

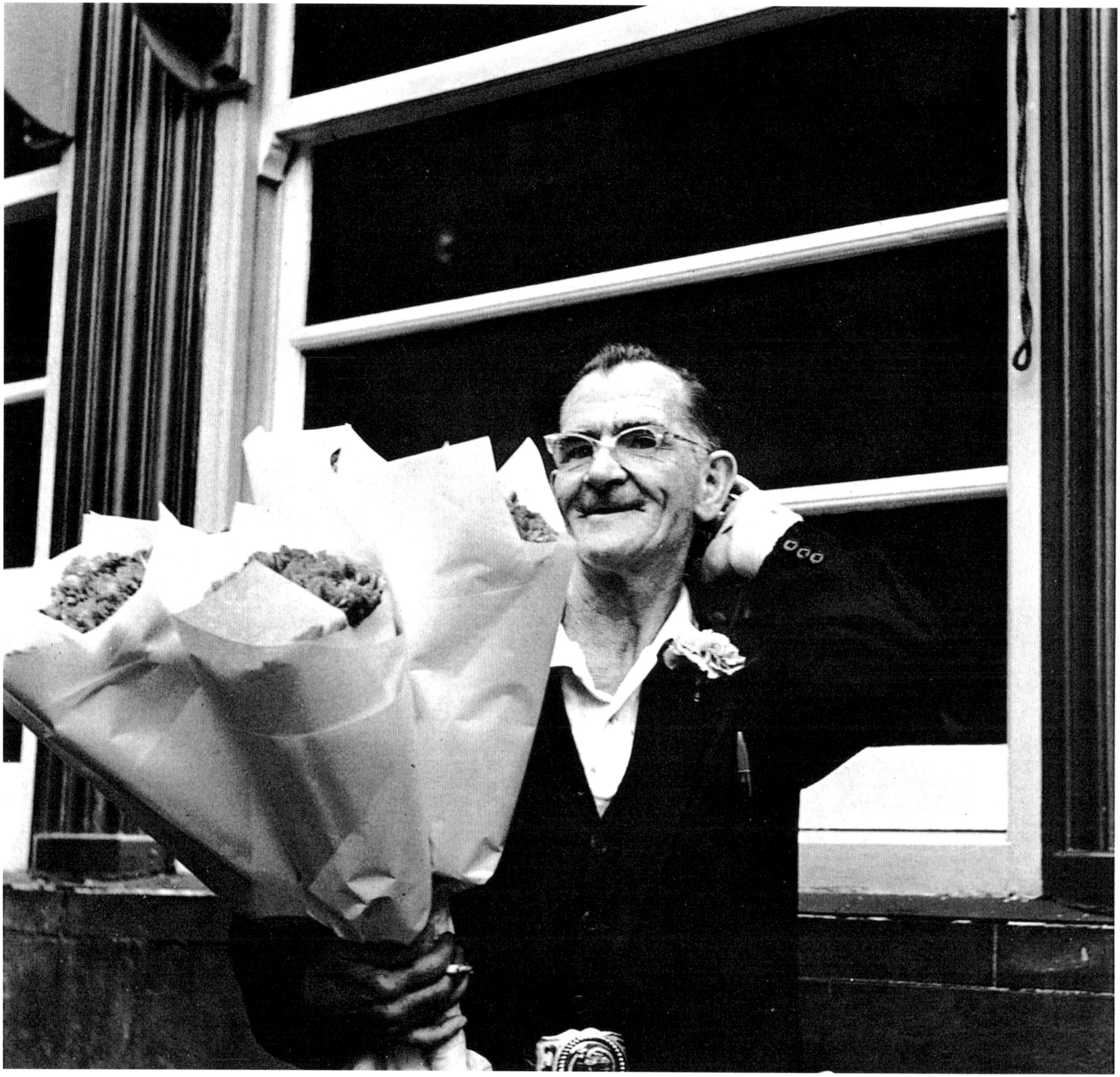

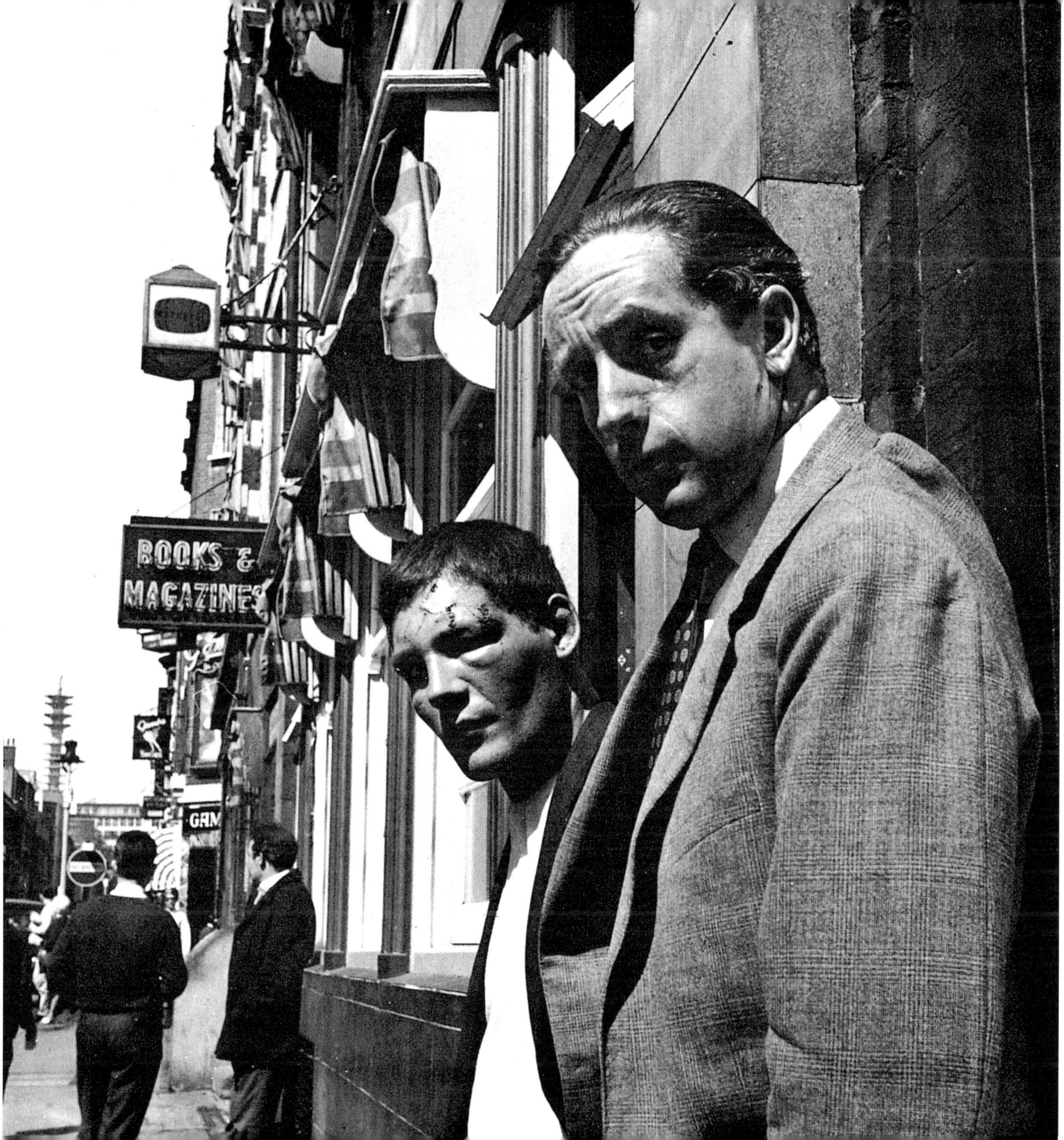
BOOKS &
MAGAZINES

ILLUSTRATIONS

ACKNOWLEDGEMENTS

With thanks to: Darren Coffield, Dan Papps, Daniel Scott, and Barry Miles.

Note from the Publisher: The aim of this edition is to make available to the reader Frank Norman and Jeffrey Bernard's evocative homage to the fast-disappearing Soho of the Sixties. With the addition of the introduction and obituary and just a few edits and corrections to literals and factual errors, this book is presented as close to the original as possible. It should be noted that the language and opinions expressed by the author reflect the context of the subject matter and the era in which they were written and do not necessarily reflect the view of the publisher.

ISBN: 978 1 78884 265 5

First published in England 1966 by Martin Secker and Warburg Limited

This edition published 2024 by ACC Art Books Ltd. with kind permission from Geraldine Norman and Isabel Bernard
www.accartbooks.com

A CIP catalogue record for this book is available from the British Library

ACC
ART
BOOKS

FSC
www.fsc.org
MIX
Paper | Supporting responsible forestry
FSC® C008047

Printed in China
for ACC Art Books Ltd.,
Woodbridge, Suffolk, UK
www.accartbooks.com

FRANK NORMAN, OBITUARY

I'd like to make a particularly personal tribute to Frank Norman who died on 23 December bringing 1980 to such a very sad end for so many of us. I don't want to harp on about the history of his career – that's been done – and we know he wrote 16 books that included *Bang to Rights* and *Banana Boy* plus four plays including *Fings Ain't What They Used to Be.* I just want to recollect and savour some of the happenings that involved us both during the 30 years I knew him and which spanned the hooligan days of the early Fifties through to the wild and successful days of the Sixties and then to the recent tongue-in-cheek mellowness which spread benignly during the Seventies. I say 'mellow' although I know you can stir up an old wasp's nest, but Frank, until very recently, looked to be cruising through middle age, happy with his wife Geraldine, one novel a year and a Friday-only visit to Soho to give a master class. That Soho is dying we know, but that one of its more distinguished features should be so suddenly and cruelly demolished makes me wonder what on earth is God up to? I doubt that Heaven knows.

Memories of Frank merge and blur. When I first met him in a cafe called the Alexandria in Rathbone Place – he was later to use it and the layabouts in it for his play *A Kayf Up West* – he caught my and everyone's attention with his aggression or at least his aggressive looks which were highlighted by a razor scar. He was pretty distant in those days, a little broody, and he made an amazing attempt to settle down at one point when he got married and set up as a newsagent, of all things, in the village of Boxford in Suffolk. Can you imagine it? Of course, he got as bored as hell with it. He'd pop up to London in his car, get drunk in the Stork Club, drive back to Boxford at four in the morning and, of course, the papers would get delivered at lunchtime. Well, that didn't last long.

What else springs to mind? The Ad Lib Club. That was in the days when it had just become fashionable to import piranha fish and keep them as pets. The tank in the Ad Lib represented a challenge to Frank, so he took off his jacket, rolled up his shirt sleeve and plunged his arm into the tank. They didn't even give him a nibble, which disappointed him deeply, but he then mounted the stage and sang 'Falling in Love with Love is Falling for Make Believe'.

...

Our efforts to collaborate on the book we did together, *Soho Night and Day* (he wrote it and I took the pictures), were something of a farce. We'd wander around Soho all day and night having hospitality heaped on us by publicans and restaurateurs who wanted to appear in the book and I suppose we were drunk for a year. When we weren't given hospitality, Frank paid for everything.

That generosity sums him up for me. We had some fearful rows but his sort of generosity would end them. He had tremendous loyalty towards his friends and was so much a warmer person than the 'scar-faced ex-jailbird' he called himself. *The Times* cut a sentence I wrote about him – not the sort of thing *The Times* would like. I said that he negated that ghastly cliche 'You only get out of life what you put into it'. Frank put an awful lot into it, and I wish he'd got a little more out of it than he did. We all knew him far too briefly.

Jeffrey Bernard

(originally published in *The Spectator*, 3 January 1981)

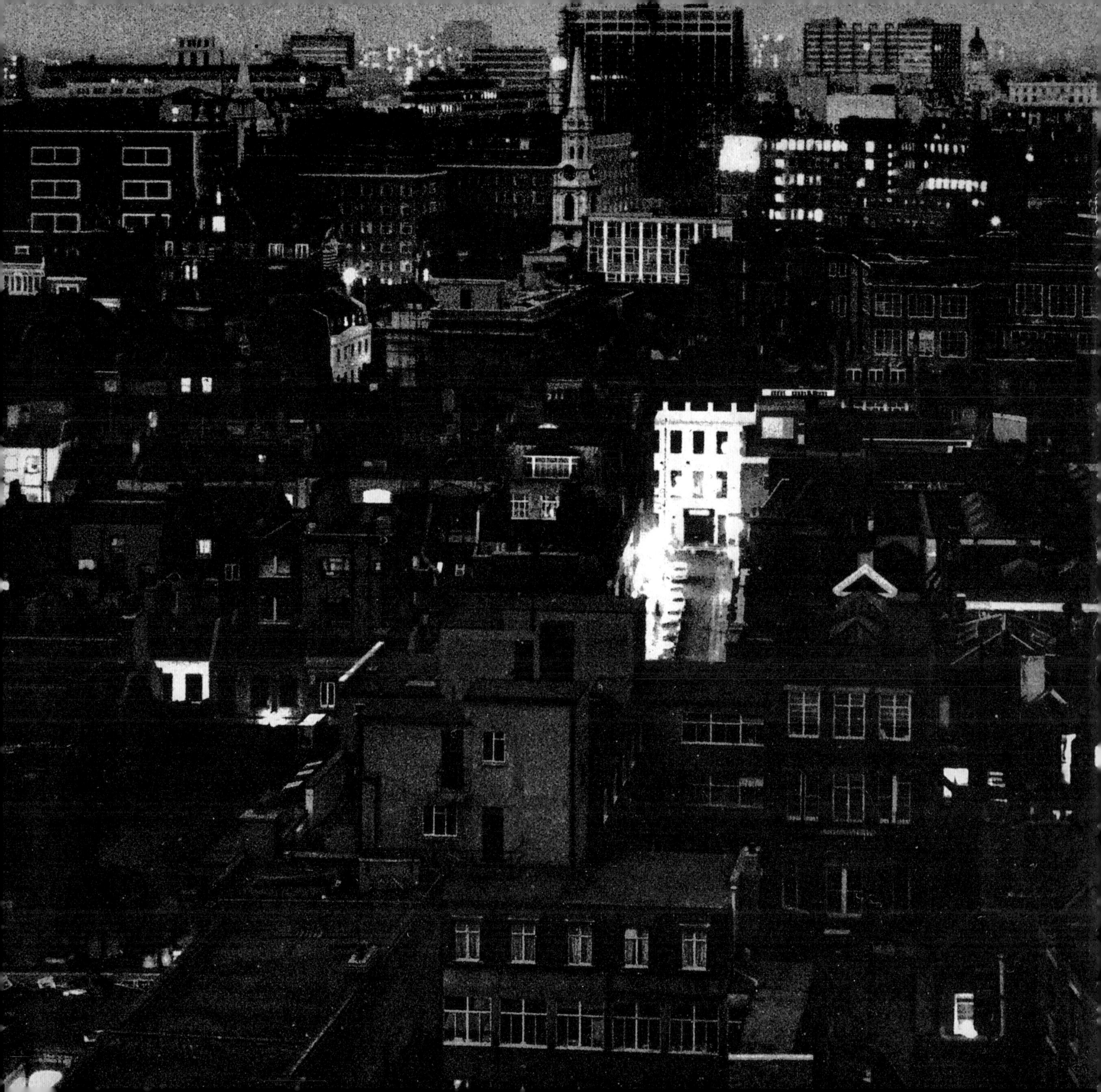